THE AMERICAN PROBLEM IN BRITISH DIPLOMACY,
1841–1861

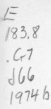

The American Problem in British Diplomacy, 1841–1861

Wilbur Devereux Jones

UNIVERSITY OF GEORGIA PRESS
ATHENS

242442

Library of Congress Catalog Card Number : 73–85870

International Standard Book Number : 0–8203–0324–0

University of Georgia Press, Athens 30602

First published in the United Kingdom 1974 by
The Macmillan Press Ltd.

Printed in Great Britain

TO ELIZABETH

To mark our Thirty Golden Years

Contents

Preface

The original name selected for this study was 'The Disorderly Art of Anglo-American Diplomacy', a title meant to convey the impression, which seems quite justified, that the techniques and tactics employed by the British and American statesmen in their diplomatic encounters during the period were often unusual and informal. Certain friendly reviewers, however, pointed out that such a title promised much too much, for the work presented not a comprehensive study of Anglo-American diplomacy but merely the British side of it. Their criticism was incontestable, so the name was changed to indicate that the work restricted itself to British diplomacy.

In offering such a study, the author had two major purposes in mind. The first was to attempt to place Britain's relations with America within the context of her domestic concerns and party politics, her relations with other nations (especially France, the one that tended to monopolise her attention), and her imperial problems. No doubt most of the motives that conditioned Britain's American policies derived from these sources.

The second purpose of the work was to discuss the diplomatic tactics used by the various British foreign policy makers in seeking solutions to Anglo-American controversies. An effort was made to discover and describe how British leaders sized up those of America, adapted their tactics to the results of this process, and sometimes learned more about the collective American personality from the success or failure of their tactics.

The contemporary British diplomats seem to have derived their impressions of the American diplomatic personality and its moods from three main sources – the despatches and private letters received from their diplomatic representatives in a few American cities, the brief items on American affairs (often reprints from various American newspapers) printed in British

news media, and their personal contacts with American diplomats, or simply casual visitors, in Britain. As often as not, the
impressions they received from these sources did not agree with
one another.

British impressions of American representatives or governments in Washington might change from time to time, but there
were certain constituents of the collective American personality
that seemed to alter very little from one decade to the next. One
such constituent was an unrelenting persistence in striving for
certain national objectives – their 'hardihood of claim', as Sir
James Graham once put it. Softly or loudly, bluntly or deviously,
the Americans would persist, always persist. Another constituent was an expanding appetite for land or national advantages,
which made America seem to British observers an 'encroaching' nation. Most British observers also noted a liberal amount
of bluster and braggadocio in the American personality.

But there was another quite different aspect to the American
diplomatic personality. For example, no American statesman
during the 1841–61 period pulled the lion's tail with more
enthusiasm than James Buchanan, yet when he was on the
threshold of the presidency in 1856, he gratuitously assured the
British Consul in New York that there was more love for 'Old
England' in America than in any other country, and that Britain
had nothing to fear from the United States. When the appropriate situation arose. American statesmen would suddenly re-
discover their ties of blood to 'Old England', and even dwell
on them with Victorian earnestness. In this mood the American
diplomatic personality took on an aspect of filial intimacy,
suggesting that the biological relationship between the two
nations had created a special status for her which entitled the
United States to special treatment. In some respects this approach could be more embarrassing to British foreign policy
makers than American defiance, for American truculence might
give rise to a similar reaction among the British people and
unite them, whereas the kinship approach struck a responsive
chord not only among the British lower classes, but even higher
up. For example, at the time of the Oregon crisis that fine old
Tory journalist, John Wilson Croker, wrote to Lord Aberdeen
that a war between the two nations would be 'almost *impious*'.

Discovering the motivating impressions of the American personality present in the minds of the British foreign policy makers was no easy task. Information of this nature was hardly to be found in the despatches available at the Public Record Office, which were written with the knowledge that Parliament might call for and publish them at any time. Under these circumstances remarks about Americans were likely to be favourable, and any criticisms would be advanced in the most measured language. The private correspondence of the British statesmen involved, being beyond the reach of Parliament, proved to be a much better source of such information, but mere chance would determine whether or not the British diplomats would reveal their thinking to colleagues when the historian was most likely to long for it. So the information required to carry out the secondary purpose of this work might or might not be available as needed. When it was not, the writer could offer little more than a partly documented guess, a possible analogy or – in the most desperate circumstances – an unsubstantiated theory.

The documentary materials used in this study were collected over a period of many years while the writer was culling information from British archives in connection with several projects in purely British history. The kind financial support of the American Philosophical Society enabled him to return to Britain a few years ago to fill in the gaps in the narrative, in so far as they could be filled at all. To the Earl of Derby (and Professor Robert Blake of Queen's College, Oxford), the Duke of Wellington, the Earl of Clarendon, Miss Margaret Sinclair, Sir William Gladstone, and the National Trust go the author's gratitude for permission to use and quote from the private collections of letters vital to the present account.

University of Georgia   Wilbur Devereux Jones

25 April 1973

1
The Diplomacy of Menace

It would be an oversimplification of history to state that two distinct schools of thought emerged in British diplomatic circles after the Revolution regarding how best to deal with America, the 'hard-line' and the 'soft-line', but, as generalisations go, it has more than a modicum of truth in it. The first of these was based on the assumption that Americans were encroaching and untrustworthy in their foreign relations; the second, in the belief that they were a rational people who would respond in kind to generous treatment. The hard-line school envisaged an indefinite period of constant suspicion and watchfulness; the soft-line, the possibility of an era of settled, friendly, Anglo-American relations. The former was the policy of most British Foreign Secretaries, including Canning; the second was limited to a precious few, especially Lords Grenville and Castlereagh.[1]

At the Foreign Office in 1839 was an outstanding representative of the hard-line school, a peerless practitioner of balance-of-power diplomocy, a highly intelligent, resourceful, imaginative individual who regarded the nation states as collective personalities which did not change much from generation to generation. The states of Latin America were anarchic and contemptible; Austria was weak and shortsighted; Prussia was stronger, but introspective; while Russia was at once stagnant and capable of violent and erratic activity.

It was the personality of France whose image had burned deepest into Palmerston's mind. A proud nation with a long memory and unstable emotions, she could never forgive the past, forget Trafalgar and Waterloo, or live long at peace with Britain, which had so often frustrated and defeated her national ambitions. Therefore, France stood out in the crowd. Palmerston's eye was always settled on Paris, and other nations simply fell within his peripheral vision.

At the moment Palmerston was engaged in the type of diplomatic operation he so often conducted with enthusiasm and aplomb – manoeuvring the states of Europe to frustrate a French project, this time in the Middle East. France, by taking up the cause of Mehemet Ali of Egypt against his overlord, the Turkish Sultan, had sought to expand her influence in that area, only to have the ever-watchful Palmerston in July 1840 form a coalition with Austria, Prussia and Russia to mediate the dispute. Though accomplished politely enough, the tactic left France diplomatically isolated, and bitterly resentful. War with France was still a possibility in the autumn of 1840, when British, Turkish and Austrian forces dislodged the rebellious Ali's forces from Syria, and the dark clouds were not entirely dissipated until January 1841, when Palmerston magnanimously permitted France to participate in the final arrangements of this stage of the Eastern Question. Palmerston wrote to the Queen on 1 February 1841, that his despatches 'virtually show that the Turkish Question is brought to a close . . . which at different periods has assumed appearances so threatening to the peace of Europe'.[2] Having administered a sharp rap on the French knuckles, and cajoled Russia into signing a satisfactory Straits settlement, Palmerston in February 1841 turned to American affairs.

Although the Viscount, like most British statesmen of the period, often referred to the ties of blood and language between the United States and Britain, in conducting his diplomacy he regarded her as another nation-state whose interests at times complemented, at times conflicted with those of Britain. The collective personality of America in his mind was that of a poor and resentful relation, envious of the wealth and power of the Mother Country, sometimes naïve, but more often cunning, and, above all a disorderly and vigorous nation whose encroachments bore watching. The European states, he was convinced, noted carefully Britain's disputes with the United States, and, if she countenanced American encroachments, those states might decide to employ American tactics in their dealings with Great Britain.[3]

After the Canadian Rebellion of 1837, Palmerston's American policy, due partly to British involvements elsewhere, and partly to his belief that the Van Buren administration was weak and pacific,[4] was simply to sit tight and let the issues between the two countries accumulate. When American blood pressure

rose over the *Caroline* incident, the Foreign Secretary turned
the matter over to John Campbell, later Lord Chancellor, who
recalled:[5]

> The affair of the 'Caroline' was much more difficult. Even
> Lord Grey told me that he thought we were quite wrong in
> what we had done. . . . I was clearly of opinion that although
> she lay on the American side of the river when she was seized,
> we had a clear right to seize and destroy her, just as we might
> have taken a battery erected by the rebels on the American
> shore, the guns of which were fired against the Queen's
> troops on Navy Island. I wrote a long justification of our
> Government and this supplied the arguments used by our
> Foreign Secretary till the Ashburton Treaty hushed up the
> dispute.

There existed, then, some disagreement in high circles regarding
the legality of the British action in this affair, but Palmerston
coldly ignored American complaints. When the United States
presented a formal demand for reparations on 22 May 1838,
Palmerston did not even bother to reply to it until 27 August
1841 – a full three years later, and then he merely termed the
destruction of the *Caroline* a justifiable act of self-defence. It
was not the orderly diplomatic procedure one would expect in
negotiations between great states. Palmerston's cavalier attitude
indicated he did not place America in that category.

During those years, while America fumed over the *Caroline*
incident, and explosive tensions were building over the disputed
boundary in Maine, Palmerston's policy of inaction was complemented by a strong show of force. The 2000 British regulars
in Canada in January 1838 were increased to 10,500 by the
spring of 1839, and a force of four steamships, some schooners
and gunboats were raised to defend the Great Lakes.[6] These and
other warlike measures were taken ostensibly to suppress the
rebellion in Canada and pacify the border, but they were undoubtedly a major factor in Anglo-American diplomacy during
those years. Some members of the Government, such as Lord
John Russell, were nervous at Palmerston's temerity, and
haunted by the possibility of another two-front war against
France and the United States, but Palmerston had correctly

accepted America's lack of war preparations as good evidence that such fears were groundless, and he continued to ignore the rising temperature in America. He would modify his policy only when there was some cogent reason for so doing.

The reason for modification arose at a most opportune moment, just after Palmerston had rearranged Near Eastern affairs to his liking. Alexander McLeod, a British citizen, was arrested in New York on 12 November 1840 and charged with murder and arson in connection with the *Caroline* affair. Henry S. Fox, the British Minister in Washington, immediately demanded his release on the ground that McLeod was acting in the public service when the alleged crimes had been committed.[7] Unable to secure his freedom, Fox reported the arrest in a despatch of 27 December 1840.

There was little notice of the incident in Britain until 8 February 1841 when Lord Stanley in the Commons and the Earl of Mountcashell in the Lords, both members of the opposition Conservative Party, called for papers on American affairs. The ensuing debates revealed how little attention the members of both Houses had been paying to American problems, and Palmerston refused to enlighten them on the ground that negotiations between Britain and America were still pending. Sir Robert Peel, the Conservative leader, no doubt urged to do so by Lord Aberdeen, had recently made an issue of Palmerston's handling of French relations, and had brought on a debate which was somewhat embarrassing to Peel for he had Radical support. Either because he wished to avoid a repetition of such a situation, or because he suspected that the cause of McLeod might be highly popular in England, Peel did not press the matter at the time, and Palmerston had a free hand in American affairs.

Palmerston was quite confident of public support for a strong stand in defence of McLeod. Although the members in the Commons were lethargic and even bored when a foreign affairs issue involved some narrow political or economic interest, one bearing on national honour would rally not only the Whig-Liberal coalition, but would bring the Conservatives to their feet *en masse*.[8] The McLeod issue could have been played up, or played down. Palmerston evidently decided that the time was right to play it up, and thereby to secure still another diplomatic triumph to add to those over France and Russia. Europe was quiet, and save for the undemanding China War and some difficulties in India, Britain was at peace.

The Viscount, therefore, called in the American minister, Andrew Stevenson, and warned him 'as a private friend'[9] that McLeod's conviction and execution would be a *casus belli*. Then he wrote to Fox in Washington that McLeod's execution 'would be a war of retaliation and vengeance'.[10] That Palmerston was not bluffing is evident from his letter to Sir William Temple, which noted : 'If they were to hang McLeod, we could not stand it, and war would be the inevitable result'.[11] Thus – at a moment when Anglo-French relations were raw and still bleeding – Palmerston raised a serious crisis in America.

It might be argued that the nature of this case forced Palmerston to adopt the extremely 'hard line' that he took.[12] A note in Greville's famous memoirs, however, shows that some eminent British figures had doubts about Britain's position.[13]

. . . the violent and bad spirit displayed in America have produced no small consternation here, though everybody goes on saying that a war between the two countries, and for so little cause, is impossible. . . . The real difficulty arises from a conviction here, that in the case of McLeod, we are in the right, and the equally strong conviction there, that we are not, and the actual doubt on which side the truth lies. Senior, whom I met the other day, expressed great uncertainty, and he proposes and has written to the Government on the subject, that the question of International Law shall be submitted to the decision of a German University – that of Berlin, he thinks, would be the best. This idea he submitted to Stevenson, who approved of it, but the great difficulty would be to agree upon a statement of facts. Yesterday Lord Lyndhurst was at the Council Office, talking over the matter with Sir Herbert Jenner and Justice Littledale, and he said it was very questionable if the Americans had not right on their side; and that he thought, in a similar case here, we should be obliged to try the man, and, if convicted, nothing but a pardon could save him. These opinions casting such serious doubts on the question of right, are at least enough to restrain indignation and beget caution.

While the opinion of William Nassau Senior, an Oxford professor and authority on economics, might be discounted when he
spoke on the niceties of international law, that of Lord Lyndhurst, twice Lord Chancellor and to hold the same position
again when Peel took office, cannot be brushed aside. Obviously
there was enough uncertainty in the situation to have justified a
less extreme course than the one Palmerston adopted.

Why, then, did Palmerston choose to present so stern an
ultimatum to the United States? The reasons would seem fairly
clear. In the first place, he knew that his case, though not air-
tight, was strong, and would receive support from almost all
political sections in Britain. Secondly, he correctly assumed that
the peace-loving Van Buren administration in America, and the
Louis Philippe government in France would hardly go to war
on such an issue. Finally, the situation permitted Palmerston to
teach the United States a 'good lesson' (British statesmen often
used the term), which would put her in a properly chastened
mood for the coming negotiations over the Maine Boundary
and other problems.

As the crisis developed, it became ever more apparent that
Palmerston had correctly anticipated the national mood. Lord
Aberdeen, who probably disapproved his handling of the
Caroline and *McLeod* incidents, saw fit to hold his peace, and
Peel, as party leader, could not let the angry crowd go by without
waving at it. On 5 March Peel gave unqualified support to the
Government in resistance to wrong. Much as he deprecated war
with a people 'united to us by the ties of ancient descent and a
common language', he declared the present difficulty should not
be settled by 'any unjust concession'.[14] It was a very strong
speech, which led Lord John Russell to report to the Queen:
'This declaration was received with loud cheers. It must be considered as very creditable to Sir Robert Peel'.[15] Two months
later, when it was abundantly clear that he might actually be in
office before the McLeod verdict came in, Peel – acting no doubt
on the advice of Aberdeen – stated '... that the question was not
whether Mr. McLeod – respecting whose arrest and imprison-
ment he would give no opinion whatsoever – ought to be released or not ...'.[16] This was a notable decrescendo, which left
him with more room for manoeuvre once he came to Downing
Street.

The McLeod crisis continued into the early months of the Harrison–Tyler administration, and the new Secretary of State, Daniel Webster, tried to balance off the McLeod incident with that of the *Caroline*, which was not illogical for both involved national honour more than any specific interest. He left no stone unturned to secure the release of McLeod.[17] One plan was to have McLeod jump bail, but the court set bail impractically high. Webster then turned to every technicality that he could conceive, all without success.

Palmerston meanwhile was kept informed of each successive failure. What went on in his mind as he watched the Federal Government, thrown into a panic by his ultimatum, struggle to make its will felt in New York we shall never know, but, if he felt any sympathy for Tyler and Webster, it was not reflected in any modification of his ultimatum.

The Foreign Secretary not only persisted with his 'hard line' toward the United States, but he seemed determined that it should be passed along to the new administration. On 27 August 1841, after three years of silence, and after the Melbourne Government had been defeated, Palmerston finally answered the American demand for reparations in the *Caroline* incident with a total rejection of the claim. This bluntly dispelled any hope the harassed Americans might have had for balancing off the incidents against each other, and made it more difficult for his successor to adopt a conciliatory policy in this matter.

To the extent that diplomacy is the art of forcing other nations to do what they do not particularly want to do, or positively loathe doing, Palmerston emerged as a stunningly successful practitioner, for his successes during this period had come not over small, weak, states, but over major powers. The public response to the McLeod incident must have impressed him deeply, and may well have inspired him to take up the case of Don Pacifico – with even more popular success – nine years later.

Lord Aberdeen, who replaced Palmerston at the Foreign Office in September 1841, was a Scottish aristocrat by birth, a gentleman both by nature and choice, a Victorian with the keenest sense of moral responsibility, and a veteran diplomat whose experience dated back to the Napoleonic Wars. This last may have been important in conditioning his attitude toward Palmerston, who was something of a parvenu at the diplomatic trade, a disciple of George Canning with whose political faction he had once identified himself; whereas Aberdeen learned the art from the elegant Castlereagh himself. Although the competition between the two statesmen stemmed largely from conflicts as to policy and tactics, Aberdeen's disapproval of Palmerston may also have been fortified by his Victorian dislike of the Viscount's questionable private life.

Aberdeen agreed with Palmerston that France should be the centre of all British diplomacy, but they viewed that country through entirely different eyes. Distrustful Palmerston took his cue from the past; Aberdeen believed that rationality and patience could create an entirely different Anglo-French future, and that the healing of their centuries-old conflict was the key to bringing a stable peace to Europe. For this reason he was not ready to applaud Palmerston's recent victory over France in the Middle East.

Toward the United States, Aberdeen's attitude was similar to that of Lord Castlereagh, who had healed the wounds between the nations after the War of 1812. Conciliating the United States was an end in itself and in the interest of general peace, but it might also be a means of obliterating for all time the tenuous Franco-American combination that had operated against Britain in two wars. Such measures he could take to win over France, and separate her from the United States seemed perfectly justifiable to Aberdeen. It was a most delicate operation indeed – to conciliate both nations, and at the same time to separate them – but Aberdeen did not consider this project outside the range of possibilities. At the moment Aberdeen took office the success of his conciliation policies seemed remote – both France and America were in high dudgeon and united in their outrage against Palmerston's policies.

Leaving aside the difficulties in the way of French conciliation, there were a number of high hurdles to be jumped before Britain and the United States could meet in the centre of the field and shake hands. One was a tradition inherited from the

last war that America had administered a 'stab in the back' to
Britain when the latter was fighting for the freedom of Europe
and that of America herself. This interpretation had behind it
the weighty authority of George Canning himself,[18] and had
some currency, but it was by no means universally accepted by
the British people even during the war.[19]

Many British statesmen, well-schooled as they were in the
history of Greece and Rome, simply distrusted republics in
general and America in particular as an example of mob government. In 1847 Henry Goulburn wrote: 'Certainly if there ever
was a moment when the effects of democratic institutions ought
to be at a discount, it must be at present when we have before us
the radical tyranny of the Sonderbund in Switzerland and the
attack upon Mexico by the United States. . . .'[20] '. . . when a
country is so mob-governed as America', Greville wrote, '. . .
there must be great danger [of war]'.[21] To Lord Melbourne, the
United States was a 'most hostile and uncontrollable com-
munity'.[22] The distrust of the democratic form of government
explains why many British statesmen could associate on cordial
terms with individual Americans, but still not trust a government that reflected the unpredictable emotions of the mob,
which were often anti-British.[23]

Less clear, but nevertheless operative as an obstacle to rapprochement was the British attitude of superiority which so
often infuriated Americans. 'I have been not a little amused
with an *American* dictionary, quite classical', Lord Lansdowne
wrote. 'What do you think of "squiggling", the definition is as
American as the word – "to get out of a bad bargain by twisting
and turning like an eel" '.[24] When Louis McLane arrived in
London in 1829, Greville observed: "Maclane [sic] is a sensible
man, with very good American manners, which are not re-
fined'.[25] Among the aristocratic upper crust, it was the fashion to
look down upon Americans in general, so the historian is left to
guess whether some of the snide remarks and criticisms of
Americans were meant seriously, or were examples of conformity.[26] This fashion was probably partly a kind of defence
mechanism unconsciously employed to prevent the 'Americanisation' of British institutions. Certainly the British could and
did look at America objectively when they really wished to do
so.[27]

Another of the obstacles to an Anglo-American accord was of a much more ephemeral nature. In 1841 some – how many is not clear – of the nobles and gentlemen in Parliament were stuck with American state bonds no longer paying interest, and so depressed in value as to be unsaleable. The Barings, probably with the advice of their paid consultant, Daniel Webster, tried to induce the Federal Government to assume the state obligations, but without success, and between June 1840 and August 1842 the American states one by one announced their financial embarrassment. Indignation reached a fever pitch. The Rothschilds in 1842 announced that America could not 'borrow a dollar, not a dollar', and one American of high character was barred from the Reform Club because his country did not pay its debts.[28] '. . . nobody loves much Jonathan', wrote Ashburton in 1843, 'more especially since he repudiates his debt . . .'.[29]

If these obstacles existed to an Anglo-American rapprochement in 1841, the economic conditions of the time worked strongly in its favour. Even before they had assumed office, Sir James Graham, who was by this time becoming Peel's closest confidant, wrote:[30]

> . . . with respect to the scale of our Naval and Military Establishments, everything must depend on our relations with France and the United States. . . . If . . . you are able to secure peace and reduce both expenditure and establishments, still the income of the country and the general scheme of taxation require adjustment. Your success in a pacific and economical policy will have rendered you both strong and popular. Then will be the time to risk something for the sake of placing our finances on a solid basis.

'This is the only pledge that Peel has given', Aberdeen wrote, '– he is bound . . . to equalise the revenue and expenditure'.[31] To cut the expenditures of the armed services, it would be necessary for Aberdeen to completely reverse Palmerston's policies, and restore some semblance of friendliness between Britain, and France and the United States.

Reconciliation did not seem outside the range of possibility because Louis Philippe and Francois Guizot in France and President Tyler and Daniel Webster in the United States were regarded as moderate men, even friendly, specially Guizot and Webster. Perhaps the most striking evidence of an Anglo-French reconciliation would be the ratification of an anti-slave-trade treaty, which gave Britain the right to visit ships flying the French flag, and Aberdeen attached much importance to the acceptance of this treaty by the French Assembly. By the end of the year he was much encouraged to find that the French had cut down their estimates for the armed forces, a pacific gesture that encouraged the British to do likewise.

Reaching a rapprochement with the United States in September 1841 was rendered impossible by the McLeod crisis, which had still not been settled, and Aberdeen was called upon to administer a Palmerstonian policy designed to bring America to heel – certainly not a promising beginning for his project, even though Palmerston himself had made some conciliatory speeches on Anglo-American relations in August 1841.[32] In the situation in which they found themselves – with McLeod's possible conviction and execution within the near future – the Government had no choice but to make certain preparations for war. There was already a sizeable force on the Great Lakes stationed there by the previous Government,[33] and Peel proceeded with other measures which he described as 'without bearing the character of menace, or causing needless disquietude and alarm'.[34]

Popular opinion in Britain had been so aroused by the McLeod incident, and the position of the Government had been so firmly established that Aberdeen on coming to office could do little to influence the course of events save to take certain precautions against the rapid development of actual hostilities. Fox was instructed not to leave Washington if McLeod were convicted, and to do so only if he were executed.[35] The new Government also made certain by sending further orders to the North Atlantic Fleet that hostilities would not commence automatically even if Fox left the American capital.[36] These measures having been taken, there was little Aberdeen could do but wait for the decision of the New York court.

Up to this point the diplomacy of the McLeod Crisis had flowed along in an orderly channel with information being conveyed formally to the governments involved through their ministers in the form of instructions and notes. But in Septem-

ber a most disorderly tactic was employed by the President of
the United States, who informed Fox that in the event of
McLeod's conviction, he would not permit Fox to break Anglo-
American relations. He would refuse to give him his passports
until his Home Government had an opportunity to mull over
American explanations of their side of the case.

On learning of this 'perfectly novel' move, 'a measure of hostile and unjustifiable character adopted with pacific intentions',
Peel hastily conferred with Aberdeen, and they decided it would
have been much better if the American President had decided to
grant the passports, and to dispatch an American mission with
explanations when Fox returned home.[37] At the same time the
news was disquieting. The panic of the American President
suggested that he feared McLeod might be convicted and
executed after all.

It is clear from this unusual sequence of events that both
governments had in mind the same tactic in the event of
McLeod's execution – to stall for time in the hope that public
opinion would cool down, and a rational solution could be
found to salve wounded national pride. Fortunately, there was
no need for either Government to employ delaying tactics.
McLeod was acquitted, and the British Government breathed a
sigh of relief to be well rid of him.[38]

Shortly after the good news of McLeod's acquittal reached
Britain, Edward Everett, the new American minister, arrived in
London, and noted in his diary:[39]

> November 20 . . . I drove to the Foreign Office where the Earl
> of Aberdeen had appointed to meet me. He received me with
> great ease and courtesy and placed me at once at my ease. He
> is, I should think, about fifty-three years of age, of middle
> stature – very slightly – lame with one leg. He expressed great
> satisfaction at McLeod's acquittal. . . . On my going away, he
> invited me to dine on Thursday.

Amid the chill of the English November, there was obviously a
new warmth to be found in the Foreign Office, where Palmerston's policy of menace had been replaced by one of friendliness
and rationality.

2

The Diplomacy of Rationality

The dénouement of the McLeod crisis merely lifted the lid from a box filled with problems and points of conflict between Britain and the United States, most of which had been virtually ignored by Palmerston. American feelings in the *Caroline* case had yet to be assuaged, and in November the *Creole* put into the Bahamas, manned by rebellious slaves. These were freed, adding another American complaint against Britain. Both countries agreed that an extradition treaty would help to discourage flights of American criminals across the Canadian border. Britain was most anxious that America carry out her obligation assumed in the Treaty of Ghent to suppress the slave traffic, as this crusade was very popular and politically important in Britain. But the most pressing problems involved the boundaries of Canada, especially the one in Maine the scene of tensions and even minor conflicts.

The negotiation of these problems provides one of the few instances in diplomatic history for which we can compare theoretical tactics with those actually employed. The former was provided by Viscount Palmerston in a three-hour speech on 21 March 1843, after the conclusion of the Webster–Ashburton Treaty, and in criticism of it.[1] So we know how Palmerston would have handled the situation had he remained in office, and can compare the relatively tidy negotiation that he envisaged with the disorderly one that actually took place.

The noble Viscount also furnished the historian with the basic diplomatic philosophy which guided him in his dealings with the United States:[2]

I remember to have seen in the writings of a clever Frenchman the remark 'that nations have no cousins'; by which I apprehend was meant, that nations in their relations with each other are not swayed by those sympathies and affections which guide the mutual intercourse of individuals, but are governed by a due regard to what they may from time to time believe to be their own particular interests. . . . [America] most assuredly will not unduly sacrifice their interests for us, so neither ought we to sacrifice for them. The permanent security of peace is not promoted by such sacrifices; for it is a maxim of international intercourse, that unequal treaties and compacts, however much they may seem to smooth temporary difficulties . . . are not in the long run consistent with reciprocal good feeling, and tend to endanger rather than to consolidate peace.

Palmerston thus did not oppose compromises as such with the United States. He merely opposed concessions that might be interpreted as an abandonment of British interests on the theory that they would be regarded by the Americans as evidence of British weakness.

Although he had not negotiated with America regarding the Maine boundary, Palmerston had during the last several years of his administration secured some evidence to support the British case, viz. a line run in 1839 by two British officers according to the terms of the original peace treaty, which substantiated British claims, and a map discovered in the State Paper Office that had the same effect. He did not, however, regard the latter as more than *ex parte* evidence because no official map had been attached to the original treaty.[3]

Armed with these weapons – how would he have proceeded? He probably would have first proposed the appointment of a joint Anglo-American team to run the boundary according to the terms of the treaty with the proviso that any disputes that arose would be submitted to arbitration. If this plan were rejected by the Americans, he would have proposed to settle the issue through normal diplomatic channels. Unless there were cogent reasons for adopting other means, Palmerston favoured the use of normal diplomatic channels because, if negotiations proved unsuccessful, the general public would not know of their failure.

Whether Palmerston would have agreed to a special mission

is not too clear from his speech. As he saw it, the publicity that surrounded a mission put great pressure upon the government who dispatched it to be successful, and the negotiation was therefore 'apt to turn out in favour of that party which is most pertinacious'. One thing is certain – if Palmerston had chosen a mission, Lord Ashburton would not have been included in it because he had too many ties with the United States. Ashburton as a mediator – yes; as a negotiator – absolutely not. Instead he would have chosen someone, such as Sir Charles Vaughan, or Lord Heytesbury, men who were 'heart and soul in our cause', and who would 'fight the battle of the country'.

Once the Palmerston mission had arrived the chess game (that was the metaphor he applied to it) would have begun. He did not believe that making the first proposition was necessarily a disadvantage, provided that the proposition was a demand for the extreme British claim. This probably would have been countered with the extreme American claim, which would be followed by a – presumably lengthy – examination of the proofs of the respective claims, and then would come the horse-trading. Palmerston believed the Americans wanted to come as far north as possible in order to menace Canada, so he would have not permitted them north of the St. John, and would have retained the Madawaska Settlements, and Rouse's Point; but he would have conceded (grudgingly, no doubt)[4] the right of the Americans to use the St. John, and ceded the land around the Connecticut River, and most of the Narrow Strip.

Palmerston would have instructed his negotiator to take a very firm stand on the suppression of the slave trade question. As he saw it, the United States had given bond to do something effective in this area in the Treaty of Ghent, and in 1824 had been willing to concede the mutual right of search, which was vital to an effective anti-slave trade programme. No treaty should have been concluded without this provision because the failure of the United States to concede the right of search would encourage France and other European nations to withhold it. On the *Creole* incident he would have given the Americans no satisfaction whatsoever.

If Palmerston would have had his way, then, the Webster–Heytesbury Treaty would have been quite different from the one which was actually concluded, and certainly would have been negotiated in a more formal and orderly manner, for neither he, nor Heytesbury, had any connections in the United States. Whether the United States would have accepted such a treaty is an interesting question for those specialising in this phase of American history to mull over.[5]

While Palmerston in his explanation took flight into the hazy realm of pure, theoretical diplomacy, Aberdeen had to operate amid the complex pressures of the circumstances of late 1841. Certainly one of the most important facts of life that Peel's Government faced was the deepening depression, beside which (Lord Brougham observed in 1842 with some exaggeration) those of 1808, 1812, and 1816–17 wore 'an aspect of prosperity'.[6] A reconciliation with the United States seemed important as a means of cutting the military budget and keeping Peel's campaign pledge to balance income and outgo, and also – it became clear in November 1841 – as a possible stimulant to Anglo-American trade, whose stagnation contributed to the depression.

The late summer and early autumn of 1841 found Peel and Lord Ripon deeply involved in a general survey of Britain's trade position, and examining the possibilities offered by the reciprocal trading arrangements with many countries considered by the previous Government. In an undated memorandum from that period, Ripon discussed the figures on British trade during the past several years, and concluded that the decline of British exports during 1839–40 'arose from the exports to the United States', which were due to the general confusion of American monetary affairs.[7]

Peel's own memorandum on the subject in December rated Russia, France and Spain as Britain's poorest customers; Prussia, Denmark and Holland somewhat better; and the Italian States, Turkey, Mecklenburg, Oldenburg and Austria as the best.[8] Many of his observations in this memorandum, however, were centred on the trade with the United States. The American 1841 tariff, he considered to be restrictive, but not prohibitive, and concluded: 'The Trade . . . with America compared with Russia, is of immense value, and the British interests involved are of great magnitude'.[9] As Congress was going to review the American tariff in 1842, Peel agreed with Lord Ashburton (who suggested such an arrangement) that an attempt should be made to promote American trade,[10] but he was unable to excogitate a concession of real value to the United States. Interestingly enough, Peel at this time did not believe a tariff concession to America on wheat would benefit her because she was not producing significant surpluses of grain for export, and Ripon agreed with him.[11] The duty on tobacco could not be reduced because it was a revenue duty. So the Government was up against a blank wall in so far as granting America economic concessions was concerned.

This inability to influence American tariff policy by economic measures may well have played into Aberdeen's hands. In the Cabinet, Peel, Henry Goulburn, Lord Ripon and Sir James Graham all thought in economic terms; Lord Stanley, a very powerful political figure, knew little about economics, but he was a strong, tight-budget man, opposed to war and imperialism. Lord Lyndhurst was born in the United States and his wife had large properties there. Aberdeen, then, could count on the support of these individuals in a conciliatory American policy, but only – this was an important restriction – if his compromises did not involve British honour. If a question of honour were raised, the Duke of Wellington would head the walk-out, and the Prime Minister would fall in right behind him.[12]

Unlike Cabinet officials today, who are summarily cashiered at times without much ceremony or explanation, Lord Aberdeen's position in the Cabinet rested not only on the fact that he was an elder statesman, but on his position in the Conservative Party. He had headed that party in Scotland in 1838, and was second only to the Duke of Buccleugh in influence in an area where the Conservatives needed to promote themselves. These two factors – experience and political importance – virtually gave Aberdeen direction of British foreign policy during these years.

In his letters Lord Aberdeen did not state exactly why he decided to send a mission to the United States once the McLeod crisis was over. The United States evidently expected the negotiations to be carried on in Britain, and Edward Everett had been sent there with this object in mind,[13] but Aberdeen rejected 'normal diplomatic channels' in favour of the method that Palmerston believed was dangerous. '. . . the great necessity for Ashburton's mission', Aberdeen later recalled, 'was in consequence of our having a Minister at Washington, who although not without ability, did nothing. He passed his time in bed, and was so detested by every member of the U.S. Government that they had no communication with him, except as it was absolutely indispensable'.[14] This explains why Fox was not given charge of the negotiation in Washington; it does not, however, clarify why it was not carried on through the friendly Edward Everett in London.

Lord Ashburton, who was one of the few prominent Conservatives outside the Cabinet to be consulted regularly on economic policy,[15] informed Aberdeen as early as 5 September that the new American Government 'is decidedly friendly to us',[16] and suggested that certain tariff concessions be made to the United States. These considerations, as well as his intimate connections in the United States, explain why Ashburton was chosen to head the mission, but they do not establish why the mission tactic was decided upon.

The mission decision certainly was the result of a number of factors. From an economic standpoint, it seemed wise to clear up outstanding Anglo-American problems while the American Government was making its decision on the tariff. The chief political factor seems to have been the accession of Daniel Webster to the State Department.[17] His long continuance in office seemed to be doubtful,[18] and time was therefore of the essence if he were to play the part of an American Guizot. Two diplomatic considerations also figured in the decision. Undoubtedly Aberdeen believed a comprehensive understanding with the United States, which could be accomplished quickly only through the employment of a mission, would improve British relations with France, and encourage the latter's acceptance of the slave trade treaty. Secondly, certain fundamental conditions existed in late 1841 which Aberdeen believed important to the success of this technique.

'At that time,' Aberdeen recalled, 'we were in a state of profound peace in all the world and acted under no compulsion. I gave Ashburton very specific instructions and was quite prepared to quarrel with the United States had it been necessary,'[19] Neither of these statements was wholly accurate. Britain was at war with China at the moment, and Ashburton's instructions were strongly tempered with discretionary powers, but the fun-

damental idea was quite true – the decision to send a mission was a choice freely made by the British Government, as a conciliatory gesture to America, without any pressures whatsoever.

This absence of pressures was deemed so important by Aberdeen – and Ashburton – that the mission was actually underway before Ashburton's official instructions had been finalised. Aberdeen insisted that his negotiator be dispatched before Parliament met, and Ashburton pointed out the wisdom of informing the American Government of the coming mission immediately so as to avoid the possibility of having it linked with the annual message of the President.[20] Thus the Ashburton mission was presented to the world as a friendly act of the British Government[21] made freely and entirely of its own volition.

What vital British interests were involved in the negotiation? Solving the outstanding issues with the United States would be convenient, even highly important to his general foreign policy, but Aberdeen regarded none of them as vital. Many times he referred to the disputed area of Maine as 'valueless'. The *Caroline* involved American, rather than British honour. Inducing the United States to suppress the slave trade was a worthy humanitarian objective, and important from the standpoint of domestic politics, but no British interest was involved in it.[22] Signing an extradition treaty was a convenience, but little more. The *Creole* was important to the Cotton Kingdom, that was all. So the issues involved were broadly negotiable. British security would not be affected by compromises on any or all of them.

Lord Aberdeen was therefore interested primarily in compromises that would appear conciliatory to the Americans, yet would not raise the hackles of patriotic members of Parliament. In Maine he would have preferred the King of the Netherlands Award[23] (improved, if possible, by some additional territory in the Quebec area) because such a compromise could be easily defended in Parliament, and he had little interest in the Madawaska Settlements, so important to the Temiscouta–Madawaska – Fredericton road, because Palmerston had offered to give them up in 1835.[24] Some sort of explanation could be made regarding the *Caroline* because most members of Parliament – and Wellington[25] – believed that Palmerston had been wrong in ignoring American notes on this subject. The extradition treaty would cause no difficulties, and almost any agreement from

the United States on the slave trade issue could be presented to
Parliament as 'progress'. Regarding the *Creole*, Aberdeen
wished that something could be done, but he could think of no
definite solution, and therefore left Ashburton to smooth the
matter over as best he could.

Lord Ashburton was the first to admit that he was a business
man, and not a diplomat. As such, he had even less interest in
the details of the negotiation than did Aberdeen. What was
important to him was that the whole mass of problems should
be compromised in a give-and-take manner so that an improved
political climate might be expected to promote quickening
commercial relations between the two countries; but any implication that Lord Ashburton had personal financial reasons
for desiring such a settlement would be unjust. As a retired
tycoon, he had little interest in further capital accumulations,
and he was evidently motivated by the strong, friendly, paternal
interest in promoting the American economy that had been
characteristic of his family.[26] His great wealth, his social prestige, and leading position in the Conservative Party gave Ashburton a degree of independence rarely enjoyed by a negotiator,
and, further, he had no ambitions to remain, much less rise, in
the diplomatic service.

There can be little question but that Aberdeen talked informally with Ashburton before he ever left England, and that
in these conversations he was much 'less guarded' than if
Ashburton had been a regular diplomatist. At any rate, Ashburton left England believing that Aberdeen, above all, wanted
a treaty. He had chosen well. Ashburton was just the man to
give him one.

The image of an international negotiation whereat the prin-
cipals exchange formal notes, carefully drawn up and sent
through proper channels, while engaging at other times in
guarded conversations, does not apply to the Webster–
Ashburton negotiations, which were among the most disorderly
on record. The informality is clearly evident in Ashburton's
private letters, and, if the whole truth were known, the goings-
on were probably even less decorous.[27]

It would probably be nearer the truth to call the negotiations
involving the minor problems the Webster–Ashburton vs. Tyler

negotiation, for the President was deeply interested in the peculiar institution, and many of the minor problems in one way or another concerned slavery. Evidence indicates that Webster cooperated with Ashburton to tone down the American President in this area.

Lord Aberdeen had been very proud of a paper he had drawn up to reconcile the Americans to the 'right of visit', which had been transmitted to the American Government before Ashburton ever left England.[28] Actually the explanation accomplished nothing, for American feelings and honour were involved in the impressment issue, and the so-called right of visit impinged upon it. No doubt to gratify Aberdeen, Ashburton assured him that this paper had done great good in presenting the issue to the Americans, but in his next letter the negotiator suggested Britain should renounce her right of impressment in any war in which America was neutral.[29] This Aberdeen was unable to concede, largely because of the British concept of indelibility of nationality, but he did observe: 'With respect to the practice of impressment itself, I entirely agree with you that it will never be renewed. . . . Practically I think the U. States have nothing to fear from this impressment in the future'.[30]

Undoubtedly Ashburton advised Webster of this statement, and Webster, in turn, informed Tyler of it, which was reassuring to the United States, but it was not a political triumph for the Americans because the statement was informal and private. Ashburton probably hoped, however, that it might improve the prospects for an effective anti-slave-trade treaty, which would include the right of visit.

The treaty negotiated with Tyler through Webster's agency fell far short of Ashburton's hopes. Its history was recounted briefly in a private letter:[31]

I had hoped to send you by this opportunity our African Cruising Convention. It has caused much discussion & some changes by the President, and at the last moment Webster hands me the rough draft as it comes from the President. I enclose it as it now stands, as it is not in a fit state to send it to you officially. . . . The President struck out an important passage. . . . The President's motive in striking out this pas-

A.P.B.D.—2

sage . . . was that he thought it might be interpreted into an engagement to agree to a right of search should the plan of a joint cruising convention fail. It was this leaning which made me on the other hand regret the loss of this point of the Convention.

Evidently Webster had agreed to this back-door introduction of the right of visit, only to have the President see through and frustrate the scheme.

Ashburton and Webster also collaborated closely in endeavouring to soothe the President's ruffled feelings over the *Creole* incident.[32] The former reported the negotiation to Aberdeen as follows:[33]

> My great plague was the Creole, and you will see how I have at last disposed of it. At least a dozen various attempts at explanation were tried and there came only yesterday a garrulous, foolish letter from the President to Webster which made me fear we might at last stick fast, and if it were not that the general object of the Mission is popular in the Country, I think this would have been the case. My settlement on this point was at last sulkily received by him. How it may be considered by you remains to be seen. I have only to beg you will recollect that it was a case attended with no inconsiderable difficulties. The Secretary of State behaved well & liberally throughout. . . .

As Ashburton knew that British law prohibited the return of slaves who reached British territory,[34] he and Webster evidently racked their brains for a formula that seemed to promise something, but was actually no more than an honour-saving device. The British pledge of no 'officious interference' with American ships taking refuge in her ports is a splendid example of burying an insoluble problem under a mass of acceptable verbiage.[35]

President Tyler seems to have been less demanding on the subject of the *Caroline*, concerning which Aberdeen asked Ashburton to exchange a note with Webster 'in conformity with the tenor of your Instructions' that would formally end the affair.[36] Aberdeen used the word 'tenor' because he knew that, if Ashburton adhered to the 'letter' of his instructions, the problem would remain unsolved.[37] Ashburton, therefore, had to

apologise without actually apologising, certainly a major challenge to a diplomatic parvenu, but in the endeavour he obviously
had the help of Webster. This interesting negotiation was
alluded to in two letters.[38]

> You will see what I have done about the Caroline. My
> letter is more wordy than it need be, but for the audience for
> which it was intended. I hope you will not think it too apolo-
> getic, the words in this part were well-weighed and I have not
> said more than I thought was honourably due. The President
> to whom this letter was confidentially communicated before
> it was sent is satisfied, and this is important because he is
> sore and testy about the Creole....
> There was a paragraph in my Caroline letter stating why
> there could be no question of any compensation to the owner
> of the vessel. This was inserted when my letter was finally
> written to please the President. He afterwards liked the letter
> better without it, as I always did, and you will see that the
> paragraph has been altogether expunged.

This retrospective apology was so brilliantly worded that there
still exists today some question as to whether it was, indeed, an
apology.[39]

The negotiation of the extradition treaty seems to have been
carried out in a perfectly orderly manner. The only diplomatic
manoeuvre of interest in connection with it was the endeavour
of President Tyler to include mutiny on the high seas as an
extraditable crime in the hope of providing for the return of
slaves such as those involved in the *Creole* affair. Aberdeen
considered the matter at length, but finally concluded that, if
the treaty contained such a provision, it would not pass through
Parliament.[40]

If the collaboration between Webster and Ashburton is
strongly evident in the solutions – or, more accurately, circum-
ventions – of the minor problems, it appears to have been even
closer in dealing with the principal object of the mission – the
Maine boundary. Among the Aberdeen papers are found a
series of letters of wholly unexpected identity – Henry Wheaton
to Webster, Lewis Cass to Webster, and James A. Hamilton to
President Tyler.[41] These letters, which reported interviews with

Louis Philippe and other prominent French statesmen, all had the same theme – that France stood solidly with the United States, and would even back her if war with Britain resulted from their current controversies. How did Aberdeen come by these private communications to high-ranking American officials? Webster gave them to Ashburton, who sent them to Aberdeen – this is clear enough from the correspondence, but why did they do so? The answer seems to be that they were applying pressure on Aberdeen to broaden Ashburton's freedom of action, and at the same time providing Aberdeen with arguments favouring compromise for use in the Cabinet.

As it turned out, the tactic was probably necessary. On the Maine boundary issue, Ashburton was originally instructed to improve the Netherlands Award, if possible, and to revert to it if improvement proved unattainable, but before the negotiation actually got under way, Wellington and Stanley demanded that Britain secure territory south of the St. John River.[42] The former's views, which favoured Britain's extreme claims, forced Aberdeen to consult four military experts to ascertain just what configuration constituted a defensible frontier in the north-east.[43]

Had these military experts agreed upon a line, Aberdeen would probably have had to accept their advice, and the negotiation would conceivably have failed, but fortunately there was no unanimity among them. The War Office particularly sought the highlands near Quebec; some of the experts desired the Madawaska area in order to protect the Temiscouata–Madawaska–Fredericton road;[44] but one of them, Sir James Kempt, believed there was no 'good military boundary' in the area. This lack of unanimity strengthened Aberdeen's ability to manoeuvre, but the objections of his colleagues forced the Foreign Secretary to lay stronger stress on improving the Netherlands Award in his instructions.

Upon receipt of his new instructions, Ashburton replied bluntly: 'If you had read to me your present instructions before I left London, I should have ventured under such circumstances to give an opinion that it was inexpedient to send this mission,' and under the same cover he sent Aberdeen Cass's letter to Webster.[45] Shortly thereafter he also sent Aberdeen the Hamilton letter.[46] The historian today, like Aberdeen at the time,[47] finds it difficult to understand Ashburton's extraordinarily negative reaction to his new instructions, which can be explained best if we assume that Aberdeen had privately assured him he would have virtually a free hand in arriving at a settlement, and that the formal instructions inhibited his freedom of movement.

Webster – and Ashburton no doubt was aware of it – decided to take up the Maine boundary indirectly with Aberdeen himself. This extraordinary negotiative tactic was accomplished by writing a letter to Edward Everett, who sent it to Aberdeen.[48] Webster offered to give Britain the Madawaska Settlements on both sides of the St. John, if Britain would cede the Americans the right to use the St. John river, and give up some purely British territory near Rouse's Point along the 45th parallel called the 'Narrow Strip'. Ashburton continued throughout the negotiation to fight for this settlement, even though he realized Aberdeen wanted not the Madawaska Settlements (which Palmerston had previously been ready to relinquish), but the territory around Quebec. Thus, whatever might be written in his instructions. Ashburton acted like a free agent in settling this important and troublesome boundary question.

These instructions were continually modified by Aberdeen in his private letters to Ashburton until he wrote on 2 July: ' . . . it is too late now to enter into elaborate argument, for any useful purpose. The matter will be settled practically by you, while we are engaged in discussion here'.[49] Two factors no doubt influenced Aberdeen in arriving at this attitude. First, evidence seemed available that Webster was trying his best to secure a settlement which would be politically defensible in both countries; and, second, the American letters and probably other information of the same type convinced Aberdeen that success in America was absolutely vital to the success of his French policy. 'A settlement of our differences with the United States'. Aberdeen wrote, 'will greatly improve our relations with France. . . . I believe that Guizot cordially wishes our success, for it will be the means of extinguishing the warlike propensities of our enemies throughout France, & will give the Govt. the power to pursue a pacific & friendly policy'.[50]

The tactics of Ashburton and Webster thus effectively brought Aberdeen around to extreme flexibility, but their task was only half accomplished, for there remained the Governors

of Maine and Massachusetts to be convinced of the wisdom of
the contemplated compromise which brought Britain south of
the St. John. The details of their collaboration on this project
are still not wholly clear despite the accounts given by Ashburton here and there in his private letters to Aberdeen.

One of these letters indicates that Ashburton, shortly after
his arrival in America, was contacted by a not-otherwise-
identified 'informant', who requested funds from the British
exchequer to send the American historian, Jared Sparks,
to visit the two American governors, whom he would show a
certain piece of evidence bearing on the boundary question.[51]
Then Webster himself went to Maine to discuss the validity of
the British claims. The story of the discovery of the famous
Red Line map is given elsewhere,[52] and Ashburton claimed in
his private letters that he was not permitted to see the two maps
involved until after he had agreed to sign the final treaty. All
that he could say on the subject in June was: 'I have some
reason to suspect that Webster has discovered some evidence
known at present to nobody, but favourable to our claim, and
that he is using it with the commissioners.'[53]

How much Ashburton learned about the two maps from Webster and his 'informant' is uncertain, but mere logic would lead
us to assume that he knew all about the maps from Webster, and
that they both depended on them to force through the compromise that had been sent by Webster via Everett to Aberdeen.
Otherwise it is difficult to explain why Ashburton believed until
late June that he could secure the Madawaska Settlements. Still
the shades of deep mystery hang over the whole transaction. An
explanation of the affair may have been included in the postscript of Ashburton's private letter of 14 June, which unfortunately is missing, for that postscript drew the following
comment from Aberdeen:[54]

> In order to ensure success, you need not be afraid of em-
> ploying the same means to a greater extent in any quarter
> where it may be necessary. In what you have done, you have
> been perfectly right; and indeed I look upon the proposal
> made to you from such a quarter, as the most certain indica-
> tion we could receive of a determination to bring the negotia-
> tion to a happy issue. In any further transaction of the same

kind, I have only to desire that it may be made the means of leading to success, as the condition of having recourse to it. If you can command success, you need not hesitate.

Whether this referred to the money given to Sparks for his mission, or to the bribery of some high American official, is wholly uncertain, but it is interesting to note that the high-minded Aberdeen did not shrink from the use of bribery in his diplomacy, providing – here a note of Scottish thriftiness – that it worked. It might be mentioned in passing that Aberdeen at this time had an obviously important Brazilian councillor of state on his payroll.[55]

As late as 14 June Ashburton wrote confidently: 'My present idea is to insist on the Madawaska Settlements and all the right bank of the St. John from the Fish River. . .,'[56] but two weeks later all this was changed. 'I shall probably give up after a little fight my cherished Madawaska settlements', he wrote.[57] The reasons assigned for his change of plan were the opposition of the Maine people to the proposed compromise, and the necessity of securing a treaty which would pass the Senate.

With the arrival of the Maine commissioners, headed by the obstinate Judge William P. Preble, the negotiation became Webster–Ashburton vs. the Maine commissioners, whom the former pair had expected to bowl over with their cartographic evidence. When Webster mentioned the proposed compromise to Prebel, instead of being bowled over, Prebel announced his group would immediately return to Maine if Britain insisted on coming south of the St. John, and it was Webster who beat a hasty retreat northward.[58] '. . . when it came to the point', Ashburton wrote, 'he joined the Maine people in wondering that we should ever have thought of coming south of the St. John and in pronouncing it impossible'.[59] Webster's change of front doomed the compromise he had worked out with Ashburton, and, in effect, hoisted Old Glory over the Madawaska Settlements.

The final compromise was worked out by exchanges – some of them none too pleasant – between Ashburton and Prebel, some made directly, some through Webster, who seems to have been the author of the plan that was finally accepted.[60] Ashburton was able to 'improve' the Netherlands Award in the

Quebec area, but he ceded in exchange the Madawaska Settlements, a slice of territory northwest of the St. John, the Narrow Strip, and some land at the head of the Connecticut River. Palmerston later charged that Ashburton had been out-manoeuvred, and had squandered his 'equivalents', which implied that Webster had made a dupe of Ashburton. But, despite momentary annoyance at having been left in the lurch,[61] the British negotiator concluded that Webster had 'behaved well & liberally throughout'.[62]

It had been an unusual and disorderly negotiation, so much so that back in England Lord Aberdeen had virtually lost all control of it my early summer, and in July he was quite in the dark regarding what Ashburton might do about the *Caroline*, the *Creole*, and the Maine Boundary itself. But from his point of view, the details were not too important. 'The good temper in which you left them all,' Aberdeen wrote Ashburton, 'and the prospect of a continued peace, with, I trust, improved friendly relations, far outweigh in my mind the value of any additional extent of Pine Swamp'.[63]

All of the British concessions in the final treaty could be amply justified both to Parliament and the country if – and this was most important – the treaty opened a new era of friendly Anglo-American relations. Aberdeen was keenly aware of this, and at this moment seemed confident that the larger goal of the negotiation had been reached. All too soon his confidence was to begin to weaken, and it continued to deteriorate until the great crisis of 1845.

3
The Crisis of Confidence

Some American historians have interpreted the Webster–Ashburton treaty as a considerable British diplomatic victory,[1] and have gone on to score Lord Aberdeen for not proceeding immediately to a solution of the troublesome Oregon question.[2] The interpretation is not accurate, nor is the criticism deserved. Whatever one might conclude today regarding the terms of that treaty, in 1842 the British certainly did not regard it as a triumph; furthermore, it is quite clear that Lord Aberdeen took up Oregon immediately after the Webster–Ashburton Treaty had been concluded.

Regarding the reception of that treaty in Britain, Ashburton himself admitted that 'nobody viewed it very thankfully',[3] and Aberdeen himself would have preferred the Netherlands Award to the boundary agreed upon.[4] The Peel Government's estimate of Ashburton's success is perhaps clarified by the mark of approval extended to him – a viscountcy, and the Bath, both of which he (probably hoping for an earldom) refused.[5] Peel's explanation for not offering an earldom, which would have stamped official approval on Ashburton's work, was rather vague.[6] Aberdeen would probably have preferred the offer of the earldom,[7] not because of his enthusiasm for the treaty, but because Peel's failure to award it indicated governmental uncertainty regarding the treaty's value.

In the autumn of 1842 Aberdeen was keenly aware that his rational diplomacy was coming under fire. Late in September he wrote:[8]

The Treaty was at first either well, or silently received, but under the inspiration of Palmerston the *Chronicle* has opened a Series of attacks, and the *Globe* has quite changed the language it had first employed. Other papers have joined in taking the same views, and we must expect a fierce hostility.

A.P.B.D.—2*

But I am well satisfied, and am not at all afraid. The more the
subject shall be discussed, the more favourable I think the
result will be.

Much depended upon whether the United States regarded the
treaty as a foundation for Anglo-American friendship, or as a
British capitulation which encouraged further demands.

The President's Annual Message was regarded by British
statesmen at the time as a sort of weathervane in Anglo-
American relations, which indicated if winds were blowing from
the chilly north, or from the smiling south. Tyler's message of
2 December, judged by the less polished standard of present day
diplomacy, seems mild, even friendly, but in 1842 it promoted
renewed Anglo-American controversies.

Tyler's statement that Article 8 of the cruising convention
removed all pretence 'for interference with our commerce for
any purpose whatever by a foreign Government' brought a
heated response from Ashburton: 'The speech imprudently
insinuated that the cruising article as founded on some abandonment, at least implied, of our right [of visit]'.[9] Aberdeen
wrote Croker: 'The manner in which he treated the subject of
the Right of Search was really scandalous'.[10] Sir Robert Peel,
when Parliament opened, felt called upon to deny that Britain
had abandoned her right of search under the treaty. Peel's statement, in turn, brought on a debate in the American Senate,
where some members spoke recklessly of war if the British continued to visit American ships.[11] So the imperfectly formed scab
over this running sore quickly fell away six months after
Ashburton had returned to Britain.

The President's remarks on Oregon placed that controversy
on the centre of the empty stage. Admitting that taking up that
issue in 1842 might have caused 'protracted discussions' and
caused the failure of 'more pressing matters', Tyler warned
Britain: 'Although the difficulty . . . may not for several years
to come involve the peace of the two countries, yet I shall not
delay to urge on Great Britain the importance of its early settlement'. Regarding this statement, Aberdeen wrote indignantly:
'When he talked of pressing us to enter into negotiations, he
had in his pocket a most friendly overture from us, which he
had already answered favourably'.[12]

These references in Tyler's speech hardly increased British confidence in the pacific intentions of the American Government, but even more disturbing was the reintroduction into the Senate on 30 December of a measure for the occupation and settlement of the Oregon territory, and the introduction of American law into that area.[13] This attracted little attention at first, but when the Senate actually passed the Oregon measure, British indignation mounted. *The Times* believed that the Maine boundary compromise had emboldened the Americans to adopt a strong position in Oregon, and it warned that American attempts to establish themselves in Oregon would 'infallibly bring about a collision with a foreign power'.[14]

Still another source of heat evaporating whatever goodwill the Webster–Ashburton Treaty had created was the failure of Congress to pass a measure to take over and pay defaulted state financial obligations. The same issue of *The Times* which announced the disheartening failure of this measure reported the *New York Herald's* explanation of its origins: 'It was set on foot by a set of wild stock-jobbers, merely to raise the price of certain stocks, and to enable them to get out of a bad scrape'.[15] To have their hopes dashed was bad enough, but to learn from an American source that their hopes had been based on a shady financial manipulation filled to the brim the cup of gall drunk by the British investors, some of whom were sitting in Parliament. This discomfited group was joined in their misery by British exporters, whose sales in America had fallen off by 50% in 1842, and who faced an American tariff of that year, which had raised duties from 20% to 30%.[16] If Peel had hoped diplomatic concessions would secure economic favours for Britain, he was bitterly disappointed.

The events evidently helped confirm Palmerston in his opinion that the conciliatory approach of Lord Aberdeen had been a monumental error.[17] This conclusion did not arise from mere party politics,[18] but from a sincere difference of opinion with Aberdeen regarding how best to deal with a vigorous and even dangerous republic. In his three-hour attack on the Webster–Ashburton Treaty on 21 March, Palmerston singled out the Maine boundary and the cruising convention for particular criticism; but the burden of his argument was that conciliatory approach was worse than ineffective, as witnessed by the trenchant attitude adopted by the Americans on Oregon. 'A fresh proof of how true it is', he observed, 'that undue concessions, instead of securing peace, only increase the appetite for aggression'.[19]

Palmerston was answered by the Prime Minister, who was somewhat miffed by the length of his speech, and chided him for failure to solve the boundary and other questions while he was in office. He also included a fairly lengthy discussion of the various maps of the Maine territory which had been discovered.[20] Peel's most effective (if debatable) rejoinder was that the House favoured the treaty, and for this reason Palmerston did not have the courage to actually move its rejection. The Prime Minister spoke well on this occasion, but Palmerston's thesis – that concessions to America merely encouraged further demands – seems to have made some impression – even on Lord Aberdeen himself.

By far the most important issue which Ashburton had been unable to settle involved the Oregon territory, a large area north and west of the Columbia River which was jointly occupied by Britain and America under a treaty of 1818. A recent writer on the subject traced Ashburton's failure to the reactionary instructions provided for him by the Foreign Office, instructions which bound him to a Columbia River boundary that was wholly unacceptable to the Americans.[21] This argument overlooks the fact that Ashburton's instructions in Maine supposedly bound him to the rejected Netherlands Award, yet the northeastern boundary dispute was, despite his instructions, satisfactorily settled.

Ashburton's private letters provide various explanations and observations regarding the Oregon question. One stressed that he knew he could not solve it within the limits of his instructions;[22] in some others, he suspected that Webster actually was keeping the matter open because he wished to come himself to England to discuss it.[23] There was also the human factor involved – the two negotiators were worn down by the efforts to lay the other questions to rest, and simply did not have the heart to tackle another involved and politically tricky question.[24] But perhaps the chief reason why Ashburton did not enter into a give-and-take on the Oregon question was that his experiences in the Maine negotiation proved that Webster, despite his good intentions, simply could not negotiate and stand by a compromise, and that he might, as in the Maine negotiation, have been left in the lurch after making concessions to the American demands.

Lord Aberdeen's hope for a quick solution of all the outstanding problems between Britain and the United States had rested upon his confidence in three Americans – Edward Everett, Daniel Webster, and President Tyler, who seemed ready, even anxious, to find rational solutions to those issues. But, as Ashburton's private letters of 1842 began to come in, the last two took on the character of honourable, but very weak men, readily susceptible to the multitude of pressures placed upon them by the 'anarchic' system of American Government, men who were utterly incapable of carrying out their good intentions. Only Edward Everett seemed to possess the firmness of personality that was necessary to negotiate rational compromises.[25] This being so, far from attempting to keep the Oregon question open, Aberdeen instructed Henry S. Fox in Washington to ask the American Government to send instructions on the Oregon question to Everett.[26] Aberdeen's request was sent three weeks after Ashburton returned to England, and was communicated to the American Government by Fox in November 1842.

These circumstances explain why Aberdeen was indignant at Tyler's charge that Britain was dragging her feet on the Oregon question. This prevarication, and Ashburton's recent experiences in the 1842 negotiations, created a genuine crisis of confidence in the American Government, a crisis that was increased by the hostile activities of the American Congress in 1843.

Ashburton's letters eloquently reveal his own collapsed confidence in the Tyler administration, and his references to its weakness are abundant, but in so far as the Oregon story is concerned, his advice given on 1 January 1843 is of vital importance:[27]

Everett has communicated some suggestions on this point which, if they satisfy you, might I think be made to work. These give up the mouth of the Columbia, & run a line from below Vancouver to the Straits of Juan de Fuca. If anybody had power to negotiate to this effect the settlement might be worth the sacrifice we might make; but if we are not careful we run a risk, in the present state of parties, of making the concession without obtaining our Treaty. I have a bad opinion of the good faith of the party likely to be in power.

This seems to suggest the solution that was arrived at three years later, but it seemed unattainable at that moment. 'The state of the government', Ashburton explained, 'always more or less anarchical, is at the present moment eminently so, and my notion of policy towards them is to leave them as much as possible to their abundant initiative . . . without giving them the useful diversion of a foreign quarrel'.[28]

This advice from an individual who liked and understood Americans better than any contemporary British statesman no doubt conditioned Aberdeen's mind to caution in dealing with them. Another limiting factor was the changed attitude of the Prime Minister, who in 1841 had looked with favour upon some sort of commercial agreement with the United States. When Everett sent Peel one of Webster's private letters suggesting a commercial treaty, he passed it on to Lord Ripon with the comment:[29]

My advice to Everett was to say nothing whatever about negotiations. I expressed a strong opinion that no good object could be obtained by entering into one – unless we are almost assured beforehand that it would be practically successful in its Result. The power of the U.S. Senate to reject a Commercial Treaty, and the miserable motives of personal resentment and party interest by which men in the United States are influenced occasionally in deciding the gravest Questions of public Concern make Caution and Reserve doubly necessary.

The President, the Secretary of State, the Senate, the state governments – the powers and interactions of these individuals and bodies, often motivated by narrow political interest, presented the British statesmen with a pattern of government so complex that in 1843 they threw up their hands in despair. Dealing with the United States required a form of diplomacy quite different from that of the centralised, monarchical government. While Britain's domestic politics were in some respects quite as complex as those of America (which meant that the British leaders were able to comprehend the pressures on a Tyler or a Webster), the conduct of foreign affairs in Britain, compared with the American system, was comparatively simple. British statesmen were also sometimes influenced by 'miserable motives of personal resentment' in domestic politics, but this rarely spilled over into the conduct of foreign policy.

Despite Peel's coolness, and Ashburton's call for caution, Aberdeen by no means shelved the Oregon issue in 1843. Given to understand by Everett and Webster that the United States contemplated a special mission to deal with the question, the Foreign Secretary waited patiently for developments until August, when he instructed Fox to query the new American Secretary of State, Abel P. Upshur, about Oregon, and to inform the American President that, if he preferred, the matter might be taken up in Washington rather than London.[30] Nothing came of this initiative beyond a vague statement that the United States would probably prefer to negotiate in Washington. This did not prevent Tyler, however, from implying once again in his message that Britain was delaying the settlement.

Meanwhile Aberdeen was involved in the truly Herculean effort of establishing a cordial relationship with France.[31] The Spanish Marriages question had arisen in February 1842, to start the year off badly, and in November Anglo-French relations were so uneasy that the friendly Guizot found it expedient to withdraw the projected Anglo-French treaty for the suppression of the slave trade, a severe setback which Ashburton seems to have blamed partly on the United States.[32] Then in March 1843 came the announcement of a French protectorate over Tahiti. The Tahiti situation was to bring Britain and France to the brink of war in 1844, while the Spanish Marriages question was to blossom into a fullblown diplomatic crisis in 1846, but in 1843 Aberdeen and Guizot persevered, and actually made some progress toward their specific goal. Aberdeen in July proposed that Britain and France 'act together' in Spanish affairs, a proposal which was well-received, and in September Queen Victoria and the Prince Consort paid a visit to France. It was at this time that Aberdeen coined the term *entente cordiale* to describe the relationship with France he was seeking to establish, a term that attracted attention in both countries. But national postures were most difficult to change, for the diplomatic corps of both countries had so long regarded each other as rivals, rather than friends, that the spirit of cordiality was manifested only on the highest echelons of both governments. To bury the past, and to establish new habits of cooperation, it was necessary for the two countries to 'act together' as much as possible in world affairs.

This situation helps to explain Aberdeen's seemingly Janus-faced American policy of early 1844, which found him adopting a hostile line toward the United States in Texas, and a conciliatory one in Oregon. The former has been discussed in some detail elsewhere.[33] Aberdeen's proposed 'diplomatic act', which would have given an Anglo-French guarantee to Texas, was designed to undermine the traditional Franco-American friendship, and to cement the Anglo-French entente by having the countries act together. That the Prime Minister was not averse to a diplomatic adventure of this nature is evident from his statement, made in May 1844: 'I hope you are preparing the ground work for the defiance of the United States in respect to Texian annexation'.[34] The terms under which the Diplomatic Act would be carried out – the granting of Texan independence by Mexico, and a Texan guarantee that she would remain independent – were obviously visionary, and there is no reason to believe that Aberdeen expected a result other than that which actually took place – a series of futile negotiations which lasted until July 1844. In so far as Aberdeen's French policy was concerned, the incident was not wholly unproductive of good, for France's very willingness to even entertain the notion of such a policy was proof of her new attachment to Britain.

Meanwhile, during these very months when the Diplomatic Act was being concocted – October 1843–July 1844 – Lord Aberdeen was endeavouring to make progress in Oregon. Less than a week after he had received Fox's despatch stating that America probably preferred to negotiate the issue in Washington, Aberdeen offered Richard Pakenham the post in the Capitol for the specific purpose of solving the Oregon problem.[35] Then he turned to Edward Everett for advice. While noting that his Government had not sanctioned such a compromise, Everett suggested that they establish the boundary at the 49th Parallel, leaving Vancouver's Island in British hands.[36] Although Aberdeen did not commit himself to such a settlement officially, he obviously left Everett with the impression that he would not oppose it, and this information must – one would expect, at least – have been conveyed to Washington.[37] If so, the issues that continued in dispute between the two nations in Oregon might be described as minuscule, and the Oregon controversy was political and diplomatic, rather than territorial.

In so far as Aberdeen's position was concerned, it seems clear that Maine and its aftermath had severely weakened him in the Cabinet, for the Prime Minister was now distrustful of the United States, even disillusioned with her. Thus, Aberdeen sent Pakenham off to America with no better offer than the old Columbia River boundary, which was obviously unacceptable, and he had to proceed toward the 49th parallel compromise with great caution. This is abundantly clear from his private letter of 4 March 1844 to Pakenham:[38]

> ... you will endeavour without committing yourself or your Govt. to draw from the American Negotiator a proposal to make the 49th degree of latitude the boundary with the proviso that all ports South of that parallel to the Columbia inclusive shall be free ports to Grt. Britain. The navigation of the River Columbia should be common to both; and care should be taken that the 49th degree of latitude, as a boundary, is to extend only to the Sea; and not to apply to Vancouver's Island. Without actually committing us, I think you might give them reason to hope that such a proposal would be favourably considered. .... If you thought that such a settlement should be practicable, you might state this to me in a publick despatch, as your opinion, even if it had not actually been proposed to you by the American Govt. In this case I might bring the matter before the Cabinet and be enabled to furnish you with contingent Instructions without delay. This is rather a nice & delicate matter to manage; but I explained my views to you respecting it before your departure from England, and I trust entirely to your judgment & discretion with which you will carry them into effect in case of necessity.

The reasons for recommending these 'nice & delicate' tactics would seem to have been – first, a fear (voiced by Ashburton himself) that Britain might surrender all of her concessions without securing a treaty unless the offer were 'drawn from' the American negotiator, and second, Aberdeen's unwillingness or inability unaided to carry through the Cabinet another concession to the United States.

Richard Pakenham, although he was part of the Establishment, and was highly regarded by Aberdeen, was unable to manage the negotiation as sketched out by Aberdeen. His difficulties arose partly because, as a professional diplomat, he attached more weight to his formal instructions than to Aberdeen's suggestions made in private, and partly because he for many months could not find a Secretary of State with whom to discuss the issue at length, let alone from whom he could 'draw forth' the proposition outlined by Aberdeen. Secretary Upshur agreed to take up the problem not long after Pakenham's arrival, but he was killed a few days later, and John C. Calhoun, who professed ignorance of the details of the dispute, succeeded him. Finally in late August 1844, Calhoun agreed to receive a British offer, and Pakenham submitted one in line with his formal instructions – the Columbia River boundary, and a free port for the United States either on the mainland, or Vancouver's Island. Instead of submitting a counterproposal – hopefully the 49th parallel with modifications – Calhoun merely restated American claims to the region, and refused, even when Pakenham specifically requested it, to submit his ideas for a compromise so long as Britain maintained she had equal rights to the territory. So the negotiations of late summer, 1844, ended in complete failure.

That the United States had delayed until August before discussing the Oregon issue might well have seemed suspicious to the British, for American settlers poured into the territory during 1843–44,[39] and the American Government began to make threatening gestures in the Great Lakes area.[40] And all this came at a time when the *Entente Cordiale* seemed threatened with total extinction. First came a French quarrel with Morocco, which Aberdeen and Guizot, acting together, managed at length to resolve, then in late July 1844 the news of the Tahiti affair broke in England.

National honour and religious considerations transformed this minor incident into almost a *casus belli*. After agreeing to respect the sovereignty of the queen of Tahiti and the rights of

British missionaries on the island, France – or, more specifically, a misguided admiral – announced the annexation of Tahiti in November 1843, deposed the queen, and mistreated the British consul, a former missionary who arrived in Britain with his tale of woe late in July. During the following month Aberdeen and Guizot worked feverishly to find some formula which would satisfy outraged British honour. How deeply the war fever had infected the British public is evident in one of Peel's letters of the time: [41]

> I would most earnestly advise that we should without delay consider the state of our Naval preparation as compared with that of France. Matters are in that state that the interval of 24 hours – some act of violence for which the French Ministry is not strong enough to make reparation or disavow – may not only dissipate the shadow of the *entente cordiale*, but change our relations from Peace to War. Let us be prepared for war. ... The first Naval Engagement may determine the question whether we are to contend at Sea with France single-handed, or whether the United States will declare in favour of France against us. It may also materially influence the decisions of the Northern Powers of Europe.

Although Peel insisted that warlike preparations would actually promote peace, Aberdeen feared that they would simply fuel the war psychology.

Deserted by the Prime Minister on whose pacific intentions he had to chiefly rely, bombarded by the warlike views of other members of the Cabinet, standing alone in the thunderstorm of morbid excitement stimulated by the irresponsible press, Lord Aberdeen at this juncture rose to the gigantic stature in defence of peace he was not to attain again until the bleak winter of 1853–4, when he single-handedly and futilely tried to prevent the Crimean War. He and Guizot resolved to resign together rather than to take steps which would render war inevitable, and amid a torrent of public criticism in both countries, they worked out a solution of the Tahiti affair. [42] This was the calibre, the character, the mettle of the man who has been accused of delaying the Oregon settlement because of fear of Palmerston's partisan attacks.

Once a *modus vivendi* had been achieved in Tahiti, Aberdeen sought to apply massive infusions of mortar into the crumbled wall of the *entente*. King Louis Philippe returned the Queen's visit in October, which gave public confirmation to the Anglo-French understanding, but Aberdeen sensed a new anti-French spirit in the Cabinet that tended to belie it. What could be done?

It was in this atmosphere of anxiety to prove to the Cabinet that all was well again that Aberdeen – rather reluctantly – yielded to various pressures and decided to act with France in the La Plata region. The details of this interesting intervention, the purpose of which was to clarify the political situation in Uruguay, have been given elsewhere.[43] Suffice it to say that Aberdeen hoped to arrive at a quick *sub rosa* understanding with Manuel Rosas, but various factors prevented it, and by the end of 1845 Britain and France were, indeed, acting together in the La Plata region in an undeclared war. One of the factors that prevented a hasty solution of the problem was the unexpected intervention of the American minister at Buenos Aires, William Brent Jr., who persuaded Rosas that the Anglo-French activities were a violation of the 'American System' – i.e. the Monroe Doctrine. The United States, however, did not choose to make an issue of the matter at the time.

Meanwhile, in September 1844, Aberdeen learned that Pakenham had at long last opened discussions of the Oregon issue, and – hoping that an American compromise would shortly be received, the Foreign Secretary decided to reveal his projected compromise to the Prime Minister:[44]

I believe that if the line of the 49th degree were extended only to the water's edge, and should leave us possession of all Vancouver's Island, with the Northern side of the entrance to Puget's Sound, and if all the Harbours within the Sound, and to the Columbia, inclusive, were made free to both countries, and further if the River Columbia from the point at which it became navigable to its mouth, were also made free to both, this would be in reality a most advantageous settlement. . . . I am convinced that this is the utmost which can be hoped for from the negotiation.

By this means Aberdeen accomplished his purpose of introducing into the Cabinet the compromise, which, as he stated it, was the absolute maximum Britain could hope for.

Then the news arrived that America would not suggest a compromise unless Britain gave up her assertion of equal rights in the territory. Far from being discouraged, Aberdeen believed that American politics was the real obstacle to a successful compromise,[45] and that he might relieve the Americans from their uneasy position by submitting the dispute to arbitration. Accordingly, on 1 November 1844, he ordered Pakenham to sound out the American Government to see if they would seize upon this lifeline. Pakenham carried out the order, only to have Calhoun reply that the American Government thought it unwise to adopt another method of settlement so long as the Oregon question might be resolved by direct negotiations.

In view of the complete failure of direct negotiations in the past, the American position seemed to be non-conciliatory, and evasive. Shortly after the news of the American rejection of arbitration arrived on 14 February 1845, Peel wrote Aberdeen a letter which reveals how completely American motives had come to be distrusted in London:[46]

The declarations of public men in the United States . . . justify suspicion and every degree of precaution on our part. . . . The Proceedings of the United States with respect to the Oregon are however the most important as immediately affecting the maintenance of amiable Relations with the United States. After what has passed in Congress, and after the refusal of arbitration, we cannot plead surprise. . . . These occurrences render compromise and concession (difficult enough before considering what stands on record of past negotiations) ten times more difficult now. The point of Honour is now brought into the foreground. . . . You seem confident that we have the upper hand on the banks of the Columbia, that the settlers connected with the Hudson's Bay Company are actually stronger than the settlers the subjects of the United States are at present. Have you carefully ascertained this fact?

The Prime Minister by this time was ready to adopt the Palmerstonian assumption that the United States was encroaching and unreasonable, and he recommended that some small military and naval forces be sent to the Oregon area.

If the colonisation of Oregon, the hostile language and measures sometimes raised in Congress, and the dilatory American tactics in the Oregon negotiations, accompanied by charges that the British Government was stalling, all contributed to British suspicions of American motives, the inaugural speech of President Polk in March, which termed the American title to all Oregon 'clear and unquestionable', seemed to confirm the worst. Criticising most of the speech, *The Times* observed pugnaciously: 'Oregon will never be wrested from the British Crown, to which it belongs, but by WAR'.[47] The Oregon issue by now did not so much involve acres, as national honour.

The speech of the American President washed away more of Aberdeen's foundations in the Cabinet. His was a most lonely, and perplexing battle during these years, trying to convince his colleagues that both the French and the Americans were really friendly and reasonable, while events seemed too often to prove the opposite. Convinced that warlike preparations undermined peace efforts, he had since late 1844 been fighting Wellington's grandiose plans for the defence of Britain against France,[48] and now he was faced by strong pressures to prepare for war with the United States. To go to war over what he regarded as an insignificant issue seemed the height of folly to Aberdeen, but by this time he began to wonder whether or not Palmerston was right in assuming that one had to bargain with America from a position of strength. 'We ought to make all reasonable preparation without delay,' he admitted late in March, 'but it should be such as may be consistent with the preservation of peace. In spite of Mr. Polk's address, I cannot believe, when they see us determined, that the American Govt. will drive matters to extremity'.[49]

Aberdeen's delicate diplomatic tactic was now to appear determined, yet not so much so as to fuel American jingoism, and perhaps to destroy the possibility for a reasonable settlement. Parliament up to this time had shown little interest in the Oregon issue,[50] but the speech of the American President made it inevitable that the topic would come up for debate. It was to be expected that Aberdeen would provide the official Government response to the American's 'clear and unquestionable' claims.

Pursuant to notice, Lord John Russell, as leader of the Opposition, made a major speech on the Oregon issue on 4 April in which he supported the Columbia River boundary, and stressed that the 'character of England' should not be lowered in the final settlement.[51] Peel in his reply refused to commit his Government to any specific compromise, and simply assured the House that Britain's rights would be maintained.[52]

In the Lords on the same day, Lord Clarendon – who was to have his innings with the Americans in the future – called upon the Government to defend British honour, and not to reward American bluster by giving more than was due to them.[53] Aberdeen, who answered him, was not one of the great contemporary orators of the stature of Lord Stanley or Lord Ellenborough, but on occasion his Calvinist, pacific convictions would transform a mediocre speech into something like an oration, and this time he could hardly have expressed his new policy more effectively:[54]

> I am accustomed almost daily to see myself characterised as pusillanimous, cowardly, mean, dastardly, truckling, and base. I hope I need not say that I view these appellations with indifference; I view them, indeed, with satisfaction, because I know perfectly well what they mean and how they ought to be and are translated. I feel perfectly satisfied that these vituperations are to be translated as applicable to conduct consistent with justice, reason, moderation, and common sense. . . . My Lords, I consider war to be the greatest folly, if not the greatest crime, of which a country could be guilty, if lightly entered into; and I agree entirely with a moral writer who said, that if a proof were wanted of the deep and thorough corruption of human nature, we should find it in the fact that war itself was sometimes justifiable.

He assured the House that Polk's speech was meant primarily for home consumption, and insisted that Britain's position and character sufficiently protected her national honour, but he assured the Lords that he would protect Britain's rights in the current controversy. Both the pacific and the more warlike parts of the speech were loudly cheered, and Aberdeen could sit down feeling that the House would support a determined, reasonable handling of the matter.

But what should he do? Virtually every avenue had been closed to him by the American refusal to make any counter-offer, or to accept arbitration. Facing a blank wall, Aberdeen wrote his pessimistic letter of 2 April, instructing Pakenham to offer arbitration again; if refused without any specific proposition being made, he would consider the negotiation terminated. 'We are still ready to adhere to the principle of an equitable compromise,' he wrote, 'but we are perfectly determined to cede nothing to force or menace. . . .'[55] This private letter crossed a despatch from Pakenham, who quoted the new Secretary of State, James Buchanan, as saying that he preferred 'giving and taking' to arbitration, an attitude which seemed to lift the shade, and to let in a ray of hope.

Aberdeen wrote Pakenham a private letter on 18 April 1845 that was to have an effect quite the opposite than the one intended, which was obviously to negotiate a settlement on the basis of the 49th parallel. If Buchanan suggested this parallel as the boundary, leaving Vancouver's Island in British hands, the mutual navigation of the Columbia River, free entrance into the Straits of Juan de Fuca, and a system of free ports in that area, Pakenham was not to regard the proposal as 'inadmissible', for with some modifications, it might be accepted. But he added a sentence which was to cause a major difficulty in the future. '. . . although I do not think it at all likely, & of course you will give no encouragement to the notion, but recur to arbitration in the events of our terms being rejected. At the same time, you might send Mr. Buchanan's proposal, if made, for the consideration of H.M. Govt.'[56] Why Aberdeen should have felt forced to add so many conditions to the 49th parallel proposal is still not clear, though the tone of his letter suggests that the Cabinet was not in a compromising mood, and that he would be unable to secure acceptance of a less favourable compromise. On the other hand, he may have been motivated mainly by tactical considerations – to draw from the Americans as favourable a proposal as possible as a starting point in the bargaining process.

If Pakenham had been Lord Ashburton, the major blunder of late July would not have been made, but he did not occupy the independent political position of that peer, and felt himself bound by the letter of his instructions. Thus, when Buchanan unexpectedly offered the 49th parallel, pure and simple without any of the other modifications, on 12 July, Pakenham delayed more than two weeks in answering him, and in his reply of 29 July asked that America submit another proposal that would recognise Britain's strong claims to Vancouver's Island, and be 'more consistent with fairness and justice'. Strictly speaking, Pakenham was not justified in sending home the American proposal as made, for it fell short of the minimum proposition that Aberdeen said would be entertained; on the other hand, his summary rejection of it without reference to his home government weakened the British case. Viewed in retrospect, Aberdeen would have done much better to have instructed him to send home any proposal that the Americans might put before him, whether he deemed it acceptable, or wholly inadequate. As it turned out, Buchanan simply withdrew the American proposal on 30 August, and the negotiations reached an impasse.

This crisis in Anglo-American relations came at a time when Aberdeen's French policy was again in peril. In 1845 the *entente cordiale* seemed to be prospering mightily—the two nations were cooperating in the La Plata region, France had signed the much desired slave trade suppression treaty on 29 May, the Queen visited France again on 8 September, and Guizot and Aberdeen worked out an acceptable formula on the Spanish Marriages question; but France seemed to be building up her naval strength all too menacingly, and Aberdeen found all of his colleagues in the Cabinet wholly unimpressed with the future of the *entente*. Strong sentiment existed to take precautionary measures against the possibility of war with both France and the United States. Late in August, Aberdeen withdrew his objections to preparations for an American war, and it was Lord Stanley who emerged as the chief opponent of warlike measures;[57] but the Foreign Secretary believed that Wellington's programme to defend Britain against France would stultify his whole French policy, and on 18 September he offered Peel his resignation.[58] Peel, of course, refused it, and tried to reassure Aberdeen without, however, admitting that Wellington's fears were unfounded.[59]

This was the situation when the Mexican minister visited Aberdeen and offered California to the British. 'War was certain with the U. States', he said, and, while he was confident Mexico could defend herself in other places, California would be quickly engulfed by the Northerners.[60] Aberdeen immediately talked over the offer with the French Ambassador, Jarnac, and sounded him out on the possibility of Anglo-French cooperation. Jarnac, who left for Paris the following day, promised to discuss the matter with his Government. Neither Aberdeen nor Peel[61] expected the project to flourish, and they both admitted it was objectionable because British grounds for intervention would be purely selfish; but Aberdeen, on receiving a friendly, if indefinite French reply, tried to use it once again as proof of the entente. '. . . he repeated', Aberdeen emphasised, 'that he was determined to act with us in America whenever it was possible, and that he would persevere in abandoning the old French policy of connection with the United States'.[62]

Peel was frankly sceptical of French assurances under this head, perhaps because France had little to gain and much to lose by formally repudiating the American connection, and in a letter of 17 October he remarked on 'the fruitful germs of War with France which will spring up in the event of War with the United States'.[63] Aberdeen replied to this latest attack upon French credibility by insisting that even the French opposition, headed by Thiers, favoured the *entente*, while the only opposition to it came from a few Radicals and Bonapartists.[64] With desperate eagerness to convince Peel of the success of his policy, he reported Guizot's request that Britain mediate a dispute between France and Mexico as 'proof of the existence of the entente'.[65] Peel's reply was an uncharacteristically rude bit of sarcasm – the anti-duelling society 'will greatly applaud' this act.

It is clear that even late in 1845 the Prime Minister was not convinced of France's desire to bury the past, and act as a friend toward Britain. Still less could he believe that she was ready to back Britain in a quarrel with the United States. Thus, the dénouement of the Oregon story has some bearing on Anglo-French, as well as Anglo-American relations.

Coincidental with the complete breakdown of Anglo-American negotiations in Washington that August was the appearance of a new American minister, Louis McLane, in London. McLane assured Aberdeen that Polk and Buchanan were as much distressed at the state of affairs as was Aberdeen, so the Foreign Secretary instructed Pakenham to ask Buchanan to withdraw their recent letters, so that the American proposal could be sent to London for review.[66] Neither Peel nor Aberdeen believed the Americans would agree to this request,[67] and they were quite right in their prognostications. 'It is *because* I think the Government of the United States dishonest, *because* I believe they are trying to find pretexts for delay and evasion, I would have put Mr. Buchanan in the difficulty in which he would have been put by not peremptorily rejecting his proposal,'[68] Peel wrote. By this time the Prime Minister was so disillusioned with American politicians that he opposed concessions in the Oregon dispute.[69] Thus, American diplomacy had temporarily isolated Aberdeen from his chief source of support.

From this point in the crisis onward Aberdeen may or may not have been guided in his policies by the advice of Louis McLane, an American in whom he had – quite correctly – implicit confidence. In late November he instructed Pakenham once again to offer arbitration. If America refused it, she must offer an alternative proposal or stand condemned by world opinion, which meant that Britain would have some support in maintaining unimpaired her rights in Oregon.[70] In early December he expressed doubt – who but McLane could have put it in his mind? – that Polk could ever secure senatorial support for a treaty he might negotiate, so a strong British stand would actually aid in the solution of the problem. This seems to be the meaning of his statement – 'as the crisis becomes more imminent, the chance of settlement improves'.[71]

The day after he had written to Pakenham to this effect some tangible proof of the *entente* in the Oregon issue at last appeared. The *Journal des Debats*, which was supposed to speak for the French Government,[72] came out with a strong plea for peace and commerce between the United States and Britain. Noting that the Columbia River boundary would probably have been a fair settlement of the issue, it observed: 'England is now prepared for any event that may arise; she has adopted precautions as if a war were to occur in 1846'.[73] The journal could hardly have penned a statement more in line with Aberdeen's current policy.[74]

The very day this article appeared in Britain, Aberdeen's tenure at the Foreign Office was interrupted temporarily by Peel's resignation, and the governmental situation remained in a state of confusion between 5–19 December while Lord John Russell unsuccessfully tried his hand at constructing a Cabinet.[75] When he returned to power, Peel was in a most curious position.[76] More powerful than ever because he was a necessity, yet keenly aware that his term as head of the Conservative Party must end with the repeal of the Corn Laws, Peel dedicated himself absolutely to the cause of eliminating trade barriers. Never before did he exercise his power so arbitrarily, even unfeelingly, almost as if he courted the political martyrdom that Lord George Bentinck and young Benjamin Disraeli were to thrust upon him in 1846.

While the Prime Minister isolated himself from almost all of his followers, he seems to have given Aberdeen, who had supported him during the Cabinet crises of November–December 1845 *carte blanche* in the conduct of foreign affairs. In late December, Aberdeen seems to have been quite confident that the United States would eventually come around to a solution of the Oregon question, even though Polk in his December message had recommended a termination of the joint occupation of Oregon, the erection of forts to protect American settlers, and had not mentioned the British offer of arbitration. He must, therefore, have had strong assurances from McLane of America's peaceful intentions. How else could he have written in late December – when no ray of hope shone through: 'I have never been afraid of the Oregon question, & feel confident that in the course of the year we shall see it finally settled, either by arbitration, or by direct negotiation'.[77]

Aberdeen four days later gleefully wrote to Peel that Polk's reference to France 'will produce exactly the effect we most desire, and will greatly promote the policy which I hope may be considered as successful – the separation of France in feeling & interest from the United States'.[78] He had ample reason for his feeling of success. The French Speech from the Throne took note of Anglo-French cooperation in the La Plata, and in the suppression of the slave trade, and noted: 'the friendship which unites me with the Queen of England, and of which she again so affectionately gave me a proof, and the mutual confidence existing between the two states'.[79] French friendship had been demonstrated at this moment of crisis in Anglo-American relations, and furnished the proof Aberdeen thought he needed to demonstrate the success of his foreign policies.

Many weeks passed before Aberdeen learned of the American response to his renewed offer of arbitration, and when the news arrived on 28 January, it sounded taps for Aberdeen's December optimism – arbitration was rejected, and no new American proposition was forthcoming. Aberdeen had no one to turn to for suggestions but McLane, and they had an interview which the latter agreed to report to Buchanan. The formalised account of this interview is given in a private letter from Aberdeen to Pakenham.[80] In all probability it was much more intimate than this account would lead us to believe. Aberdeen said he almost doubted 'the sincerity of the President and Mr. Buchanan in their expressed desire to arrive at a pacifick [sic] conclusion of the affair'. McLane replied that the President and Buchanan 'were perfectly sincere in their desire to preserve peace', if he had thought otherwise, he would never have come to England. The Foreign Secretary noted regretfully that he could not now 'refuse my assent to those measures of preparation which were considered indispensable, both in this country, and in Canada'. McLane 'never admitted for a moment that there could be any real danger', and promised to lay before Aberdeen the terms America would accept, if Britain chose to make another proposition for settlement. 'Nothing could be more friendly and cordial than the whole of our interview', Aberdeen concluded, and I am particularly anxious that your language should be perfectly free from anything like menace or anger'.

The account which McLane sent home, however, had a much more martial ring to it:[81]

He remarked further, that although he would not abandon the desire or the hope that an amicable adjustment might yet be effected, and peace preserved, he should nevertheless feel it his duty to withdraw the opposition he had hitherto uniformly made to the adoption of measures founded upon the contingency of war with the United States, and to offer no obstacle in future to preparations which might be deemed necessary not only for the defence and protection of the Canadas, but for offensive operations. In the course of our conversation, I understood that these would consist independent of military armaments, of the immediate equipment of thirty sail of the line besides steamers and other vessels of war, of a smaller class.

Although this account was quite free from the angry tone Aberdeen wished to avoid, it certainly was redolent with menace.

Which account actually stated more accurately the extent of British military and naval preparations? Stray items culled from a number of manuscript collections indicate that there was a genuine 'war scare' in Britain as early as December, when Aberdeen expressed optimism as to a peaceful solution of the crisis, until 2 March, when Gladstone wrote: 'Our belief however is that there will be no war. . .'.[82] These sources also substantiate the fact that some warlike preparations were made during these hectic weeks.[83]

One evidence of this was the increase in the estimates for the armed forces which were made as a result of the Oregon situation;[84] another was Peel's attempt to unite the civil and military governments of Canada under Lord Fitzroy Somerset 'in the present critical juncture in our relations with America', an appointment which Somerset subsequently refused.[85] Lord Ripon at the Board of Control considered the situation menacing enough to send out an alert to Aden in December,[86] and to Singapore in February.[87] If a note by Lord Lyndhurst dates to this period, 'many ships of War' were actually sent to the American coast.[88] At the request of the Hudson's Bay Company, a small detachment was actually sent to protect Fort Garry on the Red River, but this took place after the crisis had abated.[89]

The possibility of military or naval service in a war with the United States brought requests to the Government from a number of officers. George Napier asked to be included in any combined naval and military expedition;[90] Williams Sandom sought a command on the Great Lakes.[91] Lord Ellenborough selected Sir Charles Napier to command on the American coast in the event of war, but found that his colleagues were all against the choice.[92] The other Sir Charles Napier, with whom Ellenborough had been associated in India, submitted suggestions 'as to the best mode of carrying on the War with the United States', based on his experiences during the War of 1812.[93]

It would be too much to say that Britain teetered on the brink of war during these months, but she was obviously prepared for the worst in the event that the Oregon question led to first, a local conflict, then, a general war. Most of the British statesmen shared Aberdeen's view that America would not bring on a war, even though the activities of the Polk Administration created widespread uneasiness; and all of them, even the more war-oriented, regarded such a conflict as an unmitigated evil.

The end phase of the Oregon question needs little attention, as the general outline is well-known. After receiving McLane's despatch of 3 February, the Polk administration instructed their minister to inform Aberdeen that a British offer of the 49th parallel would be sent to the Senate, and that the Senate would accept it. Some time was lost while the Senate debated its Oregon policy, but in April both Houses of Congress passed a conciliatory resolution on the subject, and on 18 May Aberdeen sent along the British compromise – typical of Aberdeen, asking for somewhat less than he had envisioned in 1844 so that its acceptance was likely – with the comment: 'Without calling this Convention an *ultimatum*, it will in fact be so, as far as you are concerned. . . .'.[94] The United States accepted the compromise just as Aberdeen drew it up.

Because the impasse was broken when the Polk Government received the 'thirty sail of the line' despatch, a scholarly debate had continued for some time regarding whether or not this threat of force was responsible for bringing about the final settlement.[95] However this interesting controversy may be decided by specialists in American diplomatic history, there is a highly interesting bit of evidence which indicates that some British diplomats believed Aberdeen's 'hard line' policy forced the solution of the Oregon question. A decade later, John S. Crampton wrote to Lord Clarendon:[96]

. . . the Oregon question was settled by the launching and fitting out of certain heavy frigates at Portsmouth without a word being said. The American Government read it in the papers & Mr. McLane was sent in a great hurry to ask Lord Aberdeen what it all meant. His Lordship replied that our relations in the Mediterranean required a force there, and *added* that the way the Oregon question was taken up by the United States was not altogether satisfactory. From that moment the hope of bullying us began *retro sublata* [?] *referri*; a peace party formed itself in Congress, and Mr. Polk shortly found himself with *five* members of the Senate for his sole support in his celebrated declarition of the 'whole or none, 54 degrees-40′ or fight'.

Crampton, who took over the conduct of British affairs in America from Pakenham in May 1847, wrote an account so garbled that it would seem to have been passed on and embellished by a number of individuals before it reached him, but it seems not unlikely that some such story was told to him by Pakenham. In a letter of late February or early March (which this writer could not locate) Pakenham seems to have informed Aberdeen that McLane's despatch had had a notable effect on the American Government; at any rate, Pakenham's letter aroused Aberdeen's curiosity, and he asked McLane to send him the threatening portion of the despatch, which he did.[97] Thus, Pakenham may have been the source of Crampton's information, but this does not explain why it is so strangely inaccurate in its details. Be this as it may, the story of Aberdeen's threat of force evidently had some circulation, and perhaps had some influence on British diplomatic thinking vis-à-vis America in the future.[98]

Some specialists in American history regard the Oregon treaty as a triumph for American diplomacy.[99] Beyond such obvious objections to this interpretation as the fact that Aberdeen dictated the convention, and that most British officials, including the Queen, sent him warm congratulations for making it, there are certain objections to the evidence used to buttress the theory. One such assumption is that Aberdeen used *The Times*, and John W. Croker of the *Quarterly Review*, to prepare the British public for a 'policy of concession', and specifically that *The Times* did a *volta facie* between 2 December 1845 and 3 January 1846, switching from a 'hard line' to a 'soft line' in Oregon. It is true that *The Times* reacted strongly to the claims in Polk's inaugural address, but thereafter the paper could hardly have pursued a more objective policy. In May it presented John C. Calhoun's statement of the American case,[100] and in December it gave Webster's views on the subject.[101] When Peel temporarily retired from office in December, the newspaper observed:[102]

Very different were the circumstances under which the difficulties still pending with reference to the Oregon territory were dealt with by the Government. Mr. Polk and Mr. Buchanan had succeeded Mr. Webster, aggression and invective had followed conciliation and peace; to these manifestations the English Minister replied in a sterner language, and, if the dispute be now, at this critical juncture, transferred to other hands, we trust that Lord Aberdeen's successor may terminate it by a 'capitulation' as honourable as the Treaty of Washington.

Supporting a replica of the Maine Boundary treaty was hardly calling for an uncompromising 'hard' line. In seeking Croker's aid in presenting the facts of the dispute to the British public, Aberdeen probably was motivated by the same consideration as inspired his despatch of 28 November 1845 – rallying public opinion in Britain and the world, which would put pressure on America to compromise, and place her in the wrong if she did not, and war ensued. Much of the diplomatic correspondence had already been published in *The Times* in late December, but it appeared in such fine print that the average reader was likely to have been discouraged from reading it.

If the object of Polk's diplomacy were to create a war scare in the hope of securing a larger share of the disputed territory, a tactic not unknown in the annals of all great powers, and – used with finesse and caution – perfectly legitimate diplomacy, he was at least partly successful. He created a war scare in Britain, and secured a perfectly satisfactory settlement of the Oregon issue, though, of course, short of the extreme American demands, just as Palmerston had demanded and received satisfaction over the McLeod issue by using a similar tactic. This type of 'bullying' – to use the contemporary term – obviously did not create a cordial good feeling in either country, and a true friend of Anglo-American rapprochement, such as Louis McLane, felt that it merited some semblance of an apology. 'I am certain, too,' he wrote to Aberdeen, 'that my countrymen generally . . . however impulsive portions of them may sometimes be, ultimately think and act right. . . .' [103]

As there is no reason to doubt that Aberdeen would have accepted a compromise such as was actually made back in 1844,

A.P.B.D.—3

when Pakenham was trying unsuccessfully to draw forth an offer of the 49th parallel from the American Government, it would appear that the American 'hard line' merely intensified the crisis of confidence in British circles, which had begun to form in late 1842, and delayed the settlement of the issue. Confidence was not restored until the arrival of McLane, who was able to demonstrate to Aberdeen that firm commitments would be made by the American Government, and carried faithfully into execution.

Once Aberdeen had located this American Guizot, his personal diplomacy was a thing of beauty. For example, McLane sent him a note on the Mexican War which he later wished to revise; upon request, Aberdeen immediately returned it to him, and accepted the form that McLane felt was more suitable for the occasion.[104] The so-called 'Rough Rice' controversy had been outstanding between the United States and Britain for some time. In order that McLane's departure from Britain might be marked by further successes, Aberdeen not only arranged to pay the Rough Rice claim, but two other American claims against Britain of long standing.[105] Writing to Edward Everett concerning McLane, Aberdeen recalled a line by Vergil to properly express his feeling : 'He has fully realised all I expected of him, when we were unfortunately deprived of you. *Uno [Primo] avulso, non deficit alter Aureus.*'[106] Aberdeen's strong friendship for McLane, indeed, leads one to wonder if the full story of the Oregon settlement has yet been told.

4

The Diplomacy of the Mexican War Period

When Palmerston returned to the Foreign Office in July 1846, he found that his predecessor had disposed of all outstanding major problems involving Britain and the United States. Paramount in his thinking in so far as Oregon was concerned was the British need for good harbours in the Pacific area, where trade was developing,[1] and, although he believed the settlement to have been overgenerous to the United States,[2] he had no intention of attacking it on that account. His attention was virtually monopolised by France during this whole period, and his American policy up to a point was an extension of Aberdeen's – to speak softly, and to conciliate save when a seemingly vital British interest was at stake.

Wedding bells in Spain sounded the death knell for Lord Aberdeen's high-minded *entente cordiale* with France. How this came about was tersely summed up by a member of the Russell Government: 'The *public* in this country will not care sixpence whom the Queen of Spain or her Sister marries. They will say only 1) We *were* on friendly terms with France 2) P. comes in 3) We *are* on hostile terms, & this looks like a good syllogism.'[3] Although Lord Clarendon, as well as the Prime Minister, shared Palmerston's indignation at France's course in the Spanish Marriages affair, historians of the present day generally agree that Palmerston 'overreacted', and transformed a French diplomatic peccadillo into a national challenge.

The Spanish marriages involved young Isabella II and the Duke of Cadiz, and her sister and the Duke of Montpensier, a son of Louis Philippe of France. They were announced on 29 August 1846, and took place on 10 October of the same year. During the protracted diplomatic negotiations preceding these marriages, Palmerston and Sir Henry Bulwer (later to appear in

Washington), British minister at Madrid, worked to secure a husband for the Queen from the Spanish liberal party, or from Coburg, and it was believed in Britain that the French marriage would not take place until after Isabella II had married and had issue. Otherwise, Montpensier's offspring might inherit the throne, binding Spain to France in an alleged violation of the Treaty of Utrecht. When the French marriage took place simultaneously with the other, Palmerston's indignation knew no bounds.[4] War was not imminent, but the *entente* for the time being was defunct.

Palmerston's extreme suspicion of France – and, to a much lesser extent, his conciliatory policy toward the United States – was much fortified by the continuing advances in naval construction, which did much to shrink the Channel barrier against French invasion. In the Russell Government, the Duke of Wellington at the Horse Guards, Earl Grey at the Colonial Office, and Lord Minto, the Privy Seal, seem to have been the Cabinet officers most alarmed at the situation; the Prime Minister, whose interest during these years was focused on domestic issues, and Lord Auckland at the Admiralty were less so, and Sir Charles Wood at the Exchequer, who had to guard the revenues, was more disgruntled than panic-stricken.

As of 1846 the Duke of Wellington, continuing the line he had adopted as a member of the Peel Government,[5] was probably the heart and soul of the rearmament movement. From his memorandums it is possible to reconstruct the anticipated French invasion of Britain.[6] As he saw it, the improvements made in screw-driven ships, and the use of steam power had revolutionised maritime warfare, and opened all the coasts of Britain to French attack, which could be carried out much more rapidly and efficiently than in the past. He visualised a large French invasion fleet being gathered in Cherbourg, St. Malo, and the ports of the Bay of Biscay, and from these ports conveying large forces to be landed on the shores of St. George's Channel perhaps for an attack on Plymouth. As steam power greatly increased the mobility of the invasion force, it was clear to Wellington that the old-style blockading force would be ineffective in warding off such an invasion flotilla.

As late as November 1846 Palmerston seems to have been much less alarmed than Wellington, even noting in one letter

that Wellington and some others were encouraging the war
scare created by the Spanish Marriages crisis;[7] and his defence
memorandum of 10 April 1847 stated that there was not at
present in France 'any deliberate wish for war with England',[8]
but, as time went by, the apparent defencelessness of Britain
against a steam-powered attack increasingly impressed him,
and this fear was very much in evidence in his memorandum of
31 December 1847, a part of which probably deserves quoting:[9]

> They have at Cherbourg and at St. Mathieu Spacious
> Basins secure from observation and attack within which they
> could easily collect steamers enough to transport across the
> Channel 30 or 40,000 Men at one Trip, and 12 or 14 Hours
> would be sufficient to bring such a Fleet within their Har-
> bours to the Coast of Sussex or Kent. It is physically impos-
> sible that any Precautions which we could take by sea in the
> Channel with the naval Force with which we should be
> obliged to begin a war would be certain to intercept such a
> Fleet, which need not consist of more than 20 to 30 steamers
> which might perform the Greater part of its voyage along the
> French coast unobserved and unseen. . . . The danger then
> against which we have to guard is, that at any Time from a
> few days after a rupture with France up to the End of a year
> or perhaps Two years from that Time when our naval &
> military strength would be fully developed, we might by
> Twelve O'clock at noon of any Day of the year find landed
> upon the Southern and Eastern Coast of England a French
> army consisting of any number of men from 30,000 to
> 100,000. . . .

According to Palmerston's figures, the French already had
available in their regular navy steamers enough to transport
34,000 men.

All sorts of suggestions were made. Wellington emphasised
'block ships' – slow-moving, floating batteries – to protect the
coast,[10] and an expanded regular army, a 150,000-man militia,
and fortifications in Britain especially to protect the dockyards
and arsenals.[11] Lord Minto, who considered Britain 'inferior and
helpless in our own element', sought an expansion of the navy,[12]
while Lord Auckland investigated the money-saving possibility

of using the commercial steamers for war purposes.[13] The necessity of raising an effective militia for home defence was stressed in many of the letters and memoranda of the period.

Palmerston sought information and ideas from many sources, not excluding the United States, from whom, through his minister in Washington, he received some details concerning the American army and militia freely furnished by the American Government.[14] With an eye to the future, he requested Pakenham to secure the results of a New York experiment involving the effects of shot on iron steamers, and received the reply: 'A Plate of Iron 5 inches thick was fired at at a distance of 150 yards with 8 inch, 10 inch & 12 inch shot. The 8 inch produced but little effect, the ten inch perforated it, & the twelve inch knocked the plate all to pieces. The Plate was composed of several plates fastened together.'[15] This particular development in marine technology was to become a major source of British concern a decade in the future.

Despite all of the excitement and exchanges of views, very little was actually done to meet the French menace. A wholly ineffective armed services bill was passed, several 'block ships' were created,[16] work was begun at Dover on a harbour of refuge,[17] and work was commenced on the formation of a coast guard,[18] but the impecunious Government was unable to implement a preparedness programme of any real value. '. . . almost any expedient to face the temporary Difficulty would be better', Palmerston wrote early in 1848, 'than to proclaim to Europe that we are too poor & too much distressed to be able to defend the Country'.[19] Lord John Russell, however, was unwilling to face the taunts of both the budget-minded Whigs and Radicals, and the even more economy-minded Peelites,[20] which would greet any sizeable expansion of the budget for the armed forces.

This fear of France, born of steam technology, and the failure of the rearmament programme, due to the vocal economy blocs in the Commons, form the background for Palmerston's extraordinary ruminations in a letter of 30 January 1848 to Russell, which contemplated an *entente* with the United States.[21] He proposed a treaty pledging mediation and arbitration to solve future Anglo-American disputes, neutrality if either became involved in a war, and prohibitions against the citizens of either nation taking up the cause of a nation at war with Britain or the

United States.[22] The Foreign Secretary believed such a treaty might be of value to Britain should she become involved in a conflict with France and Russia, as, indeed, it would have been. In the final analysis this project was merely an extension of Aberdeen's policy of breaking the Franco-American tie, which was still assumed to have a hazy existence, and which was the more menacing at a time when the British Isles themselves seemed threatened. Nothing came of the project. Indeed, instead of establishing treaty relations with the United States in 1848, Palmerston began to fish in the troubled waters of Central America.

Palmerston's American *entente* letter was written on the eve of the revolutionary upheavals of 1848–9, during which the Viscount gave moral support to the European liberals, and manipulated the European Governments with a masterly hand. He won the confidence of Louis Philippe's republican successors in France, vainly sought to create a north Italian kingdom against her, and in the end was successful in preventing French intervention in Italy. When in 1849 Austria and Russia adopted a menacing posture toward Turkey, Palmerston revived the *entente cordiale* temporarily, and an Anglo-French naval squadron sent to the Dardanelles forced the eastern nations hastily to back down. Scarcely less remarkable than Palmerston's ability to maintain a balance of power in Europe was his success in enlisting France, perennial foe in his private letters, in carrying out British diplomatic policies. During these years of revolution and confusion, his attention was wholly occupied by European affairs, and Anglo-American diplomacy was scarcely more than an afterthought.

Lord Palmerston viewed the Mexican War with the cynical eye of a *real politiker*. Writing to Russell late in 1847 regarding the possibility of the United States accepting an annexation offer from Yucatan, he doubted that America would want an area so remote and different at this time, but added: 'When the Americans have absorbed, as in Time they will do, the Rest of Mexico, Yucatan will of course follow the Fate of its Confederate states'.[23] Later, after both the United States and Mexico had declined British good offices in mediating the war,[24] he instructed Pakenham, if he were called upon to assist in making a settlement, to arrange it with 'as little sacrifice to Mexico as may be possible',[25] but obstructing American territorial designs upon Mexico formed no part of his foreign policy.

The aftermath of the bitter Oregon dispute, indeed, was much more favourable than that which had followed the Webster–Ashburton Treaty. Britain quickly recognised the American blockade of the eastern coast of Mexico, and held up approval of that of Mexico's western ports only because, as the United States freely admitted, the American fleet was concentrated along the California shore, and the area was not actually under blockade.[26] Palmerston believed that the United States was perfectly justified as a belligerent in administering occupied territories as she saw fit, in seizing Mexican property,[27] and in occupying the properties of British citizens in Mexico for military purposes.[28] On two occasions approval was given to the British minister in Washington when he forwarded American official communications to their diplomatic representatives in Mexico through the British consul there.[29] The United States, on the other hand, permitted British mail packets to go through the blockade, and established favourable tariffs in the Mexican ports that she threw open to trade.

There were three occasions on which the two nations, had they so desired, could have created at least minor diplomatic crises. A British mail steamer committed a flagrant violation of British neutrality by conveying a Mexican general from Havana to Vera Cruz. Palmerston quickly discountenanced the act, and saw to it that the commander of the delinquent vessel was removed.[30] On the other hand, had Britain felt any disposition to quarrel with the United States during the war, she might have done so when Mexico accused some American naval officers of flying the Union Jack as a strategem to facilitate landings on her territory. Instead of adopting a menacing stance, Palmerston instructed Pakenham to remonstrate to the American Government 'rather as a Precaution against a possible contingency than as a Protest of an actual event, for H.M. Government wish to believe that the thing has not actually been done'.[31] This must rank as one of Palmerston's most kindly warnings! Even greater justification for a major dispute was the unfortunate habit of some port authorities in the slave states to imprison or otherwise mistreat free British Negroes, who happened to arrive in their ports on British ships. This gave rise to a very lengthy plea by Palmerston to the Federal Government to induce the slave states to modify their laws so that British citizens of the Negro race could come and go freely in American ports, but Palmerston evidently did not expect anything to come of it.[32] On one of Pakenham's despatches relating to such an incident, someone – possibly Palmerston himself – wrote: 'It would be impolitic to make a serious complaint to the U.S. Govt'.[33]

The diplomatic correspondence of the Mexican War era thus provides a welcome change from that of the Oregon crisis period. Changed also were the economic relations between the two countries.

Some opponents of the repeal of the Corn Laws had deplored the abolition of British duties on agricultural products without securing equivalents from the nations likely to profit by the change, and they predicted that such nations would accept the boon thanklessly. The American Walker tariff, passed shortly after the Corn Laws were repealed, seemed to give the lie to these prognosticators. True – it still provided ample protection, but the 'free list' of goods was enlarged, the general tariff level was reduced by about 5% and Britain could live with the duties on iron, hardware, and cotton and wool cloth, which were staples in her American trade.

These years when Palmerston held the seals of the Foreign Office were, indeed, a major turning point in the history of Anglo-American trade. The Cotton Kingdom provided more than 80% of Britain's imports of raw cotton, and the Trans-Atlantic sea lanes were clogged with both British and American ships as the United States emerged as Britain's best single customer. The recovery of British exports to the United States had begun in 1843, but the major fillip to Anglo-American trade seems to have been the Walker Tariff, for British exports to the United States rose from £6·8 (1846) to £11·0 (1847) millions after its passage. Thereafter the opening of California, and the subsequent economic boom in the United States provided increased opportunity for sales of which Britain, which could not only undersell other nations, but could advance long-term credit, could take full advantage.[34]

The triumph of the Free Traders in Britain, however, was somewhat diluted by the difficulties caused in Canada by the repeal of the Corn Laws. Before the repeal of the Corn Laws, Canada had enjoyed a tariff preference in the British corn market, and Montreal had hoped to emerge as the great entrepôt for the St Lawrence Valley, importing American foodstuffs from the interior states, and shipping them to Britain. Thus, while fires were lighted in America to celebrate the opening of the British market to American grain, they went out in Canada, and some Canadians, disillusioned by the severing of this economic bond to the Mother Country, believed that Canada might prosper only through union with the United States. This situation was a major cause of the Montreal riots of 1849.[35] Not only in Canada, but in Britain herself there was a feeling that some prominent British statesmen were not only indifferent, but actually hostile to the needs of the colonies, and looked with favour on the dissolution of the Empire.[36]

The dissolution of the British Empire formed no part of the thinking of either Lord John Russell or Lord Palmerston. Nor had Lord Aberdeen been wholly indifferent to the economic interests of the colonies. As early as 18 June 1846 Aberdeen had launched a project which was to be discussed for many years to come – the establishment of 'equality of trade' between the United States and Canada.[37] Aberdeen had instructed Pakenham to sound out the United States on the subject, but he decided to postpone acting on his instructions while the Walker Tariff was being debated in the Congress. On 13 August 1846 Pakenham reported that Congress had passed a measure which permitted a drawback – that is, a refund of a tariff charge – on certain merchandise imported into the United States from Canada, and subsequently re-exported from the United States; but this was a far cry from the equality of trade that the Canadians were seeking.[38]

The American statesmen, indeed, seemingly hoped to trade a concession to Canada for one their country had been seeking ever since independence: viz., the right of American carriers to participate both in the indirect and direct trade with Great Britain and all of her Empire. A new chapter in the serial of negotiations on this subject was opened when George Bancroft, to whom Pakenham gave an indifferent send-off,[39] arrived in Britain as the replacement for the congenial Louis McLane. Late in August 1847 Bancroft pressed Palmerston to open the indirect trade of Britain and the Empire on a reciprocal basis provided in an Anglo-American commercial treaty, and the Foreign Secretary referred him to the Prime Minister, who thereafter took council with Henry Labouchere at the Board of Trade, and Sir Charles Wood at the Exchequer.[40] Not only were revenues involved in such a project, but it called for an important modification of the Navigation Acts, which prohibited this indirect trade. Labouchere was quite ready to open the foreign and colonial trade, reserving only Britain's coasting trade and the fisheries,[41] but Wood wished to retain, in addition, the trade between Britain and her colonies.[42]

After taking his soundings, Bancroft presented a formal American proposal to Britain on 3 November 1847, which would exchange permission for British ships to trade in American ports from any port in the world, paying the same charges and duties as American ships, for the right of American ships to trade in a like manner from any port in the world to any port within the British Dominions.[43] Palmerston replied that the Navigation Acts could not be altered without the sanction of Parliament, and promised that the Government would shortly make proposals to place the matters referred to by Bancroft on the 'most liberal and comprehensive basis' with respect to powers which would act in a reciprocal spirit.[44] The official policy at the moment, then, seemed to contemplate a relaxation of the Navigation Acts on a basis of reciprocity.

Drawing distinctions between nations who reciprocated, and those who did not, proved unworkable because Britain had entered into a number of 'most favoured nation' treaties with Sweden and other powers. When he received this opinion from the Law Officers, Labouchere wrote Russell: 'It seems to me that this leaves us no option & that we must proceed in our intended changes by direct legislation',[45] Later that same month Palmerston, in outlining the project for the arbitration treaty with the United States, described above, noted that Britain and America would probably place their merchant marines 'upon a footing of mutual Equality, with the exception of the Coasting Trade, & some special matters'.[46] There was obviously still some reluctance within the Cabinet to grant America the 'perfect equality' of reciprocal trading opportunities which she had so long desired.

Palmerston himself was by no means an enthusiastic Free Trader, and there was some reluctance among the patriotic Old Whigs to abolish the Navigation Acts, which had been regarded traditionally as vital to British sea power, but the Free Trade chorus in the Commons, composed of Radicals, Peelites and Liberals in about that order, swelled in a deafening crescendo during 1847–9, and drowned out all objections. Lord Stanley and Disraeli made an unsuccessful attempt to commit the Commons to the Navigation Acts in 1848, and the following year they were repealed, throwing open the ports of Britain and her empire, and reserving only the coasting trade for British ships alone, which was perfectly agreeable to the Americans.[47]

Once before, in 1846, Britain had taken the risky course of making a major economic concession to the United States unilaterally in the hope that she would respond in kind, and in 1849 the degree of risk seemed increased by the change from a Democratic to a Whig Administration, which was expected to be more economically nationalistic than its predecessor. '. . . I am not sure', Labouchere wrote late in September 1849, 'that the new Government may not shuffle out of it'.[48] But such fears proved groundless. On 15 October 1849 the American Government informed its customs officials that British vessels coming from anywhere in the world would be subject to the same duties, imposts, and other charges as American vessels.[49]

So a long-time Anglo-American controversy was laid to rest with a minimum of fanfare. Little was mentioned either of another solid accomplishment of Anglo-American diplomacy during these years – the drawing up of a new postal agreement between the two nations. '. . . the consequence', Bancroft wrote to Russell, 'was an increase of almost three fold in the number of international letters. . . . I am glad that the mutual benefit of the result is apparent so soon & so undeniably'.[50]

Despite these successes, some problems still remained. The American Government, despite the concessions granted by Britain in the repeal of the Corn Laws and the Navigation Acts, showed no interest in granting the requests of the British Government for a liberal trading agreement with Canada. This raised suspicions in some British minds that the United States might still have some fleeting hopes of forcing Canada into the Union through economic pressures. Then certain details of the

Oregon Boundary continued to cause difficulties. The preliminary surveys of the projected boundary were hardly underway before a controversy arose regarding the meaning of the word 'channel', the midpoint of which was to form part of the new line.[51]

But, by and large, Palmerston's policies during the 1846–8 period seemed most friendly toward the United States, and were hardly distinguishable from those of Aberdeen, save that the camaraderie that Aberdeen had extended to both Everett and McLane did not characterise Palmerston's relations with Bancroft, or with Abbott Lawrence, who replaced him in 1849. The reasons for Palmerston's Aberdeenian approach to Anglo-American relations during the 1846–7 period would seem to have a combination of concern and disinterest – concern for his preparedness programme at home, and European diplomacy, and disinterest in the issues outstanding with the United States, which were primarily economic. Neither he nor Aberdeen displayed much interest in mere economics, but let an issue involving British honour or prestige arise and Palmerston leapt from his corner like the title-holder he was, put up his guard, and had another round with the Americans.

Many intrepid scholars have ventured intellectually to the coast of Nicaragua, and grappled with the maze of facts that collectively compose the Mosquito Question. Some American historians have harboured the belief that the British Foreign Office during this whole period watched carefully the direction of American expansion, and hastily interposed obstacles to block it.[52] This was the view of Mary W. Williams in her classic work on isthmian diplomacy,[53] and it was to some extent adopted by a British scholar half a century later,[54] even though Van Alstyne meanwhile had published articles to show that Palmerston did not enter the Central American area in order to anticipate the United States.[55] One scholar emphasized that Britain's motive, in part at least, 'was the desire . . . to control the routes of isthmian transit in compensation for the westward march of the United States'.[56] Just which nation, Britain or America, blocked the ambitions of the other in this area seems to provide the crux of the argument.

Britain had historically formed connections with three areas of Central America: Belize, where British log-cutters had been working for two centuries on Spanish territory; the Bay Islands (Roatan the most important) off the coast of Belize, and the Mosquito kingdom, whose areas would embrace a sizeable section of the eastern coastline of Central America.

Much has been written regarding the unusual political connections that Britain established with these areas. Although Belize was not a full-fledged British colony until 1862, it was administered by a British superintendent, and this superintendent, in turn, supervised the magistrate of Roatan and the other Bay Islands. Although the Mosquito ruler came to Belize to be crowned in 1816, he had no political connection with the British Government. Such odd relationships, it should be emphasised, were by no means unique in British imperial history, and could be found in many places from the Malay states to the tribal kingdoms of West Africa.

In areas of minor economic importance, Britain was inclined to let nature take its course, politically speaking, and merely to respond to whatever pressures happened to appear in them. Central America was certainly one of these political derelicts. Among the five republics that appeared when the Central American Federation became defunct in 1839, Costa Rica and Guatemala developed a coffee and cochineal trade with Britain important to themselves, but the other three, Nicaragua, El Salvador, and Honduras were of no economic interest to Britain.[57] The principal economic interest of Britain in the area was still the log-wood cutters, who, according to one scholar, were running out of commercial mahogany in Belize, and hoped to find a new area for exploitation in the Mosquito coast. This situation allegedly caused a sudden revival of British interest in that territory.[58] Another historian, however, has attacked this interpretation as being too narrow.[59]

In her work on isthmian diplomacy, Mary Williams sketched the major incidents associated with this revived interest in the Mosquito shore; how Palmerston in 1838 decided that Britain's historic connection with it should be retained both for commercial and political reasons; how in 1841 the British superintendent at Belize, recognising the importance of the mouth of the San Juan River, went there with the Mosquito ruler, who took possession of the town of San Juan and accepted British

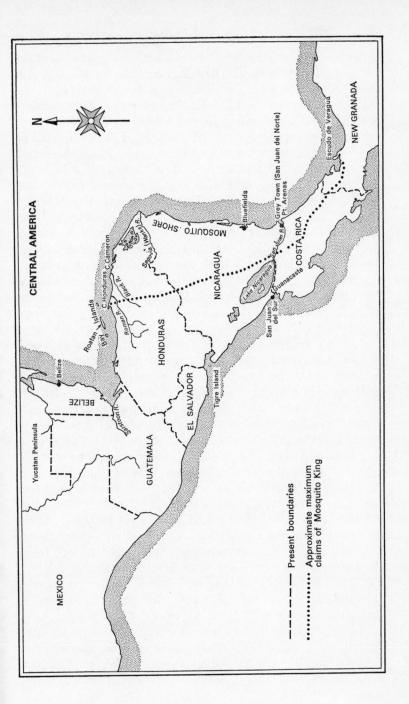

CENTRAL AMERICA

N

MEXICO

Yucatan Peninsula

BELIZE
Belize
Sarstoon R.

GUATEMALA

EL SALVADOR

Tigre Island

HONDURAS

Roatan Islands
C. Cameron
C. Honduras
Roman R.
Black R.
Segovia (Wanks) R.

NICARAGUA

MOSQUITO SHORE

Bluefields

Grey Town (San Juan del Norte)
Pt. Arenas

Lake Nicaragua

San Juan R.

San Juan del Sur

Guanacaste

COSTA RICA

Escudo de Veragua

NEW GRANADA

— — — Present boundaries

··········· Approximate maximum
claims of Mosquito King

protection; how Nicaragua protested this action, which was defended by Palmerston, and how Britain failed to mantain San Juan, and let it return to the Nicaraguans.[60]

The non-imperialistic Lord Stanley, who was Colonial Secretary in Peel's Government, did not follow up this initiative of the Whig Government. A military officer evidently applied to Peel for a government appointment on the Mosquito shore, and Stanley, returning his letter to Peel, remarked: 'I concur the only answer that can be sent is that the Mosquito Coast not being British Property, but the Territory of an independent and friendly Chief, we cannot regulate Emigration thither, still less make any Government appointments.'[61] This rare reference to the Mosquito Coast in a private letter sums up Britain's relationship with it in January 1842, when the letter was written.

Yet in 1844, Lord Aberdeen created a British residency in the Mosquito Kingdom, and Patrick Walker was sent there by the Belize superintendent to assume the office. Mary Williams traced this sequence of events to the death of the Mosquito ruler in 1842, which caused unsettled conditions in the kingdom, and led to a suggestion by the Belize superintendent to establish the residency.[62] This explanation for its establishment seems adequate enough without postulating at this moment a British interest in an isthmian canal, for no attempt to secure Grey Town, a possible terminus of such a canal, was made at this time.[63] Years later Aberdeen looked back on Britain's relations with Mosquito in a reference which is too garbled to be of much value.[64] The casual reference, however, alluded to the influence and claims of Messrs. Samuel and Peter Shepherd in the Mosquito Kingdom, who secured in all three parcels of land during and after 1839, which they valued at $274,908 in 1850.[65] Aberdeen's contemptuous description of them as adventurers 'who have obtained for a gallon of brandy, large grants of land from a drunken savage whom we have thought fit to call a King' would indicate that he held their claims in the lowest esteem, and would have been unlikely to establish the protectorate for their convenience.

The next chapter in the Mosquito story began with Palmerston's despatch of 30 January 1847, sent to Frederick Chatfield (British Consul in Central America), Patrick Walker (resident in the Mosquito territory), and an individual named O'Leary who represented Britain at Bogotá, asking them to investigate the boundaries of the Mosquito Kingdom, and to recommend those essential to the safety and well-being of that state.[66] Mary Williams traced this project to Palmerston's anticipation of the outcome of the Mexican War, which would surely provide America with territories on the Pacific, and raise Central America to new importance as an American transit route east to west.[67] There is undoubtedly some truth in this interpretation, but it is probably not the whole story by any means.

If we proceed to the 30 January despatch along the route of sequential events, we find three developments possibly relating to it: Walker's despatch of 21 July 1846, which raised the Mosquito boundary question and was received by Palmerston in the early autumn; a parliamentary report by John Macgregor on the Spanish American Republics, which was presented to Parliament on 1 February 1847, but was undoubtedly available to Palmerston before that date; and the Treaty of Bogotá between the United States and New Granada, signed on 12 December 1846. The first of these undoubtedly had a direct bearing on the decision. The establishment of the protectorate naturally raised the question of the territorial limits of the state under protection, if for no other reason than to establish the geographical limits of the new responsibility. The third of the events may or may not have been known to Palmerston; if so, the American treaty would certainly have been regarded by him as a challenge in the Central American area.

The second, however, probably played a larger part in his decision than has been recognised in the past. John Macgregor, a Joint Secretary at the Board of Trade and friend of Richard Cobden, was probably Britain's leading contemporary authority on trade statistics, and his report seems to have been a late-appearing part of the general survey of British trade undertaken by Peel's Government. He wrote a glowing account of the Mosquito territory, which had 'almost inexhaustible supplies of cedar, mahogany, santa maria, rosewood', and other timber, and where rice and Indian corn might be produced, to supply the whole of our West Indian possessions'.[68] Its climate was in many areas superior to that of the West Indies, and the territory between Cape Honduras and the San Juan River was free from the hurricanes that plagued the islands. According to Macgregor, the Mosquito kings had claims to an immense territory.[69] and he rather scored the British Government for not taking a greater interest in this potentially rich land. Another part of the report discussed the possible isthmian canal routes in some detail, but it is significant that he did not believe any of them was likely to be utilised in the near future.[70]

As the glowing Macgregor report might raise discussions of Central American policy in Parliament, what could have been more natural than for Palmerston to seek further information on which to base a Mosquito policy? This would explain his despatch of 30 January. Less easy to explain is why he should have requested information upon which to base a decision regarding Mosquito's boundaries, and then gone ahead and made his decision before the information became available. On 30 June 1847, more than a week before the reply of his principal adviser in Central America, Frederick Chatfield, reached him, Palmerston informed all three of his diplomatic officials that the Mosquito Kingdom stretched from Cape Honduras to the mouth of the San Juan River, and told them to advise the various states bordering on Mosquito that Britain would not view with indifference attempts to encroach on this territory.[71]

There would seem to be two possible explanations for this sudden decision. Chatfield's reply was not received until 8 July, almost six months after Palmerston had requested the information. Perhaps Palmerston grew impatient, and possibly this impatience was fuelled by Pakenham's despatch of 3 April 1847 in which he discussed the expediency 'of securing a passage through the Mexican Isthmus',[72] and two despatches of 28 April, which were received by Palmerston on 14 May, 1847.[73] One of these contained a public letter by Vice-President Dallas in which five possible isthmian routes were discussed, the most favoured being at Tehuantepec, which America might try to secure from Mexico by cession or purchase. The other described the proposed American peace terms, calling for a Mexican cession of her territory north of the 32nd parallel. Whether the isthmian canal proved practicable, or a mad dream, the isthmian territory was sure to take on greater importance when America secured California – perhaps this accounts for Palmerston's sudden declaration of the boundaries of the protectorate. Lacking explanations, such as are usually found only in private correspondence, one can never be certain whether he has arrived at the truth, or merely a *post hoc ergo propter hoc* fallacy when an interpretation of this kind is advanced. Indeed, Chatfield was unaware that the Mosquito decision had been taken before his advice arrived, and he assumed that Palmerston had acted upon it![74]

Upon receiving his instructions from Palmerston, Walker, alleging that the Nicaraguan commander at the mouth of the San Juan River was guilty of arrogant behaviour toward foreigners, on 1 October hoisted the Mosquito flag at San Juan, and later that month the Mosquito Council of State gave the Nicaraguan Government until 1 January 1848 to withdraw from the San Juan area.[75] The Nicaraguans protested, appealed to the United States, and withdrew on schedule, but they shortly thought the better of it, returned, and captured the British stationed at the town. A British naval commander retaliated on 12 February, retook San Juan, and liberated the British prisoners. 'The Nicaraguan Government were ignorant that the Mosquitia flag was so connected with that of England', Sir Charles Grey reported, 'as that an outrage to it should involve an insult to that of Great Britain'.[76]

Down to this point there was apparently little or no consultation by Palmerston with his colleagues regarding Mosquito, and it was early in 1848 before the Colonial Secretary, Lord Grey, and Lord John Russell became involved in the question. Grey was set against allowing 'this mock King & his advisers to pledge us to use force even against one of the petty South American republics.'[77] As the depleted armed forces in the West Indies were not strong enough to protect a British dominion on the continent, Grey proposed that Nicaragua be encouraged to purchase whatever rights the Mosquito King possessed in San Juan. There was more than a flash of prescience in his observation: 'Though this seems so trifling an affair, it is one which if not stopped at once will prove troublesome'.[78]

Just what was Russell's attitude is not clear. Probably it was unimportant, for it is obvious from his handling of the recent Yucatan affair that Palmerston was only lightly bound by the opinions of his superior. When in November 1847 Crampton reported he had been sounded out by the Yucatan commissioner in Washington regarding Britain's attitude toward

Yucatan's annexation by the United States,[79] and asked for instructions, Palmerston sought the opinions of Russell and Grey, noting: 'It would certainly not be desirable to have the United States as our neighbours at Honduras. . . .'[80] Russell wrote on the letter: 'I think we should not have anything to do with Yucatan';[81] and Grey replied: 'I think it very undesirable that we should have anything to do with Yucatan'.[82] Yet Palmerston instructed Crampton that he might 'intimate a doubt whether the contiguity of Yucatan to the Bh. settlement of Honduras might not afford valid reasons why it should not be conducive to the well understood interests of Yucatan that it should place itself in political confederation with the U.S. of N. America.'[83] So Russell's and Grey's advice was considered and ignored in this incident, which provides further evidence, if such is needed, that Palmerston was playing practically a lone hand in making Central American policy.

American reaction to British activities at San Juan was prompt. Buchanan in early February formally requested explanations from Crampton regarding British policies in Central America.[84] In his reply to the query Palmerston failed to clarify Britain's relationship with Mosquitia, simply noting that Britain had merely aided an old friend in re-establishing his control of territory wrongly occupied by Nicaragua in 1836. Britain believed that both states should have access to the Atlantic Ocean, but that San Juan was Mosquito territory.[85] Crampton reported that Buchanan made no comments concerning the British position when this despatch was read to him.[86]

The silence at the moment by no means implied American consent. The immediate result of British involvement in Central America was an intense Anglo-American rivalry during 1848–9, the details of which are recounted elsewhere.[87] The United States raised the Monroe Doctrine, which had recently been reinforced by President Polk. To this Palmerston replied: 'We are ready to vindicate our proceedings on the Mosquito coast whenever we are called upon to do so by any party'.[88] This was not so much of a threat as an expression of Palmerston's personal view that there was nothing illegal or hostile in Britain's recent proceedings at San Juan. In so far as historical connections with Central America were concerned, those of Britain were vastly superior to the American. As for the alleged Monroe Doctrine – Britain had been deeply involved in the La Plata region since 1845, and was on the eve of coercing Brazil. Why, then, did the United States single out Central America to apply the doctrine?

The strong reaction of the United States in 1848 did not immediately deter Palmerston, or cause him to change his policy. This policy, as Van Alstyne had pointed out,[89] was nothing more or less than a complete rearrangement of Central American affairs, which would give Britain a dominant position in Central America. One of the few available private letters, dated 20 December 1848, makes this very clear. Palmerston wrote:[90]

> If we could by treaty with Costa Rica secure the free use of the Magnificent Harbour of San Juan on the Pacific as a re-fitting station for our squadron, we should accomplish an object which the admiralty have long been aiming at in vain; and if we reunite the separate states of Central America in a friendly League in connexion with Mosquito and our Honduras, we might give a great impulse to civilisation and Commerce in a Part of the world eminently favoured by the gifts of nature!

On the basis of this important letter, we must assume that Palmerston, guided by the views of the Admiralty, sought a naval base in Central America of value to her Pacific operations,[91] and, guided by the views of Macgregor, expected to turn Central America into a British economic preserve. Although he may have realised the potential importance of the area as a transit and canal site, he does not seem to have been motivated primarily by these considerations. Palmerston, indeed, had objects in view of a much more extensive nature.

It is not difficult to explain why Palmerston should have conceived such a grandiose plan. On the other hand, – what led him to believe he could get away with it? One possible (though undocumented) explanation is that he thought in European diplomatic terms, which permitted nations to demand 'compensation' for friendly neutrality during a war. He had been on cordial terms with the United States during the Mexican War, and had abandoned Texas, California, and Mexico to her. Might she not be expected to repay Britain by tacitly acknowledging her sphere of influence in Central America?

As it turned out, Palmerston abandoned his scheme even more rapidly than he had formulated it. Mary Williams placed the date of his change of policy between his interview with George Bancroft in July 1849, and one with William C. Rives in September of the same year, and traced it to his new-found confidence that the United States was not planning to monopolise the proposed canal route.[92] As the canal obviously was not the major factor in causing Palmerston to project his plan in the first place, it could hardly have been the determining cause of his abandoning it.

A simple explanation of the course of events would be that Palmerston probed the possibilities of securing a British sphere of influence in Central America, was surprised at the intensity of the American reaction, and therefore modified his policy to one of cooperation with the United States in the area. Had he been able to gain his ends with little difficulty, the prize would have been cheaply purchased, but there was nothing in Central America worth a war, or even an extended controversy (which might interfere with his European diplomacy) with the United States.

There was little in the world situation to force Palmerston to back away from a diplomatic contest with the United States save for the situation in Canada.[93] The Canadian provinces needed reciprocity with the United States; a hostile America would not be expected to grant it, ergo, it was most important to conciliate her. Canadian needs, then, seemed – and rightly – to have taken precedence over Central American possibilities. Such an interpretation receives some confirmation from the fact that Palmerston had decided to send Bulwer to the United States as early as April 1849, and that he was chosen because of his interest in economic matters.[94]

The interview with Rives certainly heralded a change of British policy in Central America. Palmerston's account of it ran as follows:[95]

What Mr. Rives said to me was much to the same effect as what the President & Mr. Clayton said to Mr. Crampton. I said to Rives in reply that the British Govt. have no selfish or exclusive views in regard to a communication by Canal or Railway across the Isthmus from sea to sea – that H. M. Govt. wish that any undertaking of this sort which they may have the means of contributing to facilitate should be generally open to and available to all the nations of the world and should be a highway of Commun. for all men who may have occasion to use it, and I said that if the U. S. Govt. had any arrangement to propose which would have the effect of placing this line of Communication out of the Reach of Disturbances . . . H. M. Govt. would be glad to receive any such Proposal. . . .

This was no more than the acceptance of the American offer to discuss transit arrangements across the Isthmus, and a renunciation of any exclusive British claims to control it. Not renounced was the Mosquito Protectorate, or the British position in Honduras and the Bay Islands.

Two events rapidly disabused Palmerston of any notion he may have had that the American interest was confined to the proposed canal zone. An American agent in Central America concluded a treaty with Nicaragua which seemingly pledged the United States to oust Britain from San Juan, or Grey Town, as it was now called;[96] and the American Minister, Abbott Lawrence, on 8 November 1848 handed Palmerston a note which called for an explanation of British intentions in Central America. The latter asked Britain if she would unite with America in guaranteeing a canal or other means of communication across the isthmus, and – probably the real purpose of the note – if Britain intended to occupy or colonise Nicaragua, Costa Rica, the Mosquito Coast, or any part of Central America.[97]

Lord John Russell collaborated with Palmerston in drawing up the reply to the American note, and struck out one paragraph of the original version.[98] In its final form, the British note agreed to a joint guarantee of the canal route, and denied any intention to occupy or colonise the areas mentioned. But it noted the 'close political connection' existing between Britain and Mosquitia, and offered to secure the Mosquito king's consent to the use of Grey Town, if it should be needed as part of the communications system. So, while the reply accepted the American terms, it emphasised Britain's special position in Mosquitia, and the claim of that Indian state to Grey Town.

Palmerston in a second note, written the same day, took notice of the recent American treaty with Nicaragua: [99]

> I am sure it is needless of me to point out to you that such an engagement would involve the United States in an unprovoked aggression towards Gt. Britain; and I think I am entitled to say that there never was a Time when the British Govt. has less reason to expect so hostile a Proceeding on the Part of the United States; whether we look on the one Hand to the friendly Policy of Great Britain towards the United States, and the great measures which the Parliament of Great Britain has of late passed for opening the Markets of this Country to the Produce and the Ports of this Country to the Ships of the United States; or whether we look on the other hand to the friendly assurances which we have so repeatedly received from the United States Government of which you yourself have so recently and so frankly been the official and to us most satisfactory organ.

There is a curiously injured tone to this note, which suggests Palmerston might have expected his friendly attitude during the Mexican War, and the repeal of the Corn Laws and Navigation Acts to be rewarded by a grateful America. Perhaps he actually felt that way, or, which is more likely, perhaps he was simply advising the United States that he expected some concessions during the coming Bulwer negotiations.

Be this as it may, Palmerston had made it clear before Bulwer ever left London that Britain was not ready to relinquish the historic connections she had formed in Central America. American opposition had dissipated his dream of expanding British influence there, and forced him to recognise America's right to be consulted in matters affecting that region, but there was nothing in his notes to suggest even faintly that Britain accepted the revitalised Monroe Doctrine as international law governing the Western hemisphere.

5
The Clayton-Bulwer Formula

The Clayton–Bulwer negotiations, and the subsequent treaty, which loom so large in this area of American diplomatic history, were in that of Britain a distinctly minor occurrence, talks from which nothing much was expected, and which bore out these modest anticipations. As the United States was not prepared to grant Britain the economic favour she really wanted, and, as Britain was unwilling to satisfy the United States in her Central America policy, no treaty of a substantive nature was possible at the time, so the two countries resorted to that splendid, Anglo-American device of signing a treaty just to produce evidence of movement, which would arrest for a time the further deterioration of their relations. The conclusion of one excellent student of Anglo-American affairs that the treaty prevented 'the imminent threat of a clash over the vital interests of the two countries' seems hardly justified.[1] There was no real sense of urgency in Britain in 1849, save at the Board of Trade and the Colonial Office, such as one might expect if the two nations hovered on the brink of war. Palmerston was dilatory in beginning the negotiations, took little interest in their progress, and seemed indifferent as to their outcome.

If Palmerston took little interest in Anglo-American affairs during 1849–50, he was fully occupied elsewhere, and during this period he exercised an arbitrary authority over foreign policy such as has rarely been achieved by any Foreign Secretary. Having chastised Russia and Austria during the Turkish crisis of the autumn of 1849, he sent the fleet into Brazilian territorial waters to suppress the slave trade in 1850, and early that year he followed an ultimatum to Greece to pay the claims of Don Pacifico with a naval blockade. Stern and extra-legal measures they were, but it was difficult to attack policies that justified themselves by success, and Palmerston basked in the rising sun of popular favour.

Despite his successes (and possibly because of them), the years 1849–50 saw the emergence of an anti-Palmerston movement in both houses of Parliament, and, after the repeal of the Navigation Acts, it became the most divisive of party issues. Some of the more illustrious members of the Peelite Section, including Aberdeen in the Lords, and Gladstone in the Commons, looked to the Conservatives and Lord Stanley as a means of ousting Palmerston, while the Radicals, a small but vocal section, could be depended upon to support such a project, even though any association with the Protection-stained Conservatives was repugnant to them. On paper this was a powerful combination. Its weakness lay in the fact that some Peelites and Conservatives were unsteady on the anti-Palmerston issue, which they knew could hurt them at the polls.

Lord John Russell occupied a most uneasy position between the Court, which was affronted by Palmerston's one-man show, the Radicals and Peelites, on the one hand, and Palmerston and the mass of the Liberal Party on the other. Essentially a 'concensus-type' Prime Minister, he was increasingly dissatisfied with the stir Palmerston was making, but he was powerless to control him.

If Anglo-American relations are thrust into this tangled skein of British party politics, they would add only a few threads to it. Failure to reach an agreement with the United States would help confirm the impression that Palmerston was incorrigibile; success might be offered as evidence of his constructive statesmanship. But the fact is that Palmerston's two major opponents concentrated on wholly unrelated issues. Lord Stanley was deeply worried about the proposed extension of the franchise in Ireland; Aberdeen looked with dismay upon Palmerston's dealings with Austria, Italy, and Greece. Their thoughts were far from America.

The individual selected by Palmerston in April 1849 to replace Pakenham as British minister in Washington (Crampton, who had acted since Pakenham's departure, having been merely a chargé) was well-connected even for a career diplomat, who normally had relatives in high places. Sir William Henry Bulwer had sat as a Liberal in the Commons during the crucial age of reform years, 1830–37, but he also was on friendly terms with Sir Robert Peel, and his younger brother, novelist Edward G. Bulwer-Lytton, was a friend of Disraeli and the Conservatives. Bulwer had served at The Hague and Constantinople before going to Spain, where he had faithfully attempted to carry out Palmerston's policies in the Spanish Marriages affair, and apparently won the Viscount's complete confidence. He had no desire to go to Washington, and as late as September 1849 he almost missed his opportunity to record his name in the history books by trying to change his destination for Brussels. Toward the United States he believed a conciliatory policy, strongly tempered with firmness, was the most effective in accomplishing British objectives.[2] There seem to have been two reasons why he was appointed in April 1849 – first, he was in need of employment; and second, the change of administrations in America in March called for the appointment of a regular British minister to the post in Washington.

Yet – his departure was delayed for nine months, and the question arises – why the delay? Once again there might be two explanations of it. Palmerston seems to have held him up pending the resolution of the crisis in Turkey, a country on which Bulwer was regarded as something of an authority. This is suggested by one of Russell's letters.[3] The second factor was the appointment of a new American minister to London, Abbott Lawrence, whose arrival Palmerston awaited, particularly to learn what tidings he might bring regarding American intentions toward Canada.

On the basis of the private letters available, it would appear that the isthmian issue held a low priority in British thinking with respect to the forthcoming negotiations, and that Canada held the centre of the stage. One of Lord Elgin's private letters to Russell shows why this should be so:[4]

Let me then assure your Lordship, and I speak advisedly in offering this assurance, that the disaffection now existing in Canada, whatever may be the forms with which it may clothe itself, is due mainly to commercial causes. I do not say that there is no discontent on political grounds . . . but I make bold to affirm that so general is the belief that under the present circumstances of our commercial condition the

Colonists pay a heavy pecuniary fine for their fidelity to
Great Britain, that nothing but the existence to an unwanted
degree of political contentment among the mass has prevented the cry for annexation from spreading like wildfire
through the Province. The plea of self-interest, the most
powerful weapon perhaps which the friends of British Con-
nexion have wielded in times past, has not only been wrested
from my hands but transferred since 1846 to those of our
adversary.

In other words, since the repeal of the Corn Laws, it was in the
economic interest of Canada to join the United States, and the
economic stagnation there had by 1849 created an explosive
situation. As Elgin pointed out later in his letter, the United
States might relieve the pressure by signing a reciprocal trade
treaty with the Canadian provinces, but – would she do so?
Would she be a good neighbour, or would she refuse such a
treaty, hoping to force the Canadian provinces into the
Union?

It can hardly be coincidence that the available private letters
of the various British statesmen at this time all dwell on the
same theme. Palmerston turned aside a move by Bulwer to go
to Brussels, noting: 'Besides Bulwer will have some important
commercial matters to settle with the United States, and he is
well acquainted with those subjects, and I doubt not will do us
good service and credit to himself'.[5] Russell had quite a different impression of the new minister's qualifications:[6]

I should rather dread giving Bulwer back a commission
to concede the Newfoundland Fisheries to the Americans.
Grey wishes to please the Colonies and the Bd. of Trade
would give up anything to promote trade. Bulwer knows
nothing of these questions and would be at the mercy of our
cousins at Washington. . . . I know not the extent of our
present Newfoundland fishery, but I suspect that if our people
found that the Americans by bounties had secured the mono-
poly of the Spanish and Portuguese Market – and that this
had been done behind the back of John Bull, we should have
a great outcry.

This letter was evidently in response to a suggestion that a reciprocal trade treaty might be purchased by sacrificing the Newfoundland fisheries, buying this favour for the strongest section of Canada at the expense of the weakest.

Labouchere at the Board of Trade had a deep interest in the forthcoming negotiations, but little hope for their outcome. He wrote:[7]

> As to America, I have been very anxious that Bulwer should soon be at Washington in order that we may learn what their intentions really are. All I hear of the views of the President and his Cabinet is *unfavourable*. . . . I have promised to meet Lord Grey next week to talk over the Instructions to be given to Bulwer about many matters that relate to Canada. . . . I am afraid that America will shuffle and trick us if she can and that she is indisposed to adopt a liberal commercial policy toward Canada from political rather than mercantile reasons. If she does this and refuses to cooperate cordially with us in relaxing the restrictions on navigation, I fear it will not add to the popularity of Free Trade either here or in the Colonies.

After his first talk with Abbott Lawrence, Palmerston received the same impression. '. . . he doubted', he wrote to Russell, 'that Congress would agree to let in the Coal and Iron of our N. A. Provinces. . . .'[8]

Bulwer's personal views of the objects and prospects of his coming negotiations with the United States are found in a letter written in November, 1849:[9]

> I fear from what I have learned . . . that it will be impossible for me to prevent the imposition of higher duties on some of our prime articles of export – Iron, woollen, and cotton goods. The ad valorem duties now existing in the United States are to be changed to fixed duties, and these latter so established as to heighten considerably the present amount. I apprehend also great difficulties to the question of commercial intercourse between our American colonies and the neighbouring republic, but on these subjects I will do my

utmost. . . . The United States are determined to consider
the trade to California as Coasting Trade. I only mention
these circumstances now that I may not take you later by
surprise. I don't apprehend much difficulty about the
Musquitos.

Bulwer may not necessarily have discussed these topics in order
of British priorities of interest, but one must suspect that the
sequence – British exports to the United States, Canadian reciprocity with America, and the affairs of Central America –
probably represents British concerns in descending order of
importance.

It is clear that Labouchere, Palmerston, and Bulwer all seriously doubted that the United States would come to the rescue
of Canada; Russell, indeed, paved the way for failure in this
area in an exceedingly blunt letter.[10] Nor could Bulwer do much
to influence the course of American tariff policy, save to point
to the increasing exports of American corn and raw cotton to
Britain, and to protest that reserving California for American
exporters was not a very liberal response to Britain's repeal of
the Navigation Acts. So all that was left were Central American
affairs, and the limits of agreement in this area had already been
fairly well established. Palmerston in his letter to Lawrence of
13 November had already agreed to cooperate with the United
States in any future isthmian communications project, and had
forsworn any attempt to occupy or colonise any part of Central
America. With regard to the Mosquito territory, Crampton had
already informed both President Taylor and Secretary Clayton
that Britain considered her claim to a protectorate there (perhaps borrowing an American technique recently employed) as
'clear and indisputable'.[11]

So what was there left to talk about? Nothing much directly,
but indirectly the two nations would try to further their most
pressing projects – Britain, Canadian reciprocity; and the
United States, the removal of British influence from the Mosquito coast and other sections of the area. Yet they knew there
could be no meeting of minds on these subjects, and this made
the Clayton–Bulwer negotiations the most disorderly since
Webster and Ashburton practised their curious diplomacy in
1842.

Labouchere and Lord Grey had both been anxious to have Bulwer reach Washington before the meeting of the American Congress, but Palmerston and Russell had felt no sense of urgency. '. . . I am quite at a loss', Grey wrote Russell, 'to understand how you and Palmerston can allow him to linger so long. . . . His going on an Admiralty steamer and calling at Madeira and Bermuda cause additional delay. . . .' [12] As the British and French squadrons did not reach the Dardanelles until November, and Bulwer's advice on Eastern affairs was deemed of importance to the Government, the delay of his departure into that month can perhaps be explained, but why he should then have taken a slow boat to America is less clear unless one accepts the thesis that Russell and Palmerston expected the coming negotiations to be fruitless.

Bulwer was received well when he finally reached the American capital in December. The first business at hand was of a personal nature. John S. Crampton asked for leave of absence to settle some private affairs in England, and he was therefore away from the Capitol until August and took no part in drawing up the convention. No doubt one of his reasons for returning home was to complain of his supercession to Lord Clarendon, who seems to have taken an interest in his diplomatic career. Had the Foreign Office expected something important to emerge from the coming talks, it is unlikely that they would have permitted one of his experience and knowledge of American ways to leave the scene so precipitously.

The new minister obediently brought up quickly the Canadian reciprocity. He urged Clayton that the United States in all fairness should agree to admit the natural produce of all the provinces of Canada, except Newfoundland, at the same tariff rate that those provinces admitted American products. The only stick he could wield to force acceptance of this plan was a broken reed – British public opinion believed America should grant such a concession in view of the fact that American corn was being imported freely into Britain. Clayton replied with a political argument. He would not oppose a reciprocity scheme of this nature if it were introduced in Congress, but he did not think the moment 'favourable' to identify himself with the plan.[13] So Canadian reciprocity was for the time being outside the limits of political possibility, and the matter was dropped.

Clayton, on the other hand, had two big sticks to flourish, and because of them he was able to turn the negotiations into the channels in which the Whig administration took an interest. Elijah Hise had signed a treaty with Nicaragua which gave the United States exclusive canal privileges, and, in effect, gave her control of that state, including its boundary quarrel with Mosquitia. The United States several months before had offered to abandon this treaty providing a satisfactory solution of Central American problems could be reached with Britain. Later in 1849 another American agent, Ephraim G. Squier, had signed another treaty with the same distracted American republic, which recognised Nicaragua's claim to the disputed territory, but opened the way for Anglo-American cooperation in building the proposed canal.[14] Save for a reference to the Monroe Doctrine, the second of these treaties was not so objectionable to Britain as the first. But both contemplated ending British influence at Grey Town.

To further complicate the diplomatic picture in Central America, British subjects were also politically active. The British on Roatan had been virtually self-governing, subject to some supervision from Belize, and, tiring of their anomalous situation, they sent a petition to the Governor of Jamaica in January 1850 requesting a decision – were they a British colony, or merely British citizens resident abroad.[15] Their status was debated by various members of the Home Government during most of the year. In October 1849 a British agent in Central America ordered the seizure of Tigre Island off the western coast of Honduras to achieve a dual purpose – to forestall an American coup to take over the temporary administration of that island, and to hold it as a guarantee for the payment of the Honduran debts to Britain. The news of this seizure reached Washington about the same time as Bulwer, and, though the island was promptly released when higher authority learned of the incident, this rash act could not have aided the new British minister in his mission.

Knowing that he could give the United States little satisfaction on the Mosquito question, and disappointed at the American reception of his request for consideration of a reciprocity treaty with Canada, Bulwer tried to concentrate the negotiations on the proposed isthmian canal, a matter which had already been to some extent agreed upon by the two nations.[16] This was the origins of the most solid accomplishment of the period – the Clayton–Bulwer Convention. Bulwer, therefore, as early as 6 January, sent back the outlines of two possible conventions to Palmerston. The first, after a flowery introduction which described the proposed canal as a 'lasting monument of friendship,' had two articles, one which pledged the two states to protect the construction and neutrality of the canal and the two ports at either end of it, and a statement that neither country would seek exclusive privileges, erect forts, or establish colonies in the area. Bulwer believed this form would provide for a prompt settlement, no doubt because it applied to Nicaragua, the contested area, and would have solved the San Juan question by making it a free port. The second version contained similar self-denying statements by the two countries, but pledged them to jointly examine all possible sites for the proposed canal, not just Nicaragua.

Clayton, who professed anxiety that Congress might make him submit the Hise and Squier treaties to them, and thus much complicate attempts at a friendly adjustment, pressed for the conclusion of a convention without further delay. Whether this was sincere, or a diplomatic ploy to put pressure on Bulwer to concede to American demands, might be argued one way or another, but the fact is that Bulwer found himself under considerable pressure, fearful that the whole matter might be thrown into the Senate, fearful that the United States might take up its options to annex Central America, and fearful that Central American affairs might actually bring on a war. This tactic – frightening the British Minister – was to be employed on more than one occasion in the future by the Americans, much to the annoyance of the Home Government. Bulwer, therefore, conceded everything that he could concede, but, as he explained to Clayton on more than one occasion, specifically giving up the Mosquito protectorate involved a point of honour, and Palmerston would not hear of it.

So proceeded the disorderly negotiation described effectively by Mary Williams in her study of the question.[17] A convention was completed by 3 February, and sent back to Britain, then Clayton demanded some assurance be given to satisfy his colleagues that Britain would not through the Mosquito government do anything she had foresworn in her own name, which led Palmerston to give a formal assurance to that effect that was to be handed over to America when the convention was signed. Instead of laying the matter to rest, the receipt of this statement was followed by a counter-statement by Clayton that the United States did not recognise Mosquito's sovereignty. So Clayton and Bulwer were faced with the difficult task of putting something into the treaty which would convince the American Senate that Britain had relinquished the Mosquito protectorate without its being specifically abandoned. This led to Article I of the treaty, one of the most splendid examples of ambiguity ever penned by a British or an American diplomat, a marvel of verbiage which was to confound interpreters in both countries during the next decade, and in no way solved the problem of the pesky Mosquito Protectorate, but served the higher purpose of preventing a dangerous situation from degenerating further. This willingness to resort to ambiguity when agreement proved impossible has always been one of the uniquely civilised and effective aspects of Anglo-American diplomacy. Clayton and Bulwer showed themselves to be first-rate practitioners of the diplomatic art, covering over their difficulty with a bright-coloured brush.

It is not necessary to score either Bulwer or Clayton for some sort of unpatriotic collusion in composing this article even though they collaborated closely in drawing it up.[18] They were men of the world and politicians who understood each other's positions clearly, so that any actual collusion was unnecessary. This sympathetic understanding was displayed when Bulwer was instructed to make clear to Clayton that Britain claimed Roatan, which he did in a note of 15 April, a note that Clayton feared might have to be sent to Congress, which would doom their treaty. So he requested that Bulwer withdraw his formal note, and accept a private note from him stating the United States had no desire to occupy or settle the Bay Islands. This was done, and the reef was avoided.

Four years later Bulwer looked back upon these extraordinary diplomatic events, and left an interpretation of them which should probably be regarded as his definitive statement on the subject:[19]

Our Musquito protectorate is *de jure* a rotten affair and it would have been far easier for us to take the Mus-quito territory in our own name than in that of King Log.... I certainly did not mean to entrap the American Government into any recognition of our protectorate by these expressions [in the treaty].... The real fact is that we did not abandon our Protectorate, but we abandoned every portion of it that could directly concern the United States, and that we thereby reduced what had been a substance into a mere shadow – obtaining in return for our doing this no resignation of actual power on the part of the U.S., but a limitation of their means of extending their power, which as 3 of the 5 States of Central America were then asking to be annexed was a fair equivalent. It is also to be borne in mind that we obtained in common with the U.S. every advantage to be derived from any route by railway or canal across Central America, the 3 lines then in contemplation being in the hands of American citizens.

England doubtless gained thereby, but so did the Americans and America; for without this double protection and common advantages the lines wd. not have been constructed, nor the owners of the different grants been in a position to contemplate their undertakings. But why [when] G. Britain sacrificed all that was valuable in her protectorate over the Musquitos, in order to conciliate the interests of the U.S., did she not sacrifice the remainder? Simply for this reason – the remainder did not concern the U.S., but Nicaragua.... It was however certain that having gone so far it was our interest to go further at a suitable time and in a suitable manner....

The substance of Bulwer's interpretation was clear enough – he had exchanged all that was valuable in the Mosquito protectorate for an American promise not to annex three of the five Central American states, and what was left of the Mosquito protectorate was of interest to Nicaragua and not the United States. The shadow that was left surely could not have included Grey Town – that was of high interest to America as a possible canal terminus; he, therefore, must have been referring to the boundaries of Mosquitia other than the Grey Town area, and asserting the right of Britain, as protector, to draw them up in negotiations with Nicaragua, a right certainly of little actual value. All else had already been given up by the Clayton–Bulwer Treaty. Palmerston, however, did not interpret the treaty in quite that way.

It is interesting to read the comments, points of emphasis, and interpretations of various diplomatic historians regarding the meaning, purposes, and effects of the Clayton–Bulwer Treaty. Bemis regarded it as a compromise not in the best interest of the United States, but quite understandable in view of the domestic political scene, disrupted by the slavery issue.[20] Mary Williams stressed that the Clayton–Bulwer Treaty, though purposely vague, nevertheless violated the spirit of the Monroe Doctrine.[21] Richard W. Leopold noted that the treaty tied the hands of American expansionists, but at the same time gave substance and support to the Monroe Doctrine.[22] Bourne stressed that Britain intended the treaty to present a formal barrier to the territorial expansion of the United States in Central America.[23] Van Alstyne pointed out that the treaty gave the United States rights in that area wherein she had previously had no rights, but concluded that it was a master-instrument of British diplomacy, for Britain sacrificed no material interest, and secured the best insurance possible for peace in the Western Hemisphere.[24]

If we are guided merely by the popular sentiment in the two countries with regard to the treaty, its being hostilely received by many Americans, and readily accepted by many British, the Clayton–Bulwer Treaty would seem to have been a British diplomatic victory, but, if we turn to its long-run effect, the picture is quite different. Thereafter Britain could hardly turn around in Central America without being charged by Americans with violating its provisions, and almost immediately the Americans used it to pry Britain loose from the Mosquito protectorate and the Bay Islands – two of the three areas in which she had an interest, and eventually they were successful. Palmerston's dream of uniting the Central American states into a league in friendly connection with British Honduras and Mosquitia, and securing a powerful naval station in Costa Rica, was nothing more than a memory after the Clayton–Bulwer Treaty, and such territory as Britain managed to keep was of little value, and no threat to any nation.

The twenty months remaining to Palmerston after the signing of the Clayton–Bulwer Treaty brought him a stunning parliamentary triumph, a popular victory over the Brazilian slavers, and new frustrations in his American policy. At the end of that period Palmerston found himself unceremoniously ejected from the Foreign Office to become the newest recruit among the growing legion of critics of the Russell Government.

Students of Palmerstonian lore usually ponder long over the Don Pacifico debate, yet not overlong because its consequences were so long-lasting. His handling of the claims of Don Pacifico, at most a technical citizen of Great Britain, against friendly Greece, outraged that nation, and gave new umbrage to France, which had attempted to use its good offices to settle the matter. This situation pushed Lord Aberdeen for the time being into the Conservative camp, and he promised to collaborate with Lord Stanley on a major domestic issue in return for the Conservative leader's support for a censure of Palmerston. Stanley, at heart an isolationist and opponent of costly war, did not violate his own principles in acceding to the proposition. There was a meeting of minds, and on 17 June the two former colleagues, leading a Conservative–Peelite combination which hinted at reunion, censured Palmerston for enforcing 'unjust and exorbitant demands upon a feeble and defenceless ally'.

This censure by the Upper House did not particularly disturb Russell and Palmerston, who decided to move a counter-resolution in the Commons. The debate that followed brought to light fairly clearly the views of various statesmen as to the proper conduct of British foreign policy, as well as the outlook of the sections in the Commons. John Roebuck and Richard Cobden, both Radicals, were Palmerston's most unbending opponents; among the Peelites, Gladstone shone forth as Aberdeen's outstanding spokesman in the Commons, while Graham and Peel were much less effective. The Conservatives were lethargic, and Disraeli, though urged by Stanley to strike hard and unsparingly, made such a spiritless speech that an astute observer might have concluded that his views on foreign policy were not wholly at odds with Palmerston's. The large Liberal section, the small Whig party, and secessions from the Conservatives and Peelites gave Palmerston his majority, and a vindication that was eloquent testimony of public support both for the man and his policies.

Palmerston emerged from the debate as a highly possible candidate for the prime-ministership, having demonstrated his ability to secure widespread support from the various sections in the Lower House, and his political stock rose the higher in 1851 when Lord John Russell, leader of the Whigs, deeply offended both the Irish Brigade and the leaders of the Peelite Section by his strong stand against what was termed 'Papal Aggression'.

Among the Peelites at this time it was also out with the old and in with the new. Shortly after the Don Pacifico debate Sir Robert Peel died as the result of an accident, and Lord Aberdeen and Sir James Graham emerged as the leaders of the un-organised Peelite Section. Graham had no ambitions for the highest post, so Palmerston's chief rival in the diplomatic field now became his potential rival for the office of premier. Yet the only statesman at the time who actually commanded a large, disciplined party was Lord Stanley, with whom Aberdeen had lately collaborated.

Palmerston's general popularity was increased again early in 1851 when it became clear that his policy of pursuing slavers inside the territorial waters of Brazil was highly successful. 'If you and the Cabinet had agreed to the same course two and one half years ago when I first proposed it,' Palmerston wrote to Russell, 'many thousand Africans would have been spared the Calamities which have befallen them'.[25] It was hard to quarrel with success.

In the American area, it is clear that Palmerston interpreted the Clayton–Bulwer Treaty as an agreement by Britain to retire from the Mosquito protectorate, but not from the Bay Islands. The petition of the British subjects on Roatan for a clarification of their status seems to have caused some desultory discussion of that area during 1850. Lord Grey believed Britain should annex, or withdraw; Russell wished to preserve the status quo because the Roatan citizens were too few and poor to support a government; Palmerston appears to have supported Grey in a tentative decision to work out some sort of constitution for the Bay Islands.[26] But no step was taken to formally annex the islands during the balance of Palmerston's term of office.

Palmerston and Bulwer seem to have been wholly innocent of any attempt to delay clarifying the situation in Mosquitia. In March 1850 Palmerston advised Russell that Chatfield should be able to settle Mosquitia's boundary with Honduras, and that thereafter Britain would negotiate boundary treaties with Nicaragua and Costa Rica, the last of which would receive Grey Town.[27] Having thus provided protection for the Indian state, Britain would 'withdraw from any active interference in Mosquito concerns'.

That he could not carry out this policy of divesting Britain of the shadow of the protectorate certainly was not his fault, nor that of Bulwer. '. . . directly after the Treaty of April', the latter recalled, 'I began treating with Mr. Webster for the total withdrawal of Great Britain or British protection from Grey Town, and various plans were discussed by us relative to this withdrawal. . . . Mr. Webster was the man least likely to take a wrong view of the spirit of a treaty or of its letter'.[28] The talks mentioned began in July, when Daniel Webster, who had the complete confidence of the British Foreign Office, once again became the Secretary of State.

The official British interpretation of these negotiations, their course and their outcome, is given in one of Lord Granville's letters of a later date.[29]

Mr. C. is aware that within the last two years H. M. Minister at Washington [Bulwer] made to the U.S. Government several communications on the question at issue, whereby he explained to the American Secy. of State that, in adopting any new settlement with respect to Grey Town, it appeared to H. M. Govt. desirable to make if possible such settlement conducive to the establishment of amicable relations between Nicaragua and Costa Rica, those Republics being at variance with regard to their respective Territories and Rights. It appeared also to H. M. Govt. preferable that the two Ports at the several extremes of the projected Canals should be placed in the hands of two separate central American states rather than that those Ports shd. remain in the hands of one and the same State. Consequently the first proposition or suggestion put forward by Sir H. Bulwer was that the Mosquito Govt. shd. be induced for some consideration to surrender to Costa Rica the Port of Grey Town, and a district adjoining thereto, and that if Nicaragua assented to this arrangement, this state shd. be compensated by receiving an adequate portion of the Country claimed by her, but now held by Costa Rica. Some delay in dealing was unavoidably caused by there being no Minister from Nicaragua at Washington until the opening of /51, and when a Minister at length arrived, H. M. Minister found it impossible to induce that person to conclude any friendly arrangement on the basis above described. Sir H. Bulwer therefore suggested that instead of Costa Rica being put in possession of Grey Town, the Port and district shd. be made over to Nicaragua in the same manner in which he had first proposed it shd. be ceded to Costa Rica, and further that Costa Rica shd. cede to Nicaragua the share which she claims in the Sovereignty over the River San Juan, on condition that she should still retain the right of free navigation over the sd. river for all except Steam vessels. In return for this concession it was proposed that Nicaragua shd. abandon her pretentions to those portions of the territory now possessed by Costa Rica, but claimed by Nicaragua, it being always understood that Nicaragua and Costa Rica shd. both agree to respect the remaining territory of Mosquito. This proposal was made to the Minister of Nicaragua in the presence of Mr. Webster, who appeared at that time to consider that it offered upon the whole a fair basis for mutual agreement. But the Minister of Nicaragua declared that he had no sufficient authority to treat thereupon, and that he was therefore obliged to refer to his Govt. for further powers. In the meantime those changes and convulsions, which unfortunately took place at that period in the state of Nicaragua interposed obstacles to the negotiation.

That Britain tried to play the part of honest broker, and to free herself of her embarrassing protectorate by fair agreement is hardly contestable.[30] The effort was frustrated by the chaotic state of Nicaraguan politics.

Bulwer in August 1851 returned to Britain in search of a continental post, which was found for him at Florence the following year, and affairs in Washington were again turned over to Crampton, who had settled his personal affairs abroad, and returned to America. Shortly after assuming charge of British diplomatic affairs he discovered and seized upon an opportunity to do a good turn for his hosts. An attempt by Narciso Lopez and American adventurers to seize Cuba in August 1851 was frustrated by the Spanish there, who then called upon Britain and France to help defend the island against these repeated attacks.[31] Some of the Americans involved in the filibuster were sent off to labour in Spain; others were condemned to death, and when the news of these sentences reached America, a New Orleans mob attacked the Spanish consulate, and provoked a crisis in Spanish-American relations. Crampton quickly offered his good offices in mediating the quarrel, and he was wholly successful. Spain accepted the American explanations, and re-patriated many of the captive Americans. 'Webster wrote me a very handsome letter for his services in patching up the recent Spanish quarrel', Clarendon wrote, 'and the Spanish Government think that without him they would not have arrived at a successful issue'.[32] Certainly this was a brilliant beginning to a tour of duty which was to have so miserable an end.

While all this was taking place, the seemingly invincible Palmerston was riding to a fall. By late 1851 the Foreign Secretary was entirely out of hand. Whenever possible he simply ignored the Queen and Prince Albert, and even opened the former's private letters from other monarchs. When the revolutionist, Louis Kossuth, arrived in Britain Russell asked Palmerston not to receive him, but the Foreign Secretary was unwilling to miss this opportunity of ingratiating himself with the European liberals, and (as a private citizen) received both Kossuth and Radical petitions against Austria and Russia. The final blow to Russell and the Queen was bestowed when the Foreign Secretary, who had agreed not to take sides when Louis Napoleon in December assumed the permanent presidency of the French Republic, expressed his approval of the change to the French Ambassador.

Russell, who, earlier in the year had promised the Queen to keep Palmerston in hand, had little choice but to cashier him, which was done by offering him the position of Lord Lieutenant of Ireland. Palmerston quite naturally refused a situation for which he was little fitted, and instead retired from the Government. Nursing a grudge, he awaited an opportunity to have his 'tit for tat' with the foundering Prime Minister.

The fall of Palmerston in December 1851 would have given the seals of the Foreign Office to Lord Clarendon, who was next in line, but he hesitated to thrust himself into the middle of the Whig schism between Palmerston and Russell, and the position went to Lord Granville Leveson-Gower, a splendidly-connected Whig who had served briefly as Under Secretary for Foreign Affairs. More than thirty years younger than Palmerston, and fifteen years the junior of Clarendon, the thirty-six-year-old Earl brought the industry and the earnest purpose of youth to the Foreign Office.

Granville's position was much less difficult than that of Aberdeen in 1841. Aberdeen had faced an outraged France and a major crisis with the United States, and although the decade had by no means eliminated all sources of friction between those countries and Britain, relations seemed much improved in both areas. Palmerston's prompt approval of Louis Napoleon's coup had ingratiated him with that adventurer. Furthermore, even though Russell still continued to fret about the intentions of the French,[33] the statistics regarding the relative strengths of the French and British navies should certainly have quieted his fears.[34] Indeed, in view of Russell's continued nervousness in this area, it would seem that he had imbibed deeply Palmerston's settled distrust of the French.

The Prime Minister also distrusted the United States despite the recent Clayton–Bulwer Treaty. This is illustrated by the remarks he made (given in parentheses) on an American report of conditions in the Minnesota Territory:[35]

The policy of the Hudson's Bay Company has been to keep these people in their territories in a deplorable state of ignorance as to the value of their lands. . . . (What is this to the Yankees even if true?) A paper currency has been established among them, which from its peculiar character would be considered as savouring rather too much of fraud by the laws of the United States. (The issuers of dollar-notes or shin plasters are not the parties to complain. 'Quis tulerit Gracchus de seditione querentes?') The vast amount of peltries has to a great extent been withdrawn from the territory of the United States. . . . (How is this to be shown or proved?) Not content with their influence along the Red River of the North, the Company has established a chain of trading-posts along our northern frontier, to connect with their settlements in Oregon. (Is it meant to infer that it is within the territory of the United States? If it is not, where is the ground for complaint?) The encroachments of England upon American territory . . . would, I think, produce sufficient reasons to attract the immediate notice of our Government. (Why not condescend to particularise, as the Scotch lawyers say?) The American traders . . . labour under the most insuperable disadvantage of being compelled to observe the strict laws of the United States in reference to the introduction of spiritous liquors among the Indians. . . . (Our regulation is the same. I doubt, however, whether it is observed by the Company.) The course now necessary is the immediate establishment of a military post . . . which will manifest the intention of the Government of the United States to encourage the enterprise and industry of the people . . . (For *enterprise* we should probably read *aggression*.)

The continued refusal of the United States to proffer economic relief to Canada encouraged this British suspicion of American intentions. So did the occasional American harassment of the Hudson's Bay Company, which was excoriated in the above report.[36] American intentions toward the Sandwich Islands also occasioned fleeting concern in Britain just at this time.[37]

Despite his youthful *avant garde* opinions on some subjects, such as Free Trade, Granville had the full confidence of the Queen and Prince Albert. He could also rely on Clarendon for advice, if it were needed. His chief weaknesses were lack of experience and prestige in international circles, and he obviously sought to make up for them by going about his task with unusual earnestness and energy. Toward the United States he adopted the conciliatory policy that had been characteristic of Aberdeen most of the time, and of Palmerston (save for his Central American adventure) especially since 1846.

Two gestures made early in his administration might be considered by the Americans as a mark of his good intentions. On the advice of Clarendon, who believed Palmerston had treated Crampton badly, he gave approval to Crampton's handling of the Cuba crisis by advancing him to the rank of Envoy in January 1852.[38] The same month he recalled Frederick Chatfield, who had long been a thorn in the side of the Americans, from his consular post in Central America.

Granville's most pressing problem on assuming office – and this was to some extent solved for him before he could take action – involved the American ship *Prometheus*, owned by Cornelius Vanderbilt's recently opened Atlantic and Pacific Company, which refused to pay harbour dues to the authorities at Grey Town. Late in November 1851 the authorities there employed the British brig *Express* to force the payment, an action which brought forth angry reaction in Congress. Crampton, who suspected that certain American citizens on the council at Grey Town, hostile to Vanderbilt's enterprise, had manufactured the incident, quickly instructed the British Consul there to avoid 'all matters which cause excitement in the U.S., and give rise to grave questions between the two Govts'.[39] About the same time the British admiral in the area instructed the commander of the *Express* to refrain from enforcing the Grey Town customs regulations in the future.[40] These reactions to the incident convinced Webster of the desire of the British Government to avoid such clashes in the area.

As soon as he had received full information regarding the *Prometheus* affair, Granville addressed a note to the American minister in London in which his Government offered 'an ample apology for that which they consider to have been an infraction of treaty engagement'.[41] He also censured the British Consul in Grey Town for his part in the affair.

The United States could hardly, under the circumstances, have expected a more prompt and comprehensive disavowal by the British, the circumstances involving, as they did, an American vessel which alone (other American vessels paid the dues) took upon itself to challenge the authority of the Grey Town authorities, and create an incident.

The *Prometheus* affair inspired the second major attempt by the British to settle affairs in Central America, and retire from Mosquitia. Bulwer had failed, due to the inability of Nicaragua to come to an agreement, and negotiations had been suspended for almost six months. As soon as he learned from Crampton that Webster had expressed a wish to resume them, Granville drew up two letters to his envoy in which he outlined the current thinking of the Government on the Mosquito problem.[42]

In the first letter Granville suggested that the propositions advanced by Bulwer should again be discussed, but that, if Webster desired some other solution, the British Government would entertain it, providing that it did not force them into a dishonourable abandonment of Mosquitia. In the second letter, he suggested two alternative plans – that Grey Town could be made a joint ward of all the Central American Republics, or that Britain and the United States assume responsibility for it. Thus Crampton was given almost *carte blanche* to settle the issue, and to end the protectorate; the only strings attached were that an indemnity be paid Mosquitia for Grey Town and the territory taken from her, and that her remaining territory be respected by the Central American states. In laying down these two conditions, the British believed they were redeeming a pledge given before the signing of the Clayton–Bulwer Treaty. Uppermost in Granville's mind was arriving at a settlement that would 'secure that cordial assent and good will of the U.S.'

The Foreign Secretary had obviously studied the situation carefully. He anticipated trouble from Nicaragua, which might resist ceding any disputed territory to Costa Rica, paying any indemnity to Mosquitia, and, indeed, leaving that state with any territory at all. Arbitration was the only means he could excogitate to solve the Costa Rica problem. To circumvent the vexing sovereignty question, he suggested that Nicaragua pay Mosquitia an indemnity for her occupancy, rather than her vague sovereign rights over the ceded territory, much as the United States did in securing lands from the American Indians. Granville's proposals were statesmanlike and highly conciliatory – as he said, Britain had no selfish ends to serve in the solution of this question.

During the rest of his brief term at the Foreign Office, the news Granville received from America was not encouraging. Illegal fees were being charged British ships putting in at San Francisco;[43] the American duties levied on British coffee and tea were considered less than 'liberal'.[44] Even more discouraging was a report from Crampton that the United States had adopted a new mode of levying its ad valorem duties on articles imported from Canada, which was detrimental to trade, and seemed to indicate that the United States was increasing her economic pressure on British North America.[45]

Then came news in February that the American naval forces in Central America had been advised that Britain, under the terms of the Clayton–Bulwer Treaty, had resigned her protectorate over any part of Central America and British authority in Grey Town and elsewhere would be ignored. Granville recognised the 'critical situation' that these American instructions created, and quickly ordered Crampton to secure *de facto* recognition of the governing body at Grey Town from the United States until its status could be determined by negotiations.[46] This sudden and unexpected raising of a new and dangerous question – the meaning of the Clayton–Bulwer Treaty – at a moment when Britain was making every effort to satisfy the United States in Central America, combined with the new economic pressure on Canada, fortified the impression in the Foreign Office that America was an 'encroaching' nation even when so friendly and conciliatory a statesman as Daniel Webster was Secretary of State.

The same day that Granville sent out his instructions to Crampton regarding the *de facto* status of Grey Town, and complained about American duties on British imports, the Russell Government fell from power. The disgruntled Prime Minister charged that he had been the victim of a 'pre-arranged determination' between Lord Palmerston, and Lord Derby (formerly Lord Stanley), which was quite untrue, but Palmerston unquestionably found no inconsiderable satisfaction in thus revenging his own recent dismissal, and Derby, leading an impatient party that had been out of power for six years, was quite ready to take up the burdens of office.

6
The Derby–Malmesbury Policy

When Lord Derby took office in 1852, he did so in company with rank amateurs, who had to be sworn in as Privy Councillors before they could accept the seals of their offices. Derby himself (as Stanley) had twice served as Colonial Secretary, so he was well-versed in official routines, but the others, including Disraeli, were wholly inexperienced. For this reason, as well as because of his connections, oratorical ability, and social prestige, Derby was the directing force in all departments of the Government during this period of his official life.

The Conservatives in 1852 held office, but they had no power. Without a majority in the Commons, they were tolerated by the Peelites and others only as an interim government until an election could be held later in the year. Indeed, the Government had to pledge itself to refrain from proposing any controversial legislation before that event, which severely limited their freedom of action in tackling domestic problems.

So the only area where they had much freedom of movement was one in which Derby was not particularly interested – foreign affairs. In this sphere Derby had been deeply influenced both by Aberdeen's Christian pacifism, and Peel's dislike of the expenses of wars and armament programmes, and he might be classified as a 'big navy man', who depended on a strong navy to keep Britain out of war. The rank and file of the Conservative Party shared these views, and longed for the repeal of the Income Tax, but they were also strongly patriotic, and more than a few had a secret or open admiration for Palmerston. While desiring to avoid the bloodshed and expenses of war, the Conservatives nevertheless liked the Government to 'show spirit', and not be quite so dogmatically pacifistic as Aberdeen had been.

Lord Derby's ministerial state of 27 February 1852 called for

a 'calm, temperate, deliberate, and conciliatory course of conduct, not in acts alone, but in words also'.[1] Peace was best preserved by neither excessive arming or disarming, but by adopting a dignified attitude toward all powers, great and small, and
regardless of their forms of government. Much of this was a
criticism of Palmerston, whose enemies charged him with
bullying weak powers, using intemperate language, and favouring revolutionary governments over monarchical ones.

The one area in foreign affairs where Derby could feel at
home – unlike all of his predecessors – was in Anglo-American
relations. He had the inestimable advantage of having toured
much of the eastern United States, and having met Americans
of all social classes, as well as many American politicians. He
believed he understood Americans, how they thought, and why
they acted as they did, and his previous dealings with them had
been marked by understanding, even kindness. But he was now
Prime Minister, and leader of a Party many of whose members
openly feared the 'Americanisation' of British institutions, who
regarded the republican form of government with deep distaste,
and looked down upon Americans as misguided relatives. The
conservative *Quarterly Review* hailed Derby as Britain's 'last
chance of escape' from a 'democratic and socialist revolution'.[2]
As leader of this party, it was Derby's duty to extol British institutions, and to properly downgrade those of all republics,
including America.

Even had he been completely free to follow a pro-American
policy, it is doubtful that Derby would have done so, for in 1852
he was disgusted with the American attitude toward Canada,
an area toward which he felt a strong, personal responsibility.
During the Second Peel Administration, he had fathered the
Canadian Corn Bill, which had given Canadian wheat a preference in the British market; only to have the whole system overturned by the repeal of the Corn Laws, and the American
refusal to enter upon a trade agreement with Canada. He had
also, as Colonial Secretary, opened the Bay of Fundy to American fishermen, not as a matter of right, but as an 'amicable
concession' against the advice of the Law Officers. Derby believed the Americans had behaved badly, and bringing them
around to a more liberal attitude became a major endeavour of
his foreign policy.

For Foreign Secretary Derby selected his friend and favourite hunting companion, the 3rd Earl of Malmesbury, whose major contact with foreign policy-making had been editing and publishing the papers of his grandfather, the 1st Earl, who had been a diplomatist of some stature at the turn of the century. The 1st Earl had been one of Palmerston's patrons, and Palmerston, in turn, had been friendly with the 3rd Earl, who was a generation his junior. To help Malmesbury, and to initiate him into the routine of public office, Derby appointed his son, Edward Stanley, as Under Secretary of Foreign Affairs.

Malmesbury had one other, and quite important, qualification for his high office. He had been the friend of Louis Napoleon when the President of the French had been very much in need, a prisoner, in fact, in Ham. Now that Napoleon's fortunes had much improved, and the chancelleries of Europe nervously awaited the next phase in the life of another Napoleon, this connection suddenly loomed as of major importance. President Napoleon quickly wrote a congratulatory letter to Malmesbury on learning of his appointment, and the Foreign Secretary replied in kind to 'your Royal Highness' – a strange title for a republican leader![3]

The new Foreign Secretary had the benefit of advice from many quarters. The Queen and Prince Albert made him privy to the complexities of German politics. Palmerston presented himself at the Foreign Office to warn Malmesbury that foreign governments often sought concessions from new British Governments denied them by their predecessors, and that his primary function was to uphold British prestige abroad. Malmesbury must 'keep well with France', but never quite trust her, especially in eastern affairs, for in that area Britain and France were like 'two men in love with the same woman'. The conversation ended with Palmerston advising an increase in defence expenditures. Almost identical advice was tendered to Malmesbury by the Duke of Wellington, whom he visited shortly after assuming office. The Duke did not think Napoleon wanted war with Britain, but he might do anything in order to maintain his popularity.[4]

As was customary, the former Foreign Secretary briefed the new one regarding the state of international politics. Granville's forebears had been associated with those of Malmesbury, and the latter counted Granville among his friends. The outgoing secretary told him that the pressing questions included French demands on Switzerland, Prussian claims on Neufchatel, Abbas of Egypt's demands upon the Sultan for greater authority, and the Greek and Danish crowns. The situation that needed the closest attention was Napoleon's campaign to make himself the Emperor of France.[5] This conversation furnishes additional proof of the low priority Anglo-American relations held in British diplomacy at this time – not a word, apparently, was spoken about the Mosquito coast, nor the situation in Canada! Americans might justly complain about this lack of attention; on the other hand, the omission indicates that Granville believed the Fillmore–Webster combination was friendly, and presented no threat to Britain.

Throughout the ten months of the Derby administration, French policy was the dominant theme in foreign affairs. There was a minor incident involving Switzerland, another concerning Belgium, and a drawn-up debate regarding the proper international reaction if Napoleon adopted the numeral III when he became Emperor. There was a widespread fear that the adoption of that numeral would mean the Emperor did not recognise as valid the various agreements reached by the 'illegitimate' French governments since the fall of his uncle. How these questions were blown up to immense proportions is evident in Malmesbury's memoirs. Under the date 24 October, Malmesbury recorded: 'Universal apprehension of war if the French Empire is proclaimed. This panic is spread far and wide by King Leopold'.[6] Ten days later he noted that Disraeli, Chancellor of the Exchequer, had had a long conference with Prince Albert regarding national defences. 'Disraeli, in very low spirits, said it would destroy his budget, and ridiculed the panic'.[7] It is interesting to note that Disraeli, later to be a main pillar of the British Empire, and exponent of a vigorous foreign policy, when Chancellor of the Exchequer (and having to meet the expenses entailed by both) was both pacific and anti-imperial.

Lord Derby had a low opinion of both the French and Napoleon. 'France and Frenchmen', he wrote, 'are incapable of rational self-government, and . . . sooner or later they will give themselves a master'.[8] In October he wrote a lengthy letter to Malmesbury, which betrayed some concern, but no panic. 'Her language and her actions towards us, so far, have been perfectly friendly', he observed, 'but I cannot help mistrusting Napoleon's *patte de velours*, and we must continue to make all "snug" at home, in case of a sudden outbreak'.[9] Alone among the makers of British foreign policy at this time, Derby spent as much time thinking about the United States and Canada, as about France. At least, this is the impression conveyed by his letters.

During this autumnal crisis, when others were losing their heads, Malmesbury did a most noteworthy job of correctly analysing the psychology of the French leader. He wrote to his chief:[10]

> This general terror of what is coming is a presentiment, for none can give any reasons founded on facts to show the sinister feelings and intentions of Louis Napoleon. I believe I stand alone, therefore, in disbelieving them; and these are my arguments. – He has no natural dislike to the English. Ever since I knew him, he courted their society, and imitated their habits. Twenty years ago, when he could not have been playing a part with me . . . he always said that his uncle's great mistake was not being friends with England.

He went on to produce such a mass of impressive evidence proving Napoleon's friendly intentions that one wonders today how the panic of those months could possibly have arisen. The fact that it did demonstrates the cultural lag so often characteristic of diplomatic affairs, as opinions and prejudices change but slowly, and traditional enmities nourish themselves upon them.

Malmesbury, then, deserves the main credit for guiding his nation gently over the numerical hurdle. When Napoleon made himself the Emperor, Malmesbury was quick both to accept his new position, and his title, once he had written proof that the new Emperor accepted the validity of the engagements entered upon by previous French Governments. Many years later, when Malmesbury looked back and enumerated the accomplishments of the Derby Governments, he included 'the ready recognition of the Second French Empire under Louis Napoleon, in spite of the grudging hesitations and objections of the Great Powers to follow suit'.[11] In this recognition, Derby's disinterest and Disraeli's budget worries no doubt played a part, but the chief motive force was undoubtedly Malmesbury.

There were certain areas in which the Conservatives had had their course laid out for them by previous administrations, and they had little choice but to proceed along them. One of these was in Brazil. Anglo-Brazilian relations were much improved by 1852, and the British Consul at Montevideo had displayed confidence in Brazil, which had some claims to the area, by inviting them to occupy Uruguay to keep order after the fall of Rosas. It was merely a temporary occupation.[12] Later in the year the Brazilians offered Britain a new anti-slave trade treaty designed to end the illegal activities of the British cruisers in their waters. Malmesbury admitted that Palmerston had taken a 'high-handed line' that could be justified only by necessity, but he would not agree to such a treaty until it became absolutely clear that the Brazilians themselves were in earnest in suppressing the slave trade.[13] A Conservative spokesman the following month traced for Parliament the decline of slave importations as follows – 54,000 in 1849, 23,000 in 1850, and 3,287 in 1851.[14] Malmesbury was obviously reluctant to disturb a policy which displayed such striking successes.

Central American policy seems also to have been dictated by the policy set afoot by Palmerston and Granville. Crampton had been given far-reaching powers to end the Mosquito protectorate; Webster was conciliatory and anxious to bring it about – the result was one of the more orderly negotiations conducted during the whole period, which can be followed in detail in Crampton's despatches.[15] Orderly – up to a point, but by no means entirely so.

In order to prevent a clash between British and American naval units at Greytown, Crampton and Webster quickly agreed to send instructions to their respective commanders to recognise the government there as *de facto*, but by the time these instructions had arrived, the commanders had left the scene, and an unruly body of citizens, mostly Americans, threatened to take over the town and expel the British agents. Once again Crampton and Webster collaborated on instructions to preserve law and order. Malmesbury approved Crampton's 'judicious proceedings' in both cases.[16]

Late in March 1852 Crampton and Webster began to negotiate an agreement to dispose of Grey Town, and end the protectorate. Crampton brought forth what might be termed

Britain's maximum demands; Webster replied with a similar assertion of the American position. No meeting of minds took place, and Webster told Crampton to outline terms which would be accepted by his Government, and he would submit them to the President. Crampton, therefore, drew up and sent home an eight point project which gave Grey Town and a modest share of the Mosquito territory to Nicaragua for an unstated sum of money, provided for the voluntary annexation of all Mosquitia to that state if the Indians desired it, and gave the District of Guanacaste and the south bank of the San Juan River to Costa Rica. He also asked to be able to detain Charles L. Wyke, the new British Consul to Central America, who was passing through Washington, so that he could accompany an American agent to Central America and secure the assent of Costa Rica and Nicaragua to the terms eventually agreed upon. Malmesbury approved both the project, and the method suggested by his Minister.[17]

Late in April Webster discussed the terms of the agreement, and secured some sweeping modifications of the original project. Convinced that Nicaragua would not accept Crampton's proposal, he secured most of the Mosquito territory for her, and left the Indians with a reservation; whittled down the compensation to the Indians, and provided for its payment from Grey Town port duties; and considerably abridged the territorial settlement south of the river to accommodate eight large sections of land which Nicaragua had granted to the Atlantic and Pacific Canal Company. This project was much less favourable both to the Mosquito Indians and to Costa Rica than Crampton's original plan, but Crampton considered it similar to the terms accepted by Bulwer the preceding July. Yielding to Webster's plea that time was of the essence so that the matter could be cleared up before Congress rose, he sent it off with Wyke and his American counterpart without Malmesbury's having even seen it. Crampton, however, emphasised that Wyke would insist on an indemnity to Mosquito as a *sine qua non* for British acceptance.

Malmesbury was presented with this *fait accompli* in a despatch which reached his office on 16 May. The Foreign Secretary was disappointed by the sweeping changes, and perhaps a little piqued by Crampton's arbitrary handling of the matter, but he put a good face on it. '. . . I conclude you found it impossible to obtain the sanction of the United States Government to the project as it stood', he wrote, 'and that, in order to close once for all, while yet practicable, a difficult and hazardous question, you preferred to admit less favourable terms rather than to leave the question still open. If such was the case, Her Majesty's Government could not refuse their assent to the correctness of your decision'.[18] It was a paragraph that would read well if presented to Parliament and the world at a later date. Malmesbury agreed to stand by the version if Nicaragua accepted it, but (as seemed probable) if they did not, he suggested certain changes in any later revision, tightening up the wording so that Nicaragua could not expand her territorial claims even farther, and providing for a more definite means of paying the Mosquito indemnity. The Foreign Secretary also noted the omission of any reference to a Honduran claim, and the Black River grant that had been made by the Mosquito king to certain British subjects.

To all intents and purposes, however, he had lost control of the negotiation, and the Anglo-American project was again proceeding in a disorderly fashion. Perhaps Malmesbury was not too wroth at this development. All sensible observers realised the Mosquito protectorate had to be ended by concessions, and if, at a later date, some chauvinist criticised the project as knuckling under to American pressure, Malmesbury could transfer the weight of obloquy to his representative in Washington.[19]

In July Malmesbury learned that the citizens at Grey Town, now predominantly Americans, had adopted a constitution and completely reconstituted the government there, making it a free town under the nominal sovereignty of the King of Mosquitia. Far from disapproving these proceedings, Malmesbury quickly wrote to Crampton that the new government of Grey Town probably would not want to be annexed to Nicaragua, and that Britain had no desire whatsoever to give the town to her; therefore, if Nicaragua rejected the current offer, Britain would arrange with the United States almost any settlement she suggested including (what Britain most desired) a joint Anglo-American protectorate.[20]

As Malmesbury had expected, the joint Anglo-American project was accepted by Costa Rica, and summarily rejected by

Nicaragua. Crampton therefore informed Webster that he considered the negotiation as broken off. The American Secretary of State asked for time to consider the subject, and opined that America and Britain might have to arrive at a solution themselves without the adherence of Nicaragua, a tactic which would have been eminently acceptable to Britain.[21]

So, for the second time, Britain had made a major effort to settle the Mosquito question, and to withdraw from the area. She had accepted an American-made compromise of which she really disapproved simply to bring an end to the unfortunate situation. It would seem that one would have to be a strong partisan of Nicaragua not to saddle that state with the full blame for keeping open a source of irritation between these two great Powers.[22]

In another area of Central America, which is much less documented, the Government completed a project which had been far advanced by their predecessors. One authority traced British interest in annexing the Bay Islands, the largest of which was Roatan, to the rising commercial importance of these islands off the coast of Honduras.[23] Actually, the annexation seems to have been virtually assured if and when the settlers there could afford to support a magistrate. Following their request for a status clarification, the Russell Government went to work on a constitution, which was adopted, and on 20 March 1852 the Colony of the Bay Islands came into existence. This was the work of the Colonial Office, and Malmesbury at the time apparently was not even informed of it.[24] Nor did Webster see fit to challenge, or even ask for explanations from Crampton on the subject. No one in the Government seems to have anticipated that this action would be blown up by the Americans into a breach of both the Monroe Doctrine and the Clayton–Bulwer Treaty.

The very same month that Roatan was formally annexed, Malmesbury showed a nice appreciation of American sensitivities regarding Latin America. The same commercial-based pressures that had forced Aberdeen into his disastrous intervention into La Plata affairs in 1845 were brought to bear on Malmesbury to secure by treaty the opening of the rivers of that region once Manuel Rosas was overturned in early 1852. The day after learning of this event, Malmesbury contacted the French Government with an invitation to send a joint Anglo-French nego-

tiating team to secure the opening of the Parana and Uruguay
Rivers to general trade.[25]

This was not a hostile mission, nor was Britain seeking any exclusive advantage in the La Plata. It was only because haste
seemed advisable that Malmesbury, who considered such a step,
did not invite America to join in the intervention, and Lord
Derby saw fit to call in the American Minister, and explain to
him the plans of Britain and France in detail. To make doubly
sure that America would not take umbrage, Malmesbury
ordered Crampton to explain the situation in Washington:[26]

> It is the wish of Her Majesty's Government that you should
> mention this . . . to the Government of the United States,
> stating at the same time that we desire no commercial advan-
> tages for ourselves in particular. . . . We have reason to
> believe that the Government of the United States will receive
> the information with favour; but if you should find any dis-
> satisfaction expressed at our not having invited it to join with
> us and France in this mission, you will account for the fact by
> representing that our success depends upon the most rapid
> movements. . . . Should any question be asked you respecting
> the primary proposals, you will not fail to state that we can
> only demand the opening of the Parana as a privilege and not
> as a right. You will at once see how this point touches our
> rights to the navigation of the St. Lawrence, and the impor-
> tance of our not appearing to hold different principles on
> different sides of the Equator.

This letter was in itself an admission of the special interest of
the United States in Latin American affairs, if not an acknow-
ledgement of the Monroe Doctrine.

The mission seemed to have been successfully completed
shortly after the Conservatives left office. 'Sir C. Hotham has
written to me to say that he has signed a commercial Treaty with
Paraguay obtaining everything laid down in his instructions',
Malmesbury wrote in early 1853. 'The Treaty is based upon the
English form & has been signed by France, Sardinia & the U.S.
The Parana below having been opened before we are now free
to go right up to Bolivia. *We ought* to have the credit of
this. . . .'[27] It appeared to have been a major accomplishment of

the administration. Unfortunately, however, Malmesbury could not anticipate the vagaries of Latin American domestic politics.

By far the most daring and imaginative venture into foreign affairs by the Derby administration was in Canada. Lord Elgin, the Governor General, early in 1852 complained about American encroachments in the Newfoundland Fisheries area in violation of the Treaty of 1818. He also stressed the importance of an American-Canadian reciprocity treaty, and suggested that Britain might cede America the right of navigating the St. Lawrence River as a bribe to secure such an agreement. The able, efficient Colonial Secretary, Sir John S. Pakington, broached these subjects in a letter to Lord Derby in April, and posed the possibility of dispatching a more efficient naval force to police the fisheries.

Good fortune and the Prime Minister's affection for the sport of kings have provided an historical record of Derby's reaction to the situation. After the day's races at Goodwood, he sat down and penned a fairly long letter about Canadian affairs in general, and noted the importance of 'bringing Brother Jonathan to his senses'.[28] As he saw it, Britain ever since the repeal of the Corn Laws had made a series of humiliating advances to America 'beseeching them as an act of favour & bribing them by most liberal offers, to do a mere act of justice to our Colonial possessions. . .' .[29] Reciprocity would bestow no boons on Britain, on the contrary, it would bind her colonies more closely to the United States. Furthermore, he was convinced that previous British Governments had used the wrong tactics in dealing with America. Instead of offering the navigation of the St Lawrence as a bribe to the United States, Britain had better employ some form of coercion, such as closing Canadian canals to American ships.

The various Canadian colonies, he pointed out, differed widely upon the fisheries issue, but all of them seemed to forget that there was an imperial interest in the matter – the United States was Britain's greatest maritime rival.[30] Subject to further reviews by the Foreign Office, Board of Trade, and the Admiralty, Derby tentatively approved a plan to send small cutters to police the fisheries area, but he very wisely insisted that the fleet should be composed of British, not colonial, ships.[31]

Derby had some reason to hope that this tactic would jar the Americans into action. Bulwer had more than once prodded the President about both the fisheries and reciprocity questions, and the latter had finally referred both subjects to Congress in 1852. The Congress, however, had chosen to ignore them.[32] Meanwhile, Francis Hincks, a principal agent of the Canadians, had visited Britain early in the year ostensibly to secure British support for a railway project, and perhaps to obtain authority to lay bounties on fish, both of which were denied to him. Some American observers later traced the origins of the fisheries crisis to Hincks, who denied it, and the part he played in it is still not wholly clear.[33] It seems likely that the chief motive force was Derby's determination to show the Canadians, wavering in their loyalties because of Britain's trade policies, that the Mother Country could protect colonial interests. While no imperialist, Derby took pride in the British Empire, and regarded Canada as the most important part of it.

What more effective gesture could be made than to force the United States to grant reciprocity? The fisheries crisis was obviously brought on intentionally with this end in view. Malmesbury noted in August: 'In fact I understand our decision to defend our fisheries as having for its principle object the attainment of other privileges denied to us'.[34] Derby and Malmesbury evidently concluded that the only way to secure action from the American Government was to bring on a crisis.

In a study centred primarily upon diplomatic tactics, the rights and wrongs of the fisheries issue need not detain us at any length. At issue was the renunciation clause of the Treaty of 1818, which was subject to legalistic interpretations. Perhaps the most telling American argument was based on customary rights, on Britain's having tacitly accepted a broad interpretation of the treaty for thirty years before suddenly switching to a narrow interpretation. The British statesmen, on the other hand, could argue that the treaty had always been enforced – 35 American vessels had been seized and brought into the Admiralty Court at Halifax between 1821–51 –, and that they were simply asserting their treaty rights more effectively in 1852.

In the argument between the two great powers, the maritime Canadians were often more or less overlooked. Their fishermen faced the competition not only of Americans, who benefited from a $300,000 bounty on fish, but of French fishermen, who enjoyed a bounty so large that they could undersell competing fishermen everywhere in the world.[35] There can also be little question but that both their French and American competitors poached upon the vital mackerel area, which lay within the three marine mile limit off the Canadian coasts.[36] The struggling and impoverished Canadian seaboard colonies undoubtedly had stronger claims to British attention than had previously been given to them.

When the Derby Government decided to take action, timing was very important, and, save for one glaring error, their timing was well conceived. As the fishing season began in late spring and ended in mid-October, they took action on 26 May which would disrupt the American fishing for about the whole year. If they had informed the United States immediately of the plan to send an additional force to the fishing area, the Derby Government would probably have found itself involved in a diplomatic wrangle with America that would have held up the dispatch of the fleet, so they delayed advising Webster of their policy until early July, when it was on station and in operation. With their forces already on patrol, they could negotiate with the United States from a position of strength.

The circular letter to the Governors of the Canadian provinces by Sir John Pakington, issued on 26 May was skilfully drawn up to accomplish its purpose. It explained that the British Government, in response to the constant complaints of the colonies regarding American encroachments, had decided to send 'a small naval force of steamers, or other small vessels' to police the fishing area, which, of course, lay the whole blame on the Americans. The letter stated further that the British Government was reluctant to permit the Canadians to lay fishing bounties 'especially pending the negotiation with the United States of America for the settlement of the principle on which the commerce of the British North American Colonies is hereafter to be carried on', but they were disinclined to exercise imperial authority to prevent the Canadians from taking steps they deemed conducive to their prosperity.

Placed in less diplomatic terms the threat was clear enough – if the United States did not enter upon a broad negotiation on Canadian economic problems, they would have their fishing rights circumscribed, and Canadian fishermen would be aided by bounties.   ·

The Government could now sit back and await developments. Only later did an awful truth break upon them. 'Our American demonstration was ill-timed', Pakington wrote, 'as regards that confounded election. . .'.[37] Even the less-informed British statesmen realised that electoral considerations would heat up the fisheries question far beyond the degree they had planned, and commit many an American candidate to an Anglophobe policy.

Upon receiving official notification of the British action, and a copy of Pakington's instructions to the colonial governors, Webster's reply was obviously framed for home consumption. He published the instructions, along with his views on the fisheries question, in a State Department release of 6 July, which for some reason was not printed in the *New York Times* until 20 July.[38] The Secretary of State mentioned the case of the *Coral*, recently taken by the British in the Bay of Fundy, and noted that the new British interpretation of their rights would lead 'to constant collisions of the most unpleasant and exciting character' which threatened the peace between the two countries. Then in a speech at Marshfield on 24 July, the peace-loving Webster declared in the best American electioneering style that the American fishermen would be protected 'hook and line, and bob and sinker. . .'.[39] Neither the speech, nor the press release impress an historian today, accustomed to the irresponsible language of contemporary diplomacy, as being warmongering in tone, but in the mid-nineteenth century both were regarded as strong statements, especially in Britain. Abbott Lawrence, the American Ambassador, told Malmesbury and Pakington early in August that 'Webster is creating this excitement that he may have the credit for *settling* it as United States Minister here!'[40] Poor Webster, conciliatory and good friend of Britain that he was, was shortly to keep a prior commitment which would prevent his appearing in London, or anywhere else.

Webster's reactions, however, were practically bloodless when compared with some American statements pieced together by the *New York Herald* and reprinted in *The Times* (London) on 11 August.⁴¹ The general theme was 'Let us have war with England!' British 'bullying' of the United States had provided an excellent *casus belli*, and 'when we emerge from the smoke and dust of the conflict, the British North American provinces will be ours, their fisheries will be ours, and the absorption of Mexico and Central America will be left wholly to our discretion'. The United States would launch 200 of the swiftest and most powerful ocean war steamers, 300,000 men would rise up for an invasion of Canada, and 'a hundred thousand fighting Irishmen from the United States would hasten across the sea to aid their countrymen in wiping out the disasters of the Boyne, Vinegar-hill, and Slievegammon'.

While the American newspapers were fulminating, Webster and Crampton were discussing the crisis. The former asked that Britain suspend partially any hostile acts against American fishermen until the question of fishing rights could be cleared up, indicating meanwhile that the United States was ready to negotiate 'all the Commercial Questions at issue between us'. 'As the season is nearly over', Malmesbury wrote on 5 August, 'I think it will be better to follow the suggestion of the American Govt. . . .' ⁴² The commitment of the United States to negotiate a reciprocity treaty seemed to have crowned the Derby–Malmesbury venture with instant success. But the crisis was not quite over.

Malmesbury next brought the situation before Disraeli. 'We are quite right in the American question of fisheries', he wrote. 'We have claimed no new principle & worked no Aberdeenian concession. . . . *The Coral* was seized poaching within ½ *mile of our shore*. Lawrence is very civil about it & the result will be I think that we shall open our Fisheries for countervailing advantages. With these & the St. Lawrence we ought to get something'.⁴³ Evidently disturbed by the crisis, Disraeli replied in terms which reflect his view through the Exchequer windows. 'The Fisheries affair is bad business', he complained. . . . 'These wretched colonies will be independent too in a few years and are a millstone around our necks. If I were you, I would *push matters* with Fillmore, who has no interest to pander to the populace like Webster, and make an honourable and speedy settlement'.⁴⁴

How to respond to the American request to suspend the

surveillance of the fisheries? Malmesbury and Derby decided to send Crampton two despatches, one to be read to President Fillmore stating that the British cruisers would only capture vessels that were manifestly violating the treaty; and a second informational despatch, which suspended for the season the execution of the treaty by the British cruisers. It appears that the latter instruction had meanwhile been carried into effect, so as to remove any possibility of collision with the United States, but Malmesbury especially did not want the United States to know about it, lest they believe Britain was abandoning her diplomatic position.[45] He was convinced that the only real threat to peace lay in violence among the fishermen.[46]

Having sent these despatches, Derby and Malmesbury waited confidently for the good news that the United States had formally agreed to the broad negotiation they were seeking, but a letter from Crampton early in September conveyed a threat by Webster to start a tariff war with Britain, rather than the expected detente.[47] To make matters worse, despite all efforts by the Government to secure their support,[48] the gentlemen of the press were castigating its American policy.[49]

Malmesbury, pained with disappointment when success had seemed so near, almost lost his head. In his letter to Derby of 8 September he declared that '*Come what will* we cannot in my opinion yield an inch of our exclusive right to the three mile waters', and posed the grave question: 'Will you fight for the right of the 3 miles if necessary?'[50] In a letter written the following day, he asked: 'Are our Canadian fortresses well mounted & provided?'[51] The Foreign Secretary nevertheless was not excited enough to forgo his autumnal pastimes, and his next letter to the Prime Minister was written from his estate following his return from a successful hunt. Word had been received from Crampton – 'Mr. Webster says he is ready to enter upon a broad negotiation'.[52]

Derby, who visited the Royal Family at Balmoral in September, replied to Malmesbury in a letter of 15 September:[53]

Crampton's private letter, which you left for me here, was not altogether satisfactory; but I do not see anything to be uneasy about in his public despatches, and this letter from Seymour appears to negative all probability of any collision.

We must hold very temperate, but very firm, language; and assuredly, though God forbid it should come to that, I am prepared to fight for our undoubted rights, rather than yield to a spirit of democratic encroachment, which, if not steadily resisted, will have no limits to its demands.

This is probably the best available insight into contemporary Conservative thinking on the subject of how best to deal with the American Republic, and at this moment there would seem to have been little to distinguish it from Palmerstonianism. Derby assumed that America was an encroaching nation with whom negotiations must be carried on with great care and firmness; Malmesbury specifically renounced 'Aberdeenian' concessions. Like Palmerston in 1841, they were ready to approach the 'brink' if a vital British interest were involved.

Yet, one who reads the letters of these men senses that there was a considerable difference not so much in matters of policy between Derby–Malmesbury and Palmerston as in the personalities who administered the firm policy. Derby and Malmesbury were unwarlike men, strongly religious, and opposed to the expenditures for military purposes;[54] Palmerston was much more dashing and adventuresome, less orthodox in his religious views, and one of the chief proponents of preparedness programmes.

From Balmoral Lord Derby went on to Goodwood then to Knowsley, his beloved estate near Liverpool. Malmesbury had meanwhile maintained the firm policy agreed upon,[55] and by 3 October he could write: 'You will have seen that I directed that the President's wish respecting the place and manner in wh. our negotiations with the U.S. should be carried on was to be complied with if pressed by him'.[56] By now the crisis was in the past, and the Prime Minister could review what had been accomplished:[57]

I think our American affairs look well; but we have evidently got the Yankees in hand, and the three-mile limit, which is what they really want, is so clearly and absolutely ours, that negotiate they must, sooner or later; and in the meantime I have no doubt that the part we have taken will do us good in our most important colonies, and will have widened the breach between them and Jonathan, so as to afford little apprehension on the annexation question. *If* we did go to war with them, however, which God forbid, I cannot say that I should look without uneasiness on the state of Canada. We have a large and undefended frontier, and I cannot but fear that recent events have greatly shaken the loyalty, more especially of the West Canadians, the first to be invaded and the most distant to be succoured.

The Prime Minister suggested that Crampton should manifest 'every readiness' to negotiate, but should not show 'too great anxiety' on the subject. He approved the Washington locus for the negotiations under the circumstances mentioned by Malmesbury.

The letter has an incidental interest in its description of the 'large and undefended frontier' of Canada in the light of some recent writings on this topic.[58] If one makes a distinction between 'undefended' and 'unguarded', then the assumption that the Canadian frontier was not 'unguarded' would seem to be a valid one; but, if one assumes that the British Government during this period believed the Canadian frontier was adequately defended, he is far wide of the mark. The frontier defence was so token in nature that Derby was quite right in considering the boundary 'undefended'.

As it turned out, the unexpected death of Daniel Webster held up the negotiations Derby and Malmesbury anticipated in early October, and by the end of the month, there was a brief flurry of excitement over the Cuba issue. Early in October the Spanish authorities refused entrance at Havana to the American mail ship *Crescent City*, forcing her to proceed with her mail and passengers to New Orleans. This was not the first insult of this type sustained by Americans in Cuba, and public indignation in parts of the nation was running high. Fearing a Spanish-American war, Malmesbury in October wrote to Derby that France would join Britain in protecting Cuba against the United States if the need arose.[59] Instead of forming an anti-American coalition, however, Malmesbury approached the United States with the offer of an Anglo-French-American protectorate of Cuba, which Edward Everett refused in a note that lauded the benefits of the United States bestowed on its acquired territories. If Malmesbury had in mind substituting collective action for the Monroe Doctrine, he was unsuccessful.[60]

By the time this brief flurry of excitement had arisen, the Derby Government was fully occupied with other matters not relating to foreign affairs. The British general election had been held that summer, but its results, because of the extraordinary confusion of parties, could not be judged with certainty until Parliament had met, and an important division had been recorded. In the Speech from the Throne on 11 November 1852, the Government took credit for having opened the rivers of the La Plata region, and announced that friendly negotiations of some importance were currently underway in the United States.[61] Neither Derby, nor Malmesbury took note of American affairs during the debate that followed. Later in the month, Lord Wharncliffe, who had been for some time a resident of the United States, called for some papers regarding the fisheries dispute, which brought Malmesbury to his feet, and from him a brief account of the incident ending with the statement: 'There had not been a single word said by an official personage in the United States which did not give her Majesty's Government sanguine hopes that these negotiations would be brought to a satisfactory conclusion, and that every cause of dispute between the two countries would be amicably settled'.[62]

Malmesbury sounded in 1852 almost as triumphant in the cause of Anglo-American peace as Aberdeen in 1846, and he had ample cause for satisfaction. Though the Mosquito negotiations had proved abortive, they had been carried on in an exemplary spirit of Anglo-American cooperation. The United States had not challenged Britain's formal annexation of Roatan, and, after a flurry of excitement, she had agreed to a broad negotiation on the reciprocity question. Malmesbury could be satisfied that his Canadian policy had restored their confidence in Britain, and made annexation to the United States more remote.

The Conservatives had also reverted to and revived the Aberdeen policy of securing French cooperation in American affairs. France had been friendly toward Britain during the fisheries crisis, had cooperated with her in opening the La Plata area,[63] and had shown willingness to join forces with Britain in protecting Cuba against American aggression. Malmesbury's prompt recognition of the Empire had further cemented good relations between the two nations. So the Aberdeen policies of conciliating America and France, and at the same time dividing them from each other, took a major step forward. Later administrations were to proceed along the same lines.

But a successful American policy carried little weight in contemporary British politics. The long-awaited division in the Commons took place on the night of 16–17 December over Disraeli's budget, and the Conservative Government crumbled under the combined weight of the Whigs, Liberals, Peelites, Radicals, and Irish. The next government was to find the perennial rivals, Aberdeen and Palmerston, sitting in a coalition Cabinet composed of Whigs, Peelites and Liberals, a coalition that never quite managed to coalesce, and which was to break down under the accumulating problems of a questionable war.

7
The Aberdeen–Clarendon Period

'I assure you that often, in the silence of the night, this fatal decision weighs heavily on my conscience. I am aware that much may be said in justification of it, and God knows, it was reluctantly consented to by me; but, nevertheless, when a man acts contrary to his own clear conviction, he cannot escape from severe self-reproach'.[1]

These lines, written by Lord Aberdeen long after his country had entered the Crimean War, serve to remind us that the art of diplomacy is not practised by automatons, but by flesh and blood human beings who feel responsible (and in Aberdeen's case, accountable to God) for their decisions and actions. During the period 1853–4, when the crisis mounted in the Near East, the man who had compromised the Maine and Oregon boundaries, a sincere pacifist, in theory held the reins of the British Government as First Minister. His thoughts, and those of the other British statesmen in his Cabinet, were further from America than the three thousand odd miles that separated the two countries, and were centred upon those narrow necks of water that separate Europe from the Middle East. Aberdeen could foresee the coming of the catastrophe, and his struggles to prevent it provide one of the more intimate insights into the difficulties and failures of the diplomatic art.

To a certain extent, Lord Aberdeen was himself responsible for his untenable position. Although he could take such Whigs as Russell, Clarendon, Palmerston and Lansdowne into his Cabinet and feel perfectly at ease when they drew up reform measures or budgets, when it came to the conduct of foreign policy he belonged with Lord Derby. 'I look back with regret on the vote that changed Lord Derby's Government', the Radical pacifist Cobden wrote. 'I regret the result of that motion, for it cost the country a hundred millions of treasure and between thirty and forty thousand good lives'.[2] Had Aberdeen chosen to cast his lot with the Conservatives, he could have conducted his foreign policy for peace within a Cabinet of rock-like solidarity, and the Crimean War might well have been avoided; but the glittering prize of the Prime Ministership, as well as his liberal leanings in domestic affairs, brought him into a divided Cabinet some of whose members were much more powerful political figures than he.

The Whig-Liberal-Peelite Government that Aberdeen formed following the ousting of the Derbyites found Sir James Graham at the Admiralty, William E. Gladstone at the Exchequer, the Duke of Newcastle at the Colonial Office, the Duke of Argyll as Privy Seal, and Sidney Herbert at the War Office, all staunch Peelites who might be expected to back Aberdeen in the Cabinet; but in the Commons they could command scarcely fifty votes. The bulk of the Government's voting power looked to Viscount Palmerston, who took the Home Office, and Lord John Russell, who agreed to accept the Foreign Office temporarily on condition that he should have the succession to the Prime Ministership. Russell abandoned the Foreign Office to his Whig friend, Clarendon, in February 1853, and thereafter waited somewhat impatiently for Aberdeen to relinquish the headship.

Aberdeen could not, of course, have anticipated the crisis in the Near East that arose early in 1853. During its early phase, involving a dispute between France and Russia over control of the Holy Places, he advised Clarendon not to back France, and to cooperate with the other Great Powers in protecting Turkey. Clarendon was deeply suspicious of Russia, and was pleasantly surprised when that nation receded from its position, and admitted it had behaved 'foolishly for themselves, & improperly towards us'.[3]

The Franco-Russian crisis was followed immediately by increased tensions between Russia, which would have gladly given Britain a share of the spoils from the dismemberment of Turkey, and the Ottoman Empire on an issue involving the Russian protectorate of the Orthodox Christians of that Empire. After some weeks of fruitless negotiations on the subject, the Russian Ambassador on 21 May left Constantinople.

There could be little question but that Russia would have liked to carve up Turkey, and in that situation the British Cabinet faced a choice of means of preventing the dismemberment. Should they seek the assistance of all the Great Powers of Europe, and force Russia to negotiate; or should Britain immediately adopt a menacing position that would leave no doubt of her intention to contain Russia? While not mutually exclusive, the two tactics, one looking toward peace, and the other, war, did not fit well together. Clarendon later looked back upon this as perhaps the decisive moment in the crisis.

The crisis found the Cabinet sharply divided, Aberdeen and most of the Peelites looking toward a negotiated solution, and Palmerston, Russell, Clarendon, Lansdowne, and Newcastle calling for strong action. Under threat of their resignations, Aberdeen was forced to take the first major step toward war by consenting to the dispatch of an Anglo-French fleet to Besika Bay near the Dardanelles. Those who anticipated that a show of Anglo-French strength would force Russia to back down were disappointed when she occupied the Principalities on 2 July, and held them as a guarantee that Turkey would meet her demands.

This brought on another rift in the Cabinet. Palmerston demanded that the fleets be moved into the Bosporus, and that the British Ambassador at Constantinople, Lord Stratford de Redcliffe, be granted discretion to move them into the Black Sea, if further pressure on Russia were needed. Aberdeen, on the other hand, chose to ignore the occupation of the Principalities, and emphasised the mediation efforts of Britain, France, Austria, and Prussia, who were meeting in Vienna that July. The Great Powers there drew up the Vienna Note, an instrument of the Clayton–Bulwer type – that is, one which could be interpreted rather differently by the two contending powers, and which might smooth the matter over if a will for peace existed in St. Petersburg and Constantinople. Aberdeen's contention that Russia was seeking a graceful way out of the situation seemed to be confirmed when that country accepted the Vienna Note on 5 August and he stressed the importance of Lord Stratford's pressuring Turkey to acquiesce to it. This the anti-Russian Lord Stratford did not do. Turkey would not accept the note without an important revision that destroyed its essence.

Both Clarendon and Aberdeen in late August blamed Stratford for the failure, and when Russia on 17 September revealed her own interpretation of the note, it was dead as an instrument of conciliation.

Although desultory negotiations between Austria and Russia continued, the Aberdeen formula for peace was damaged severely, if not wholly discredited. A new and pressing crisis arose in October when Turkey ordered Russia to evacuate the Principalities within fifteen days, and on 23 October, following the expiration of the ultimatum, declared war. Lord Aberdeen's policy was now to try to localise the war – Russia and Turkey had fought a number of brief wars in the past – and to force Turkey to come to an adjustment that would remove its basic cause. Palmerston insisted instead on full support for the Porte. While public opinion in Britain on the question was pacific, or indifferent, there was still a balance of power in the Cabinet, which aided Aberdeen in his peace efforts. Hence the 'massacre at Sinope' on 30 November, a perfectly legitimate act of war which involved the destruction of a Turkish fleet by the Russians, was a decisive factor in the situation, for public indignation forced many of the Peelites to go over to the Palmerston approach. The Cabinet was now in a sad state of disunity, divided not only on the Russo-Turkish War, but on the issue of parliamentary Reform, which caused Palmerston to resign and rejoin the Government in December.

Public opinion backed a Palmerston project to move the combined fleets into the Black Sea to prevent future Sinopes, but such a move would bring Britain and France to the border of actual hostilities, and Aberdeen opposed it, still hoping to find a negotiated way out of the situation. By this time he was virtually alone in the Cabinet, and was unable to contend with his colleagues, who asserted that moving the fleets into the Black Sea was merely a precautionary measure to protect Turkey pending a negotiated settlement. So on 4 January 1854 the order was given to move the fleets.

The Russian reaction to this new display of power was to demand explanations, and, failing to receive satisfaction, on 4 February 1854 she withdrew her diplomatic representatives from London and Paris. Ten days later, Aberdeen could still write: 'I still say that war is *not inevitable*; unless, indeed, we are determined to have it, which perhaps for aught I know may be the case'.⁴ What tenuous hopes he clung to! By this time the war fever had taken over completely – Aberdeen had no support, save, perhaps, from a few Radicals. Even his close Peelite friends, such as Graham and Gladstone, had deserted him. In this situation there was no staying the descent into war. Austria suggested an ultimatum be sent to Russia calling for the evacuation of the Principalities. Britain and France sent the ultimatum on 27 February, setting a 30 April deadline, and when it was rejected, declared war on Russia on 27–8 March.

This brief outline of the origins of the Crimean War provides merely the pivotal events in the tragedy. Beginning with the mild crisis of March 1853, the Cabinet faced the May crisis, when Russia broke diplomatic relations with Turkey, the July crisis when Russia occupied the Principalities, the September crisis when the Vienna Note failed, and then a succession of events – the Turkish declaration of war on 23 October, the Sinope affair of 30 November, the ordering of the combined fleets into the Black Sea on 4 January 1854, the breaking of Anglo-Russian relations early in February and the Franco-British ultimatum of 27 February, and the declaration of war on 28 March. 'Lord Clanwilliam . . .', Malmesbury wrote early in 1854, 'says there is no doubt that Lord Aberdeen's timid policy is the cause of the war with which we are threatened, and that a little determination at first would have stopped the Czar'.⁵ This interpretation has been widely accepted by diplomatic historians, who assume that Russia would have submitted to coercion in 1853.

Lord Aberdeen explained his failure in quite a different way. 'It is quite true, as you say', he wrote to Brougham, 'that the Press having made the war, is now unable to control the spirit it has raised. But other causes have also contributed to bring about this calamity. These are at present very imperfectly known and appreciated, but they may perhaps be more clear hereafter. I can only say for myself, that I never before really understood the full force of the expression of being *dragged* into war'.⁶ Unfortunately, this high-minded, tragic statesman left historians to speculate regarding the 'other causes' that he had in mind.

During the period 28 December 1852, when Malmesbury relinquished the seals of the Foreign Office to Lord John Russell,
and 21 February 1853, when Lord John insisted on turning
them over to Lord Clarendon, the direction of foreign policy
was in the hands of an ex-Prime Minister whose chief concern
was to fill that office again in the near future. Diminutive in
stature, Liberal by nature, and a politician to his fingertips,
Lord John Russell during this brief term of office spent a sur-
prising amount of time on American affairs, despite his pre-
occupation with domestic politics.

The Conservatives by their skilful, even daring, tactics had
brought the friendly Fillmore–Everett administration in Washington to the conference table, and left a claims convention, a
reciprocity treaty, and a settlement of the Mosquito issue to
their successors. The first of these, which settled all claims between Britain and America that had arisen since 1814, was
signed on 8 February 1853, and ratified in July. Outstanding
claims were to be negotiated by a British and an American
commissioner, whose decisions would be final. If they disagreed,
the decision would be turned over to a neutral umpire.[7] This
agreement gave a promising beginning to 1853 in the Anglo-
American area.

Responding, perhaps, to the discussions regarding Roatan in
the American Congress, Lord John decided to reopen negotiations on the touchy Mosquito issue. His proposal, sent to
Crampton on 19 January, viewed in the light of past failures
seemed perfectly logical – that Britain and America should
settle all aspects of the Mosquito question by bilateral negotiations without reference to Nicaragua, which had caused past
negotiations to be abortive.[8] Edward Everett in February expressed regret that too little time remained to the Fillmore
administration to negotiate such a settlement,[9] but he revealed
Russell's proposals to the American Congress to forestall any
charge that Britain was unwilling to abandon the protectorate.[10]

The Canadian reciprocity question, which the Conservatives
had linked with the Fisheries issue, was to some extent merged
by the Aberdeen Government with a third question – Canadian
defence. The crisis of the summer of 1852 seemed likely to be
repeated when the fishing season opened the next year, so the
moment seemed auspicious to force the Canadians to give

greater attention to their own security. The Colonial Secretary took up the question with the Governor General, Lord Elgin, who argued the case of the Canadians eloquently, noting that Canada absorbed the first shock 'whenever John Bull and Jonathan quarrel',[11] but Newcastle insisted on the reduction of British forces from 5239 men to 3219.[12] Like Lord Derby, Newcastle regarded the border as an undefended frontier. 'If we kept forces to defend its frontier against the Un. States,' he argued, 'we must have at least quintuple the present number of men.'[13] In the end the Canadian legislature was induced to appropriate £10,000 for a militia force, hardly enough to turn aside a possible invasion by an American army hardened in the Mexican War. Ultimately, Canada's defence depended on the threat of the British Navy to American coastal cities.

While reducing the British forces in Canada, Russell and Newcastle took up the reciprocity and fisheries questions with vigour. They had on hand a draft treaty, which had already been amended by the Americans, and had been reviewed by Lord Elgin and Francis Hincks for Canada, but there were still some vital areas of disagreement. The Americans wanted the reciprocity and fisheries issues to be separated; the Canadians opposed this, lest in the future the Americans should abrogate the former, and retain their advantages under the latter agreement. The Canadians also wanted a provision that would place British-built ships owned by Americans on the American registry, another that would exclude the Newfoundland fisheries from the agreement, and an expansion in the reciprocity items, especially coal from Nova Scotia, which would concede its inshore fisheries to the Americans.[14] The Americans opposed most of these concessions, and looked with disfavour on suggestions by Elgin and Hincks that skins, furs, and pelts be added to the free list, and that the United States concede her inshore fisheries.[15]

After extended discussions the ideas of Russell, Newcastle, and Hincks were embodied in new instructions as amendments to the amended draft treaty. 'I hope that the U. States govt. may adopt it', Newcastle wrote, 'but I have my fears'.[16] Lord Elgin, who was one of the more astute observers of American politics, replied: 'It is very clear that we shall get no reciprocity treaty from the Yankees during this session of Congress. The question, like most others in the United States, is used at present by the different political Jobbers for their own purposes'.[17] Elgin proved right. The Fillmore administration left office without taking action on the reciprocity treaty, and the two countries faced another period of tension in the fisheries of the North Atlantic.

While Lord John Russell was unable to solve the more difficult problems between Britain and the United States during his brief term, he could tell his successor and Whig friend, Lord Clarendon, that the line to Washington was open. Clarendon had had lengthy experience in official life, and was not an untried rookie like Granville, but this was his first venture into major league diplomacy, and he approached the pitcher's mound with caution. Surrounded as he was by experienced coaches like Aberdeen, Palmerston, and Russell, Clarendon actually had most of his diplomatic pitches called for him by the others. Aberdeen was particularly useful when America came to bat.

Advice was needed, for Clarendon had the misfortune of coming to office only two weeks before the expansionist Franklin Pierce became President, and William L. Marcy, a former intimate of the troublesome Polk, became Secretary of State. The tone of the next three years was set by the President's Inaugural Address, which stated that 'certain possessions not within our jurisdiction' were important to American defence. Cuba and Santo Domingo seemed likely candidates for annexation. Lord Elgin wondered if Canada were included,[18] and one of Clarendon's friends wrote bluntly: 'Pierce's attention is directed to the Sandwich Islands'.[19] To make matters worse reports came in from various parts of the Empire, which suggested that the United States was a subversive influence, either intentionally, or simply by example. Poor, depressed Newfoundland had cause to consider connection with the United States as a way out of her economic stagnation.[20] Reports about Australian disaffection were so numerous that Crampton saw fit to investigate and report on them later in the year.[21] To Britain, America seemed to be a growing threat to her thalassocracy; to the United States, Britain was a roadblock in the way of her legitimate territorial expansion.

Actually 1853, despite the alarms, was a fairly quiet year. The chief irritant was the Mosquito protectorate again. During a debate in Congress that spring, Clayton raised the dangerous question of interpreting the treaty he had signed with Bulwer by declaring that it prohibited Britain's retention of the Mosquito Protectorate.[22] Clarendon quickly suggested in late April that the question be adjusted on the basis proposed by Russell.[23] When no reply was forthcoming from Washington, Clarendon wisely or unwisely transmitted to the United States an official interpretation of Article I of the Clayton–Bulwer Treaty. While indicating Britain would abandon Mosquitia once agreement had been reached, Clarendon asserted the British right not only to retain it, but all of her other Central American possessions as well.[24] Crampton read this despatch to Marcy, who said he was 'not yet able to say what the opinion of the United States Government in regard to the interpretation of the Treaty would be'.[25] Crampton concluded that this touchy matter would be turned over to the new American minister to Britain, James Buchanan, the same individual who had carried on the Oregon negotiations so unsatisfactorily, and acrimoniously.

The next word Clarendon received on the subject was delivered to him by Joseph R. Ingersoll, the American minister, in the form of a testy note from Marcy regarding a minor incident at Grey Town. In a despatch of 22 July, Clarendon expressed regret at the tone of this communication.[26] Then the clouds cleared away. Marcy denied that he was unfriendly, and even acknowledged the validity of the British claim to Belize. Buchanan, armed with full powers to negotiate a Central American settlement, finally arrived in September, and began to hold exploratory talks with Clarendon the following month. The lack of urgency in his approach indicated that the Pierce Government did not place a high priority on the solution of this issue.

Meanwhile another fishing season had come and gone without incident. To avoid the excitement of the previous year, Newcastle kept his instructions to Sir George Seymour, commander of the British patrol, out of the newspapers,[27] but British vigilance was by no means relaxed. An American fisherman who went to the area late in July reported that gun barges had been stationed at strategic points along the Canadian shores, and that American ships carrying more than two guns were subject to seizure. However, the patrol acted with courtesy, and a seized ship had the right to have its distance off shore measured at the time of the seizure.[28] An American squadron under Commodore Shubrick arrived on the scene in July, not to challenge the British, but to aid in preventing clashes.[29] Crampton marked the end of this period of tension in October when he noted: 'You will be glad to see that the Fishing Squadron has returned to the United States and that Commodore Schubrick [sic] has had no pretext for complaint'.[30] Seymour was subsequently awarded a good service Admiralty pension for his work. Neither Britain nor the United States wished such an explosive situation to continue, and the stage was set for the successful negotiations of 1854.[31]

The same year the United States, impressed by the success of the Great Exhibition, staged its own Great Exhibition at the Crystal Palace in New York. Prince Albert especially was interested in sending a distinguished British representative to its opening, and Clarendon concerted with Lord Granville the means of 'doing honour to the Yankees and their exhibition'.[32] Despite their militant republicanism, Americans harboured a secret admiration for nobility, and, knowing this, the Government dispatched Lord Ellesmere together with his family and collection of paintings and objects *d'art* to America on one of the better frigates. En route the Earl proved the authenticity of his pedigree by suffering an attack of gout, but upon arrival he played his role of good will ambassador effectively. A 'sensible, moderate man' was the American verdict.[33] Returning home Ellesmere was chagrined to discover that his contribution to Anglo-American good will went unnoticed.[34]

Anglo-American relations during the year 1854 brought an accumulation of disputes and incidents which increased tensions between the two countries and led the British Government in the autumn of the year to resort to the tactic Aberdeen had used with some success in the Oregon boundary negotiations. Whether or not the Americans so intended it, their diplomacy seemed to follow the fortunes of the British war effort, to be smiling in fair weather, and disagreeable in foul.

The only friendly gesture made by the United States during the period – and even this might be interpreted as strictly self-interest – was the conclusion of the long-sought Reciprocity Treaty with Canada. A feeble initiative in this area was taken by Marcy in January when he informed Crampton he would like to have the matter settled before the next fishing season.[35] After some informal talks, Crampton concluded in March that the United States was ready to bargain, save on the matter of the registration of British-built ships on the American registry.[36] Clarendon was nevertheless so distrustful of the Americans that he was unwilling to take an open initiative in the negotiation, and instead resorted to a stratagem.

Lord Elgin, who was seeking advancement in his profession, had turned in his resignation as Governor General of Canada in December 1853.[37] With European diplomacy in such a menacing state,[38] the Government attempted to dissuade him, and after an extended argument Elgin consented to return to Canada for the next session of parliament there. Late in April Clarendon decided to turn over the reciprocity-fisheries questions to him, and in a letter the following month provided him with instructions flexible enough to satisfy most of the American demands.

Before returning to Canada Elgin was instructed to visit the United States, not as a negotiator, but merely as a friendly tourist. Clarendon continued:[39]

> The mere suspicion of such a purpose would of itself suffice to render the Government of the United States still more inaccessible than heretofore to reason on the subject, inasmuch as it would conclude, however erroneously, that the British Government was prepared to make sacrifices for the sake of averting a discussion with the United States while engaged in an arduous warfare with an European Power. . . . Your Lordship will also steadily keep in mind, as a principle never to be lost sight of in negotiating with the United States, that no concession can safely be made to that Government except in return for a corresponding concession on its part . . . and that so far from being likely to arrive at a permanent and satisfactory settlement by the adoption of a yielding tone, the result in all probability would be the reverse.

Thus, Clarendon embraced wholeheartedly the Palmerston tactical assumptions in dealing with America. Telling Lord Elgin, long a favourite in that country, about American psychology, however, was like sending the traditional coals to Newcastle.

The titled tourist engineered informal talks with Pierce and Marcy on 29 May, and on 12 June he was able to send home a treaty![40] This most orderly and effective negotiation in Anglo-American annals was made possible by Elgin's acute understanding of Americans. They had to believe they were getting a bargain. So Elgin constantly stressed the importance of the Canadian concessions to America, and he sometimes expressed doubts that even his well-known prestige in Canada would suffice to secure them for the United States. Thus, when the treaty was concluded, the Americans could wish him well in Canada, as one acting in their interests. As late as August, after the American Senate had approved the treaty, Elgin wrote Marcy: 'I trust that whatever legislation may be necessary for giving effect to the Treaty, in so far as Canada is concerned, will be adopted by that body without delay. Of the other Provinces I cannot yet speak with the same confidence'.[41] It was in the concessions of the other provinces that the United States had its greatest interest. When back in Canada Elgin's tactic was to encourage some opposition to the treaty so that the Americans would be encouraged to ratify it.[42]

That Elgin, despite his manipulations of public psychology both in America and Canada, acted as an honest broker there can be no doubt. Reciprocal free trade between Canada and the Maritime provinces and the United States in the 'natural products' of the sea, farm, forest, and mine, including the mining produce of Nova Scotia, was probably more of a boon to the Canadians than the Americans. Canadians also secured admission to the inshore fisheries of the United States north of the 36th parallel, and a right to navigate Lake Michigan. On the other hand, the Americans were admitted to the inshore fisheries of New Brunswick, Nova Scotia, and Prince Edward Island, and obtained the right to navigate the St. Lawrence and its canals. Canadians were disappointed over the denial of the right of colonial-built vessels to the American registry, and the Americans failed in their efforts to include Newfoundland in the agreement.

For Great Britain the treaty meant the loss of some of her trade with Canada.[43] Increasing sales to the United States, however, more than made up for this loss,[44] and the Anglo-American trade continued to flourish during the Crimean War.[45] The Mother Country also gained the good will of the Canadians by negotiating the treaty, and it undoubtedly helped to undermine such annexationist sentiment as existed among them.

The Reciprocity Treaty was negotiated during the early phase of the Crimean War not long after the British fleets had been dispatched, and while the public still awaited the good news of naval victories. In some other areas, however, it appeared that the American Government was not unwilling to stir up animosities, and to secure advantages from British involvement in Europe.

The Gadsden Purchase, made in December 1853, caused no stir in Britain, as she had long since abandoned all of Mexico to America, if she wanted it.[46] More disturbing were Crampton's reports in February 1854, which told of Russian efforts to secure American ships and crews to prey on British commerce.[47] After investigation, Crampton reported in April: '. . . these ideas are gradually being abandoned, on the true American principle that on the whole such operations would not be likely to pay'.[48]

After some months of tranquillity on the subject, America chose to heat up the Central American issue just two days after the British Cabinet in January had ordered the fleet back into the Black Sea, bringing on a crisis which was to lead to war. James Buchanan, delivered an official American interpretation of Britain's obligations under the Clayton–Bulwer Treaty in a starchy note of 6 January. These obligations involved withdrawing from all Central America, save Belize. Complaining that Britain had not taken the 'first steps' to meet her obligations, Buchanan warned that the United States would maintain the Monroe Doctrine whenever her 'peace and safety' required it.[49]

Clarendon turned to Bulwer to interpret the American interpretation. The former negotiator admitted that Britain had given up the substance of the Mosquito Protectorate under the treaty, retaining only a shadow, and that Britain had a right to keep Roatan only if it were a true dependency of Belize. His advice was not to attempt to answer Buchanan point by point.[50]

Clarendon did not respond to the note immediately. Crampton's private letters of 15 and 23 January stated that the

Nicaraguan minister in Washington had done a *volta facie*, and had agreed to compensate Mosquitia for her territory and to work out a boundary with Costa Rica.[51] His attitude was conditioned by fear of American aggression which, in turn, was inspired by a spate of American fillibusters in Central America. Such a solution would have been a godsend to Clarendon, but, alas, it was not to be. The Nicaraguan government was subverted by another civil war.

The Foreign Secretary delayed answering Buchanan until after the announcement of a generous policy toward neutrals during the war, which he learned was pleasing to Marcy.[52] His rejoinder insisted that the British presence in Mosquitia did not violate the Clayton–Bulwer Treaty because it was a protectorate, not a sovereignty, and that the only question concerning Roatan was whether or not it were a dependency of Belize. The Monroe Doctrine he described merely as a dictum of Monroe, not an international axiom regulating the conduct of European states.[53] But he called for a peaceful settlement of the Mosquito question, and not long thereafter he instructed Crampton to offer to negotiate all outstanding differences with the United States.[54]

The extent of Clarendon's distrust of the current American Government is clear from a May letter to Aberdeen. 'The union won't last forever, but I doubt its being dissolved in our time', he wrote. 'Buchanan pretends to be friendly, but I believe he is as ready as the dishonest Govt. he represents to make political capital out of a quarrel with us'.[55] This outburst was no doubt occasioned by his resentment of America's taking advantage of the war to press her interpretation of the Bulwer Treaty, and her apparent willingness to raise a crisis to serve political purposes at home. Whatever they might have thought of the diplomatic advantage that the balkanisation of the United States would bring, British statesmen rarely mentioned it, much less recorded it for future generations to read.

As the weeks went by the reports of the expected naval victories failed to materialise, and the overage admirals commanding the Baltic and Black Sea fleets remained curiously inactive. '. . . one is always praying and the other always swearing',

Malmesbury noted, 'but they, however, seem to agree on one point – namely in not fighting'.[56] Public attention then turned disgustedly from the sea war to the campaign to take Sebastopol, and by autumn there were probably few Britishers who could not locate that stronghold on the map. Lord Derby in October anticipated that its rapid fall would make up for previous 'remissness'.[57] but late the same month reports of incredible mismanagement began to arrive. 'All of these speak of the dreadful mortality amongst our troops from cholera', Malmesbury wrote, 'arising from want of tents; all our men having slept on the bare ground since they landed'.[58] As the weeks went by the public mood changed from disappointment to anger and humiliation. By the end of the year Lord Aberdeen's Government was clearly doomed.

It was against this background that the United States raised new and more menacing crises. Marcy in July penned a sharp note protesting the British patrols around the Falkland Islands, fearing, perhaps, a repetition of the tactic Malmesbury had employed in the Canadian fisheries, but Crampton was able to reassure him that Britain was not trying to exclude American whalers from the area.[59] About the same time President Pierce told Crampton he was considering offering mediation in the war,[60] an act which might be friendly or unfriendly depending on the wishes of the powers concerned. Clarendon provided Crampton with a statement telling why mediation at that moment was unacceptable to Britain, but the rumours concerning it continued.

The major development of July, however, was the Hollins incident, which, under other circumstances might easily have brought war. The Grey Town government, which had *de facto* recognition both in America and Britain, attempted to arrest an American at Point Arenas for killing a Negro. The American minister to Central America refused to turn him over to the Grey Town authorities, and in a demonstration was hit on the arm by a broken bottle. The report of this incident brought American instructions to Captain George N. Hollins of the American ship, *Cyane*, to protect the Americans at Point Arenas. His interpretation of these instructions transpired on 13 July. 'It appeared', Crampton wrote, 'that the marines landed by Captain Hollins pulled the English flag down from the house of our Consul, and burned the house. . . .' [61] Grey Town was reduced to rubble.

This was not merely a challenge to the Mosquito protectorate, as one writer stresses.[62] It was the type of general challenge which Britain rarely allowed to go unpunished, as her international prestige was involved. The graceful way out of the situation was to secure an American disavowal of Hollins' activities. Buchanan was quick to assure Clarendon that such a disavowal would be forthcoming, but when Crampton applied for it, Marcy was indefinite and evasive. As of early September all Crampton received from Marcy were complaints about the activities of the citizens of Grey Town.[63]

To make matters even worse Marcy at the same time informed Crampton that the annexation of the Sandwich Islands was a 'fixed point' in the intentions of Pierce's Administration. Back in 1849 the United States and Britain remonstrated with France when she seemed to threaten the independence of these islands, and in 1852 Fillmore had discussed the possibility of a tripartite treaty among America, Britain, and France to protect them. This seemed to bind the United States to the independence of the Sandwich Islands – hence the consternation in Britain at this abrupt change of American policy.

Thus, a major if indefinite Anglo-American crisis took shape in September 1854. Crampton recommended that Britain employ a naval threat against the United States. Clarendon was uncertain, even bewildered. 'Will you have the goodness to send Crampton's letter to Graham?' he asked Aberdeen. 'I am getting uneasy about our relations with the United States. The Government is weak & unprincipled & ready for any foreign outrage to give a turn to opinion at home'.[64]

Earlier in the year Aberdeen had once again exercised his benign influence on behalf of peace in the Western hemisphere.[65] Now his mood was somewhat changed. 'Considering the transactions which took place between us some years ago respecting the Sandwich Islands', he wrote, 'the present proceeding is outrageous. . . . We shall come to disgrace if we permit this encroachment. I think it more important than the Greytown affair, which although a scandalous outrage, does not appear to me to be of the same national consequence.'[66]

The Prime Minister, Clarendon, and Graham all seem to have

agreed that Crampton's suggestion had merit. At any rate, Britain again resorted to a naval threat to buttress her diplomacy with the United States. A special box in *The Times* entitled 'Naval and Military Intelligence' made public Admiralty announcements designed especially for American eyes. '*The Termagant*, 24, screw frigate' was reported to have left Spithead for the West India station in both the 13 and 16 October issues. Those of 16, 17, 18, and 20 October gave wide publicity to the '*Colossus*, 81, screw two-decker' before its departure for 'the West India station to reinforce Rear Admiral Fanshawe's squadron'. Later issues between 23 October and 7 November told of the '*Eurydice*, 26', the '*Harrier*, 14 screw sloop', and the '*Dauntless*, 33, screw-frigate' all of which were dispatched to Fanshawe on the North American station. Two other ships were reported to be in readiness.[67]

Clarendon reported to Aberdeen on 24 October Sir James Graham's opinion that Britain was 'fast drifting into a quarrel' with the United States, and he was at a loss regarding how to prevent it.[68] Aberdeen replied that it was well to be prepared, but that he would regret extreme measures on account of the Mosquito protectorate 'where our right is very questionable, and the importance of which has been much exaggerated'.[69]

At this point in the growing, indefinite crisis Russell proposed that the Earl of Carlisle be sent to Washington to negotiate. Clarendon welcomed the suggestion, but was uncertain what might be negotiated. 'It is the general state of things', he wrote Aberdeen, 'the aggressive tendencies of the Govnt., the insolence of their subordinates & the domestic projects they are seeking to advance by a foreign quarrel that we have to complain of. . . .'.[70] How did Aberdeen view a special mission?

There was much of the old Aberdeen left in his reply.[71] He said he never could discover a British title to Grey Town, while their claim to the Bay Islands was 'manifest usurpation' and 'worthy of the Government of the United States'. In normal times he would not oppose 'making a graceful concession of the matters in dispute'. But to make them 'under the pressure of the present moment, our motives would be intelligible to the whole world'. So the creator of the Ashburton mission vetoed the Carlisle mission, and advised that they 'hang up all matters in dispute by means of civil negotiations for some indefinite period'. Aberdeen did not believe the United States desired to quarrel with Britain, and he feared that Carlisle's failure to solve all outstanding issues might simply complicate Anglo-American relations. Such was Aberdeen's advice, and one leading American authority seems to wonder why he adopted such a posture.[72]

Why he did so is probably to be found in Aberdeen's experiences, both remote and recent, in his attempts to pursue a foreign policy that was rational and pacific, experiences which had made his name synonymous with weakness and concession, even with lack of patriotism. In late 1854 he was involved in a war that many blamed on his weakness, in alliance with a French adventurer whom he disliked and distrusted, and being harassed by a nation with whom he had walked the second mile to conciliate. Nothing seemed to have turned out right. Disillusioned? Perhaps, but more probably simply weary, tired and unwilling to involve himself in a project of such dubious prospects. This year he had reached his three-score years and ten.

On receipt of Aberdeen's letter, Clarendon replied: 'Your letter about Carlisle is *quite* conclusive. I agree with every word of it'.[73]

So a policy of diplomatic immobility was adopted by the Government with respect to American affairs for the duration. The policy would be simply to react cautiously to Trans-Atlantic events, and to undertake no determined initiatives to settle the accumulating problems.

This policy was possible because Aberdeen, and to a certain extent Clarendon, was convinced that the United States would avoid an armed conflict. America had had to be warned not to press too hard, or go too far, and this had been accomplished through the reinforcement of the fleet on the American station.

Crampton, for one, was convinced that the reinforcement tactic had been an outstanding success. He wrote a year later:[74]

Nothing that I have ever seen since I came to this country ever did the slightest good but such a measure as that I took the liberty of recommending last year and which you so promptly acted upon, viz., the sending out of three heavy screw men of war to Admiral Fanshawe – quietly & without a word being said it did the business. Precisely the same thing occurred in 1845 ...

Having taken credit for suggesting a tactic which undoubtedly involved some expense to the Home Government, Crampton may have exaggerated the effect that it had on American diplomacy.

It is true that the United States shelved their unacceptable Sandwich Islands annexation project, but Crampton himself traced this to sectional opposition in Congress, rather than to the naval menace.[75] President Pierce also gave up his mediation project, and told Crampton that he would not undertake it even if asked to do so by Congress.[76] No new American demands for evacuation of the Mosquito protectorate were forthcoming during the balance of the year. These facts and circumstances might be advanced to prove that the naval threat had forced Pierce and Marcy to reconsider their attitude toward wartime Britain.

On the other hand, it is clear that the Americans did not run for cover as soon as the notices began to appear. They still did not disavow the proceedings of Hollins; indeed, President Pierce defended the American position in this affair in his address of 4 December. 'The elaborate defence of the Greytown outrage is disgraceful and false', Crampton observed, 'but the very pains taken with it betray the weakness of the case'.[77] The precise nature of the American response to the threat might well be considered in depth by specialists in American diplomacy.

By the year's end, the Aberdeen Government was thoroughly discredited by the terrible mistakes made in the Crimea. In January 1855 John Roebuck, a Radical, gave notice of a motion to enquire into the conduct of the war, and Lord John Russell – to the consternation of his colleagues – promptly resigned from the Government. Deserted by the Russell Whigs, the Radicals, and some others, the Government was beaten, and on 30 January 1855 Lord Aberdeen resigned.

A complex cabinet crisis followed. Lord Derby was called in and attempted to strengthen his minority position in the Commons by securing the services of Palmerston, Gladstone, Herbert, and some others. Palmerston would not join without Clarendon, whose strong Whig ties prevented any junction with

the Conservatives; Gladstone and Herbert sought the approval
of Lord Aberdeen, and were relieved when it was not given.
After Derby's failure, Lord John Russell tried his hand, but his
desertion of Aberdeen's Government during the January crisis
had discredited him, and he was forced to give up his attempt to
form a government.

The only remaining possibility was Lord Palmerston to whom
the Queen next turned with reluctance. Palmerston formed his
Government with the aid for a time of the Peelites, but they
resigned from it within three weeks. 'Bad as Lord John's conduct was', Malmesbury observed, 'this is a thousand times
worse'.[78] Among the major British political leaders, the new
Prime Minister was the only one to come through this lengthy
cabinet crisis unscarred.

8
The Palmerston–Clarendon Period

It would be an exaggeration to say that in contemporary Britain the only ardent followers of Palmerston were the British people. Lord Clarendon remained at the Foreign Office, and Palmerston's Whig rival, Lord John Russell, took the Colonies for a few months, but the Radicals loathed him as a reactionary who had stolen the leadership of the Liberal movement, the Peelites shared Aberdeen's distrust of him, and the Conservatives regarded him as the major obstacle to their return to power. Hence, his Government was as weak in Parliament as it was strong in the affections of the country.

The tradition he had created in Anglo-American diplomacy was not such as would cause the Americans to hail his elevation to power. He had been the author of the McLeod ultimatum, and the chief architect of British Central American policy that was still clouding the diplomatic skies. Lord Aberdeen later noted that he had tried to persuade Buchanan 'that Palmerston was not personally an enemy of the Union. Whether I succeeded or not I can scarcely say.'[1] Judging from subsequent events it would appear that Aberdeen had failed also in this project.

Palmerston adopted the Aberdeen policy of 'hanging up' all matters of dispute with the United States for the duration of the war, but there was one bequest of the previous administration that arose to force his attention to Trans-Atlantic affairs. A note in Malmesbury's diary provides an insight into the British difficulties that brought on the new and alarming crisis. He wrote: 'The accounts from the Crimea are dreadful. Only 18,000 effective men; 14,000 are dead, and 22,000 sick'.[2] With so many garrisons scattered around the world, British man-power was stretched to the breaking point.[3]

As early as November 1854, Clarendon had written to Crampton requesting him to contact the British consuls in America regarding the prospects for recruiting in their areas. Crampton was not sanguine, and pointed out to the Foreign Secretary that many Americans would like to bring charges against British officials, but he agreed '. . . there can be no harm in trying the ground'.[4] It is clear from the very out-set that Crampton was aware of the dangers inherent in the procedure.[5]

The following month Newcastle introduced the Foreign Enlistment Bill into the Lords, where it met a hostile reception from the Conservative opposition, who disliked many of its features, especially the vagueness about where the foreigners would be recruited. Newcastle explained that, as no foreign government had yet been contacted on the subject, he was unable to say where the troops would be raised, but left the impression they would come mainly from Switzerland and the German states.[6] Beaten in the Lords, the Conservatives attacked with equal lack of success in the Commons.[7] The bill received the Royal Assent on 23 December.

These were the preliminaries to the most unusual and extra-ordinary development in Anglo-American relations during the whole period.

How poorly considered the project had been, despite the debates in both houses of Parliament, is obvious from the re-port of a Cabinet session early in January 1855 written by Argyll:[8]

Clarendon says that all the authorities abroad now write that we will never get 8000 men to form a Foreign Legion, or respectable officers unless with the consent of the Govts. . . . Then Gladstone opens their eyes for the first time to the violation of public law in sending to Foreign countries a recruiting sergeant to get men agst. the will of the Govts. He says he never contemplated such a course. In short the Foreign Legion is at dead lick & we shall look like fools – having staked our existence on it. . . . . Clarendon is to try Hanover for leave to recruit.

It would appear that the violation of international law entailed by illegal recruiting was not even discussed until this meeting. Why it had not been brought up in Parliament, on the other hand, is quite clear – Newcastle and the others stressed that the foreign governments involved would be contacted before the recruiting began.

Leave to recruit was never given by the Government of the United States, and Clarendon and Crampton must have known from the very outset that their course was likely to lead to trouble, but they seem to have convinced themselves that if they confined themselves strictly to resident aliens in the United States who voluntarily applied to be recruited, and who were sent to Canada for the actual recruitment process, then they would skirt the confines of both international law and the American Neutrality Act of 1818. Crampton's early private letters have a definite (if amateurish) conspiratorial air about them. 'The subject you allude to', and the 'principle subject of your letter' were used by the British minister rather than the word 'recruitment'.[9] By April he seems to have gained confidence, and came right out with the phrase 'With regard to the recruitment. . . .'[10] When he used such a phrase as this, it was difficult to maintain that he was not actually recruiting soldiers without the permission of the country that was his host.

The recruitment, such as it was, took place between March 1855, when the network was perfected, and 7 August, when Crampton received and acted upon instructions from Clarendon to put a complete halt to it. The way it worked was this. If any American residents, especially aliens, expressed a desire to help Britain in the war, the consuls at Boston, New York, Philadelphia, and Cincinnati would arrange for their trip to Halifax, where they would be greeted by Sir Gaspard Le Marchant, who worked under the supervision of Sir Edmund Walker Head – the Governor General himself – and enrolled in the armed forces. A very prominent Nova Scotian acted as Crampton's go-between in his relations with the consuls in the seaboard towns, but Charles Rowcroft at Cincinnati seems to have worked directly under Clarendon.

Although it was claimed that the people were volunteers, not actually recruited, who were, in effect emigrating from America to Canada, some of the minions of the British officials involved recruited quite openly. One named Angus MacDonald actually placed the following advertisement in an American newspaper:[11]

> Highly important to the Unemployed! The British Government having concluded to form a Foreign Legion at Nova Scotia, and to raise several regiments for duty in the Provinces, offer a bounty of £6, or thirty dollars, together with the pay of 8 dollars a month, good clothing, and warm quarters, to every effective man fit for military duty, from nineteen to forty years of age; to join are invited English, Irish, Scotch and Germans.

If this were not recruiting, then Crampton's name was Mr. Buchanan.

Perhaps the most interesting part of the story is the interpretation that Crampton and later, Thomas Lumley, put upon the activities of Secretary Marcy and an unknown number of others in the American Government. Ever since the onset of the Anglo-Russian crisis Crampton had been worried about Russian intrigues in America, and he picked up news and rumours regarding them from a variety of sources, probably mostly from British citizens residing in the United States. 'I do not mean to say that there are not many people . . . who neither think nor wish that we shall be defeated by the Russians – but as usual, I am sorry to say, they do not dare to express such an opinion now that the word has been passed that sympathy with Russia is the popular cry.[12] The editor of the *Albion*, a New York publication, later told Crampton that the Russians had bribed 'eight or ten of the principal papers in New York, Boston and Philadelphia' to abandon their pro-British attitude, and to sympathise with the Russians.[13] The only proof that Crampton could offer for this charge was that so many American newspapers 'within a single fortnight' in late 1854 had abandoned the allied cause and gone over to the Russians.

The conspiratorial hand of Czarist Russia was spotted by Crampton in the recruitment situation. In June, when the recruitment was not going well, the British minister charged that Russian agents had bribed the New York police to slow it down.[14] Shortly after the plan was abandoned, Crampton complained that Marcy had employed spies and informers directed by District Attorney McKeon, whose 'zeal against England knows no bounds. That he is in continual communication with the Russian Legation, I know, & that the money for *extra expenses* of the proceedings comes from that source is indubitable.' [15] Then later in September, Crampton made his most sweeping charge of Russo-American collaboration: [16]

> Although I am not disposed to credit reports of an effective offensive & defensive alliance between Russia and the United States because I know this Government will not, and indeed could not venture upon such a step; their late conduct, nevertheless, taken with other symptoms, convinces me that they are acting more or less upon an understanding with Russia to annoy & thwart us; and to create the impression which Russia naturally wishes to exist in Europe that we are in a most critical position with regards this country. . . . . Some time ago one of my German colleagues told me *confidentially* that he knew positively that Mr. Marcy had promised . . . the Russian Charge d'affaires, that he would 'make a business' with the British Government about the recruitment as soon as he had collected materials for the purpose.

The implication in this interpretation was that Marcy laid a trap for the British recruiters with the intention of creating a crisis that would embarrass Britain and aid the Russians.

Just what credence Clarendon and Palmerston placed in this charge of Russo-American collaboration is not clear from the correspondence. It is perhaps significant, however, that even the friendly Aberdeen had suspected Russia of meddling in Anglo-American affairs the year before.[17]

The year 1855, like the previous two years, began on a cordial note. President Pierce adopted a more conciliatory manner on the Hollins dispute, promising further investigation, which led Crampton to suggest that they agree on some provision for the Mosquito Indians and submit their differences over interpretation of the Clayton–Bulwer Treaty to arbitration. The President left the impression that Buchanan had somehow appropriated the Central American issue, and that no action would be taken until he returned to America.[18]

In March Crampton mentioned the recruitment problem to Marcy. Explaining that he had received many applications from American residents who desired to enter the British service, Crampton said he told them they could not be recruited in the United States without violating the neutrality law, and that they would have to go to British territory if they wished to enlist. Marcy did not display much interest in the matter. He noted that Americans had a right to go wherever they pleased, but at the same time he would enforce the neutrality law with strictness.[19] Crampton later asserted he would have revealed additional information to Marcy if the Secretary had asked for it. But the fact is, he did not tell him that arrangements had already then been made to send applicants to Canada for formal enlistment.

In May 1855 Crampton reported that Anglo-American relations were very peaceful,[20] and the following month he interpreted Marcy's expressed willingness to collaborate with Britain in securing the free navigation of the La Plata and other South American rivers as a very good sign, for it showed the Pierce Administration was not afraid to associate itself with Britain.[21] In July he planned to talk with Marcy about Grey Town, but the holidays interfered. 'We have as you justly remark', he wrote Clarendon, 'been most brotherly indeed in regard to Hollins, Lynch, and other matters which might have afforded too good materials for a shindig'.[22]

There was no such deceptive calm in Britain during these months. The Palmerston Government, weakened by the desertion of the Peelites in February began peace negotiations in Vienna on 15 March 1855. Public hopes for peace were raised – and dashed when Russia would not agree to a demilitarisation of the Black Sea area. Disraeli, anxious to restore some fighting spirit in the Conservative Party, which had been grievously disappointed by Derby's failure to take office in January, collaborated with his chief on a major assault on the Government in May. Derby and many of the Conservative Lords were none too certain of undertaking such a partisan attack in wartime, and the debate in their House was listless and dull, but in the Commons Disraeli on 24 May moved a curious resolution which at once pledged 'every support' in the conduct of the war, and scored the Government for its 'ambiguous language and uncertain conduct' with respect to it.[23] The debate lasted until

11 June, during which time the Disraeli resolution was amended into one which merely pledged support for the war effort.

Palmerston had hardly survived this attack when Lord John Russell, since February a member of the Government, let it be known that he differed with his colleagues on the demilitarisation issue.[24] Sir Edward Bulwer Lytton, Conservative brother of the negotiator, immediately gave notice of a motion regarding the divided state of the Government, which seemed to promise another extended debate on the war, and by this time Palmerston was reduced to courting the Irish Brigade to secure votes to sustain his Government.[25] It was temporarily rescued by Russell's announcement on 16 July that he had resigned his post.

Lord Palmerston was now beleaguered and isolated. Almost all of the prominent statesmen of the time were out of office and to some degree hostile toward his Government. Even though he had survived the crises of May and June, another threat appeared on 17 July, when John Roebuck, a Radical, basing his resolution on the findings of the Sebastopol Committee, moved that the calamities that had befallen the British forces in the Crimea were the responsibility of the Aberdeen Government, all of whose members should be censured.[26] To further weaken Palmerston's position, the war was going badly. A June offensive against Sebastopol had met with a bloody repulse.

This was the moment selected – by intention or chance – by the Americans to spring the trap in the recruitment issue, and to revive that of Mosquitia. In July Buchanan made a formal enquiry regarding British recruitment activities. Clarendon on 16 July gave assurances that any British efforts which might be interpreted as enlisting Americans would forthwith cease. After so doing, he dispatched a letter to Crampton ordering him to immediately dismantle the network set up for this purpose. 'On receipt of your letter of the 20th ult.,' Crampton replied, 'I immediately put a stop to *all* proceedings in the business which forms the subject of your correspondence with Buchanan'.[27] It was then too late. Even while the Americans were presenting their enquiries, they were taking action. The morning of 10 July Charles Rowcroft, British Consul at Cincinnati, was arrested by a United States marshall for his recruiting activities.

Attention to the situation was drawn in Parliament on 2 August when Milner Gibson put a general question to Palmerston about the recruiting. The Prime Minister denied illegality, but said the Government had ended the enlistments that 'used to take place at Halifax'[28] in order to avoid misunderstandings with America. Nothing in the correspondence contradicts the statement that Clarendon's promise had been kept, and the recruitment ended.

To add to Palmerston's troubles, Buchanan in August demanded a formal British statement regarding its position in Central America, and the American policy was now to remove Britain entirely from the area, including Belize.[29] Clarendon replied that the Clayton–Bulwer Treaty was prospective, not retrospective in its application. This interpretation naturally gave no satisfaction to the Americans whatsoever. So lines were drawn, and a new phase of the Central American struggle had opened.

In September 1855 the American Government took determined action on the recruitment issue. Crampton found himself in receipt of a letter from Marcy, a skilfully-worded document which was definite in its assertion of the wrong done America in the recruiting episode, and indefinite regarding what might be done to rectify it.[30] Crampton at once suggested that Clarendon recall him, rather than force him to wait for an American dismissal.[31]

The diplomatic sins of which Crampton was undoubtedly guilty were quite atoned for by his subsequent sufferings. As Palmerston had denied in Parliament any wrong-doing in the recruiting, it was difficult for him suddenly to recall Crampton, and he was forced to sweat through the months of diplomatic manoeuvring that followed. To make matters worse, Crampton was instructed to maintain silence on the recruitment issue.

Thomas Lumley, who was Crampton's subordinate in America, later interpreted the events of these months for the enlightenment of Clarendon. He believed that Marcy sought to force the recall not only of Crampton and some consuls, but also of the Governor General of Canada and the Governor of Nova Scotia![32] This grandiose plan began to unfold in September, when Henry Hertz and Emanuel C. Perkins, both American citizens, went to trial for 'hiring and retaining persons to go beyond the jurisdiction of the United States, with intent to enlist in the British Foreign Legion for the Crimea'. The main witness against them was a questionable character named Max F. O. Stroble,[33] whose main purpose seemed to be to implicate as many British officials as possible and thereby to shock the American public. The conviction of Hertz, and the acquittal of Perkins on 29 September were really of no importance. What was important was that the evidence seemed to prove that British recruitment had taken place, that high British officials had been involved in it, and that it had not even ceased after Clarendon's promise of 16 July to end it.

But Marcy – according to Lumley – was chagrined to find that his timing had been faulty, for that same September the fortunes of war changed markedly.[34] Sebastopol fell, and it was now apparent that Britain would win the war. Lumley believed that this circumstance, and a reinforcement of the British fleet in October, forced Marcy to pause and alter his plans.

The reinforcement of Admiral Fanshawe's fleet was not accompanied by the piecemeal press releases as in 1854. On 13 October *The Times* simply announced that the 'line-of-battle ships *Powerful*, *Pembroke*, and *Cornwallis* [!], and the sloop *Rosamond*, were being sent to the West Indies.[35] There was no crisis atmosphere. The *Powerful*, 84, proceeded at a leisurely pace to Jamaica via Lisbon, and the *Pembroke*, 60, *Cornwallis*, 60, and *Rosamond*, 6, slowly wended their way to Bermuda.

Crampton believed that these ships had been dispatched as a coercive measure designed to strengthen his position.[36] Yet the only private letter available connects them not with Crampton and the recruiting issue, but with Cuba, where American aggression was feared.[37] Clarendon's official explanation to Buchanan – that they were sent in response to a rumour that some privateers were being fitted out for the Russians in New York – finds no confirmation in the available correspondence. About all that can be concluded is that the sending of the fleet was a measure of warning to America.[38]

This measure of coercion was accompanied by a major effort to compose Anglo-American differences in Central America.

That October Crampton took up the Mosquito question with
the Nicaraguan minister in Washington, seeking an honourable
means of ending the protectorate.[39] Then in November Clarendon proposed to Buchanan that their countries submit their
differences regarding the Clayton–Bulwer Treaty to arbitration,
and send a despatch to Crampton instructing him to communi-
cate this offer to Marcy. Unfortunately, Crampton assumed
that Buchanan had transmitted the offer to his Home Government, and he failed to make it formally to Marcy, though he
let it be known that Britain would 'not shrink from arbitration'.[40] As it turned out, as the offer was not formally presented,
Marcy did not feel called upon to respond to it.

Once again the historian in 1855, as in 1846 and 1854, is
called upon to assess the effect of a British naval threat to the
United States, and to evalute it as a tool in contemporary
diplomacy. Crampton again believed it had been highly successful. '. . . everything reminds me of 1846', he wrote, 'when the
alarm spread by the warlike Polk was met in exactly the same
manner'.[41] Those arguing for its success might also point out
that although a true bill was brought in against Charles Rowcroft on 23 October 1855, the American Government did not try
him, and reap the propaganda benefits that such a trial might
have created.

On the other hand, Crampton himself later concluded that
the calm was deceptive. The United States was no longer content merely with dismissing him and the consuls, or even the
governors of the Canadian provinces. They were out for bigger
game – Palmerston himself.

The story of the alleged American plot to overthrow the Government of Great Britain is told in two of Crampton's letters
dated 27 January and 11 February 1856, and the account was
not only believed by Lumley,[42] but by Clarendon himself. To
quote from the earlier of Crampton's letters:[43]

They are no longer content with dismissing me and the
consuls and appointing my successor but they intend to turn
out Lord Palmerston's administration into the bargain! This
is now the programme and it is discussed in the most select
political circles with the utmost coolness and self-com-

placency. They'll have no war of course . . . but Mr. Buchanan has been instructed so 'to time his action' that it may coincide with the meeting of Parliament and thus ensure 'Palmerston's dismissal' if he hesitates to satisfy the 'just sensibilities' of the great country, Sir!

The second letter explained that the Administration, Caleb Cushing, and William H. Seward, hoping to secure anti-British votes in the 1856 election decided to pursue the same course 'as in the Oregon question'.[44] The idea was to heat up both the recruitment and the Central American issues just before the meeting of Parliament, as the former especially might be used by anti-Palmerstonians to overturn him.

Such a plot had no chance of success just at that time,[45] but the American plotters – if such there were – could not have known this. On the other hand, they could very well have known how fragile was the political base upon which the Palmerston Government stood. The debates of the preceding year had made this very clear.

The plot theory has at least two bits of evidence to sustain it. President Pierce delivered his annual message excoriating the British Government for its recruitment and Central American policies without waiting for the House to organise itself, which might be interpreted as assuring that the text of his speech, and the acrimonious debates and newspaper comments that would inevitably follow it, would be available in Britain in advance of the meeting of Parliament on 31 January. The second piece of evidence is that Marcy's note charging that Clarendon had personally approved the violations of American sovereignty in the recruiting programme, though dated 28 December 1854, was delivered on 29 January on the eve of the assembling of Parliament. Thus, an Anglo-American diplomatic crisis of considerable dimensions suddenly took shape.

If there were such a plot, it was unsuccessful in its initial phase. Palmerston omitted all reference to Anglo-American problems in the Speech, and Lord Derby, noting this omission, called upon the United States to accept an apology on the recruitment issue, and to submit the Clayton–Bulwer Treaty to arbitration.[46] So long as this patriotic man led the Conservative Party, and the war lasted, Palmerston was safe.

As the war entered its final phase, American policy became seemingly more conciliatory. When an American adventurer named William Walker seized control of Nicaragua, Marcy seemed to be hostile toward him.[47] The American Government, at the request of Crampton, took steps to break up certain Irish societies in American cities whose purpose was to promote revolt in Ireland on the ground that they breached the American neutrality act.[48]

The American Government also attempted on 3 March to end the recruitment issue by requesting Britain to recall Crampton, Charles Rowcroft, and two other British Consuls implicated in the recruiting programme. This request was a conciliatory gesture, for such a course would relieve the United States of the task of bringing Rowcroft to trial, and the diplomatic officials involved would be relieved of the embarrassment of outright dismissal.

Crampton immediately attempted to resign his post, but the war was now nearly over, and Lord Palmerston's American policy hardened considerably. It was decided to maintain the innocence of the diplomatic officials, and to challenge the United States to dismiss them.[49]

Palmerston's position was enormously strengthened by the signing of the peace treaty on 30 March 1856. It was not a brilliant victory, but the general public accepted peace gratefully, and, although Lord Derby attacked the Declaration of Paris in the Lords, it was viewed with satisfaction also in Parliament.

There was still the recruitment issue to be settled, and there was also a possibility that Walker might try to seize the Mosquito Protectorate, or that the British and American navies in Central America might come to blows over some minor issue, so Palmerston decided once again to try coercion in April 1856, though Clarendon seems to have favoured a special mission to the United States.[50] The Prime Minister announced that 4,000 troops would be sent to Canada to replace the garrisons denuded by the drafts of the Crimean period. He noted that this could hardly be considered an invasion force (even 10,000 men could not be regarded in that light), and denied that he planned to send troops to Costa Rica to protect that country against Walker.[51] For the third time in eighteen months, reinforcements were sent to Admiral Fanshawe's fleet, which the Prime Minister described as intended to protect British lives and property, not to raise a conflict with the United States.[52] Whether or not this latest attempt at coercion were successful depends upon just what its specific objects were, and these, beyond warning America to walk softly, are not entirely clear.[53] If the primary object were to prevent the dismissal of Crampton, the measures were a total failure.

When the French minister in Washington, consciously or unconsciously supporting the British position, warned Marcy that the cashiering of Crampton might mean war, the American Secretary laughed and noted that steps of this nature were often taken.[54] On 28 May Crampton was handed his passports, and the exequaturs of three British consuls were withdrawn. The Home Government had unofficial word of their disgrace as early as 5 June.[55]

If Marcy had taken the situation light-heartedly, the reaction of the new American minister in Britain, George M. Dallas, was in sharp contrast to that of his chief. Whom to turn to in such a crisis but the man whose moderation, kindness to America, and rationality had been so often demonstrated? Deeply perturbed, Dallas took a step unprecedented even in the disorderly history of Anglo-American diplomacy – he contacted Lord Aberdeen, who was not only out of office but in opposition to the Palmerston Government. He explained to Aberdeen that America accepted British explanations regarding the innocence of the Home Government in the recruitment affair. but that Crampton and the others had had to be dismissed as 'objectionable residents' who had disregarded their instructions and misrepresented the conduct of American officials to their superiors.[56] Dallas even offered to show Aberdeen the official American note for 'perusal' before it was delivered to Palmerston.

That Dallas would have accepted such changes in the note as Aberdeen suggested, there can be little doubt. So we have the situation of an American minister seeking advice from a member opposed to the Government in an effort to maintain peace with that Government. Aberdeen refused to read the despatch, but noted that its contents as described led him 'to entertain a sanguine hope that means may still be found to

avert for our respective countries the calamity which seems to
be impending over us'.[57] This cautious comment combined a
note of friendliness with a warning as to the gravity of the situation, which was evidently added so as to avoid undermining
Palmerston's posture at the moment.

Palmerston on 6 June told Parliament that he had indirect
information that Crampton had retired from Washington, and
that the issues between Britain and the United States were of a
'very grave' character, but there was no real cause for collision.[58]
Two days after Dallas had delivered the despatch on the recall
of Crampton, and another on Central America, Palmerston
simply announced these facts to the Commons, and refused to
state what Britain would do about it.[59] Lord John Russell expressed dissatisfaction at his answer, and vowed to put the
question to Palmerston again the following Monday.[60] Despite
Palmerston's requests that the House refrain from pressing
American questions at that time, it was obvious that he could
not postpone indefinitely a debate on them.

As Bourne has shown in his work,[61] Palmerston was in favour
of a 'hard line' policy early in June, involving the dismissal of
Dallas in retaliation, as well as additional threatening gestures,
but Clarendon feared that British public opinion would not
support this line, and the Duke of Argyll warmly opposed it. By
13 June Clarendon was sure that dismissing Dallas would cause
the censure of the Government – in other words, the alleged
American plot to overthrow Palmerston would be crowned with
success. Faced with Russell's question on 16 June, the Cabinet
decided to abandon the hard line, and simply delay replacing
Crampton.

Russell put the question to Palmerston on schedule, com-
menting that precedent did not force Britain to retaliate in kind
by dismissing Dallas, to which Palmerston replied that America
had not intended to break diplomatic relations with Britain,
so his Government did not consider it their duty to suspend
relations with her.[62]

Thus the recruitment dispute came to an end, resolved by
adopting the splendid fiction that Crampton, Rowcroft and the
others had breached American municipal law on their own
initiative without Clarendon or the Palmerston Government
being implicated at all. This saved both British and American

honour, and was eminently satisfactory to everyone except the four subordinates.

Palmerston's Government, however, was now wide open to attack on the issue. The war had ended, all the excluded sections of Parliament were restless, and the feeling was widespread that the recruitment procedure had been badly bungled. The attack made on 30 June–1 July was largely unplanned,[63] and those who joined it did so for a variety of motives, the chief of which was probably distrust of Palmerston.

An analysis of the debate reveals just how widespread was the existing opposition to the Prime Minister. The hostile resolution stating that the Government's conduct in the recruiting did not 'entitle them to the approbation of the House' was moved by a Liberal, George H. Moore, against the wishes of many members of his section. He was supported by the Conservative, Sir John Pakington; a Peelite-turned Conservative, Sir Frederic Thesiger; the most prominent Peelite, William E. Gladstone; an equally important Radical, John Roebuck; some members of the Irish Brigade, and it had the blessing of Lord Aberdeen. Russell and Disraeli, probably to avoid committing their followers officially, both skipped the division, even though Russell had forced Palmerston to take a stand on the issue, and Disraeli had launched a strong attack on the Government's handling of the recruiting two weeks before.[64]

The resolution was snowed under by a 274–80 margin. Clarendon celebrated the occasion with a revealing letter to Granville.[65]

> You will have seen how satisfactorily the Amern. question was disposed of. It was as great a mistake for the Tories as Cass & the utter impossibility of their agreeing was made even more manifest. The majority will have a good effect in the U. S. & teach the Cushing Gang both there & here that they can't kick out Palmerston whenever they please.

This indicates that Clarendon gave credence to Crampton's plot story. America's intervention into British domestic politics, and the violent anti-British statements of the election year in that country, had for the time being alienated some of her better friends in the British Government.[66]

The second six months of 1856 produced such a marked change in Anglo-American relations in contrast to the first half of the year, that one American writer discerned a major change in British foreign policy. Her strong economic connections with the United States now took precedence over her interests in Central America.⁶⁷ This is probably exaggerated. Ever since the signing of the Clayton–Bulwer Treaty Britain had been trying to withdraw gracefully from the Mosquito Protectorate, which could have been resolved by bilateral action with the United States, if she had chosen to cooperate. Belize she was determined to retain; there was no concession there. The only real change involved the Bay Islands, which Clarendon was ready to abandon.

What prompted this decision? Certainly the major factor was that the British claim to Roatan, never strong, had become progressively weaker. Bulwer wrote to Clarendon that while only Palmerston and Abbott Lawrence, who had inserted the 'intend to occupy and colonise' phrase in the Clayton–Bulwer Treaty, knew what was meant by it, he believed that it meant neither nation then occupied any part of Central America, and would not occupy any part of it. So the British would have to claim that the Bay Islands were attached to Belize (and thus a part of Mexico), or were part of the British West Indies.⁶⁸ About this same time, newly publicised evidence proved that the Bay Islands were not attached to Belize,⁶⁹ which meant that the British claim would have to be based on a West Indian connection that was quite tenuous.

Another factor which influenced Clarendon was the coming presidential election, which would probably bring the major defender of the Monroe Doctrine, 'Old Buck', as the British called him, into the White House. 'There is, I believe, little doubt', Lumley wrote, 'that Mr. Buchanan, if elected President will carry out this doctrine in its fullest extent'.⁷⁰ The Duke of Argyll predicted: 'I think that Old Buck will be more difficult to deal with in Central America than Pierce – who is going out & may wish to settle matters before he does so. Whereas the Old Buck has his pride & feeling in the C. American crotchet & is far more committed'.⁷¹ Curiously, as the White House began to come into focus, 'Old Buck' began to place a new value on the British connection,⁷² but, in view of his past activities, the British Government felt more confident dealing with Pierce. The fact was that none of their Central America possessions was worth a week of war, and, if giving up the Bay Islands would satisfy the Americans, they could still emerge from the lingering fracas in possession of Belize.

One historian stresses that a convenient excuse for gracefully withdrawing was presented at this time.[73] Ephraim G. Squier, formerly a decided opponent of Britain in Central America, came to England at this time seeking financial help for a railway whose terminus would be dominated by Roatan. As it was British policy to neutralise terminals of this type, this could be used as an excuse to give up the Bay Islands.[74] One of Bulwer's letters sheds a little more light on this scheme. A prominent Liberal member of Parliament, William Brown (Lancashire-South), had a financial interest in the railway project.[75]

Also conducive to a quick settlement of the whole Central American problem was the friendly attitude of the American Minister, George M. Dallas, and the suggestion by Marcy that the two nations should employ direct negotiations, rather than arbitration. Once underway Dallas and Clarendon proceeded apace. 'I hope that I have settled the Mosquito & Ruatan issues by treaties with the U.S. and Honduras', Clarendon wrote to Aberdeen in September, 'but Dallas has no full powers & does not feel sure his Govt. will ratify what he has agreed to'.[76] The Dallas–Clarendon Convention, signed in London on 17 October, abolished the Mosquito protectorate, and ceded the Bay Islands to Honduras, but both of these British concessions were subject to certain conditions. Honduras had to sign a treaty with Britain prohibiting slavery, and safeguarding British interests in the Bay Islands. The territorial interests of the Mosquito Indians had also to be recognised. So marked had been the change in Anglo-American relations during the past four months that Palmerston was thought to actually be courting the Americans.[77]

Left over from the recruitment crisis was the problem of replacing Crampton in Washington. '. . . I am rather for sending a new man & not seeming to sulk',[78] the friendly Duke of Argyll had written back in June, but Palmerston thought otherwise and was very slow to restore normal diplomatic relations with

Washington. Lumley meanwhile had kept the British legation open, and continued to send back hostile reports to his superiors, including a theory that Walker was the agent of the United States in Nicaragua.[79] Once President Pierce had approved the Dallas–Clarendon Convention, and recommended it in his December message, Palmerston was ready to appoint a new minister. The choice was a peer, and friend of Aberdeen, Francis, the 9th Baron Napier, whose lofty social position was expected to please the Americans.[80] Offered the position late in December, Napier readily accepted it.[81]

At Clarendon's suggestion, Napier had a long talk with the friendly Dallas not long after he had accepted the appointment. Dallas advised that he arrive about a fortnight before the Buchanan administration took office. What he said about the Dallas–Clarendon Convention is not recorded, but in his letters to Clarendon during this period, Dallas doubted that action on it would be taken before Pierce went out of office.[82] This proved correct – the Senate voted to postpone consideration of ratification until 5 March.

Lord Napier's arrival seemed, indeed, to open up a new era of friendliness in Anglo-American relations. The Tariff of 1857, reducing duties to an average rate of 20%, was passed, and marked a solid gain for Britain. Napier carried with him a personal letter written by Clarendon to the new President, who replied that the Queen, because of her noble and pure domestic character, was very popular in America. Though Buchanan admitted the convention was 'no great favourite of mine', he hoped that an amended version would end 'the Central American difficulties',[83] and he seemed quite unlike the 'Old Buck' who had once demanded the lion's share of Oregon, and ordered Britain out of Central America forthwith.

Central America was important to the Americans. But at the moment Napier had quite another area in mind. The preceding October, following a minor incident involving a ship named the *Arrow*, the scholarly Sir John Bowring, governor of Hong Kong since 1854, had ordered the bombardment of Canton, and the Second Opium War with China was on. Britain sought no exclusive privileges in the Far East. Indeed, her policy was to secure the aid of the United States in chastising China hopefully to promote the trade of both countries.

Such a project was by no means wholly chimerical. Welcoming the Americans into the China trade had gone back at least as far as June 1847, when Palmerston had advised them to set up their own tribunals in China, a suggestion readily acceptable to the American Government.[84] When the Taiping Rebellion broke out a few years later, Aberdeen had written: 'It would be very desirable that France and the United States should view these matters in the same light; and I should imagine that a policy of neutrality would be that which under the circumstances they might probably adopt'.[85] When Bowring learned of Perry's successful mission to Japan, he informed Newcastle: 'I am bent on going North – to Japan if the Admiral can spare one ship, as no time ought to be lost in following up the Americans'.[86] A rivalry was there, but it was a very friendly rivalry. The Americans in China in 1855 gladly accepted Bowring as their arbitrator in the settlement of their commercial claims.[87] In the Far East the two countries tacitly accepted the assumption that what was favourable to trade in general would be favourable to each of them individually, so a firm basis for cooperation had been laid.

At the moment Napier arrived in Washington, Palmerston was waist-deep in political problems at home. The Conservatives, Peelites, and Radicals, whose devotion to peaceful coexistence much surpassed their political acumen, launched a massive attack on Palmerston for his cavalier treatment of feeble China, and the very day that Buchanan was taking his inaugural oath, the British Prime Minister found himself in a minority in the Commons. Rather than obligingly resigning, the resilient, septuagenarian premier decided to hold an election. Although he was not particularly worried about the outcome, Palmerston would have found an American adhesion to his China policy gratifying at the moment.

It was not to be. Napier had to tread lightly, well aware that 'if an English Minister is very prominent and zealous on behalf of any cause, that is sufficient to make opponents to it,'[88] and the best that he could obtain from the Americans was the sending out of a Plenipotentiary with 'good instructions'. '. . . armed cooperation', he explained, 'that is against their constitution, which they only violate on greater occasions, and for purely selfish purposes. . . .'[89] So America would play the role merely of a friendly observer. This failure to enlist the open support of the United States for his China policy did not affect the election results. Palmerston won a thumping victory in April 1857.

Napier failed in Central America, as well as in China. The Senate did not like the provisions attached to the British cession of the Bay Islands to Honduras, so they struck them out and provided simply for the cession. With this change the Dallas–Clarendon Convention was ratified on 12 March 1857.

Faced with the question of to insist, or not to insist, on the conditional cession of the Bay Islands, Clarendon chose the former course, and his convention was returned to the United States in its original form. 'I cannot measure your difficulties in England', Napier wrote disappointedly, 'and the importance of the vested interests for which the treaties with Honduras were designed to provide. What I fear is that the opportunity for confirming the Clayton–Bulwer Treaty is now gone by, and that an irresistible movement may be set on foot against the Treaty itself'.[90] By insisting on the anti-slavery provision, Palmerston (rather than Clarendon) doomed the Dallas–Clarendon Convention.[91]

As Napier feared, the amended treaty was unacceptable to the Americans, and to complete the debacle, the British treaty with Honduras failed to be ratified by that country. This led to an interview between Napier and Buchanan in late June 1857. The President observed that the best method of terminating the difficulties that had arisen was by abrogating the Clayton–Bulwer Treaty. Napier replied that, under such circumstances, Britain would be left with her interests in Belize, the Bay Islands and the Mosquito Coast, and this would place the United States at a decided disadvantage in any future talks. Buchanan was unconvinced. So Napier played his last card to preserve the Clayton–Bulwer Treaty. '. . . if Her Majesty's Government before the meeting of Congress should by direct and independent negotiations with Central America bring our position into conformity with the American recorded construction of the Clayton–Bulwer Treaty, would he then abet or encourage an attempt to break that Treaty?' Napier asked. 'He said he would not'.[92]

Thus a new chapter in the lingering, tedious Central Ameri-

can story was opened up. Britain, to save the Clayton–Bulwer
Treaty, was now ready to accept the American interpretation
of it.

The time limits Napier had set in his conversation with
Buchanan could not begin to be met. On 11 May 1857 a
garrison of mutinous Sepoys murdered the Europeans in Delhi,
and proclaimed a surprised descendant of the old Mogul Emperor as their ruler, after which the uprising spread to Oudh.
Then came the massacre of Europeans at Cawnpore, and the
siege at Lucknow. It was not until late December, when the
news of the British victories in India in November reached
home, that the Government could breathe a little easier.

Although Britain's initial experiences with President
Buchanan and Secretary of State Lewis Cass, long regarded as
raucous enemy of Britain, had been fairly favourable, it
appeared that they could not let the Sepoy Rebellion go by
without making some political capital out of it. Buchanan now
sought a restriction of the boundaries of Belize, as well as withdrawal from the Bay Islands and Mosquitia.[93] Rumours were
rife that Congress would abrogate the Clayton–Bulwer Treaty
even if Britain concluded acceptable treaties with the Central
American states. An American project to separate Panama
from New Granada was said to be afoot. Clarendon could think
of nothing better than to renew the offer of arbitration again.

Meanwhile William Gore Ouseley, whose job it was to negotiate treaties with the Central American states, arrived in
Washington on 18 November. Napier, who was sometimes
accused of out-Aberdeening Aberdeen in his relations with
America, promised Cass that the details of Ouseley's mission
would be revealed to him prior to Ouseley's departure. Ouseley
therefore felt called upon to inform the United States that the
transfer of the Bay Islands to Honduras would be unambiguous,
if not wholly unconditional; that the Mosquito solution would
follow the terms of the Dallas–Clarendon Convention, and that
the boundaries of Belize would be arranged by treaty with
Guatemala.

The United States did not reply to the renewed offer of arbitration, nor did they react immediately to the plans which
Ouseley obligingly revealed to them. President Buchanan in his
message of 8 December admitted that he would have preferred

to abrogate the Clayton–Bulwer Treaty, and had accepted the British plan for settling the Central American issues with the understanding that it would be consistent with the American interpretation of that document. His remarks left Britain free to proceed with the Ouseley mission, or simply to agree to the abrogation of the Clayton–Bulwer Treaty.

It was upon receipt of this information that Palmerston wrote one of his most revealing letters regarding Britain's difficulties in dealing with the United States: [94]

> These Yankees are most disagreeable fellows to have to do with about any American Question; They are on the Spot, strong, deeply interested in the matter, totally unscrupulous and dishonest and determined somehow or other to carry their point. We are far away, weak from Distance, controuled by the Indifference of the Nation as to the Question discussed, and by its Strong commercial Interest in maintaining Peace with the United States. The result of this State of Things has been that we have given way Step by Step to the North Americans on almost every disputed matter. . . .

Palmerston went on to state that America would undoubtedly in time become master of all of the hemisphere, but that it was in Britain's interest to delay it as long as possible. The Clayton–Bulwer Treaty shut America out of Central America, so it was in Britain's interest to maintain it even if she had to accept the American interpretation of its meaning. He concurred with Clarendon that Buchanan should be sounded out regarding a substitute for the Bulwer treaty, if Britain consented to its abrogation, but it might be better from a tactical standpoint to force him to give reasons for refusing arbitration. '. . . the Yankees are such Rogues', he wrote gloomily, 'and such ingenious Rogues that it is hardly possible to hope that even if the present questions were settled to their liking . . . some new cavils would not be found. . . .''

The choice of the word 'cavil' was a good one. Although the United States might dignify her policy under the name 'manifest destiny', and Britain lift trivial obstructionism to the level of grand strategy, seldom had two great nations quarrelled so much over so little. Once they came to admit this, then a rational solution of the Central American question became possible.

9
The End of the Mosquito Controversy

Looking back on the events of February 1858, more than two years later Lord Palmerston observed: 'My former Govt. had fallen by reason of the narrowness of the Basis on which it stood, and the combination of influential Parties arrayed against it'.[1] Politics, not a real issue, overthrew him in 1858. Just too many luminaries among the parliamentary sections had been left standing in the wings, while Palmerston alone held the centre of the stage. While the out-of-office sections could agree on little else, they were convinced that the ageing Viscount had too long excluded them from power.

How make-believe was the issue that brought his downfall is obvious from its very nature – the most prominent upholder of British national honour was condemned for a failure in that very sphere. The way it all occurred was this. In January 1858 some Italian nationalist-terrorists, who had been staying as refugees in England, crossed the Channel and made an attempt on the life of Napoleon III. The angry Emperor sent an intemperate despatch to Palmerston through his minister, Walewski, demanding that Britain take steps to prevent aliens from hatching such plots in the future, and the Prime Minister brought in a Conspiracy Bill to accomplish that purpose before protesting the tone of the despatch. So it appeared that he had weakly given in to French pressure. The Radical, Milner Gibson, assisted by his colleague, John Bright, the office-hungry Russell, and the ex-Peelite (that section having been routed at the 1857 election) Sir James Graham, now a supporter of Russell, gave notice of censure on 16 February. The Conservatives joined in the attack, and on 19 February Palmerston, muttering not inaccurately about political chicanery, resigned office.

Thus, Lord Derby again took the helm, bringing his boon

companion, Malmesbury, to the Foreign Office, and the two ventured forth on the rough seas that must be the lot of minority office holders. Palmerston attempted a 'tit-for-tat' in May, and came close to succeeding, but the Derby Government received some aid from the remains of the Peelite section, and Lord John Russell. So long as Palmerston and Russell were at odds, the Conservatives could govern Britain, and, as a corollary to this statement, whenever the two Whig leaders decided to patch up their differences, the Derby Government was doomed.

The diplomacy of the Second Derby Administration was conducted within the atmosphere of a rising fear of France. '. . . if unfortunately any more attempts are made on the Emperor's life by refugees from England', Malmesbury wrote, 'war will inevitably ensue'.[2] The confidence that Malmesbury had possessed previously of the pacific intentions of the Emperor gradually dissipated as the latter involved himself in various and sundry European intrigues and incidents. 'The Portuguese business', he wrote in October, 'proves to me that the Emperor had lost all his sense of right and prudence, and is acting on passion'.[3] So the mutual confidence that had existed between Malmesbury and Napoleon in 1852 was no longer present six years later.

The Conservatives could hardly escape the conviction that the Emperor was keenly disappointed when they came to power. The French minister in Britain was so openly and vocally hostile to them that the Emperor saw fit to recall him, But in November he invited Palmerston and Clarendon to visit him, an unusual departure in Anglo-French diplomacy. Why he should have turned a cold shoulder on the Conservatives, and catered to Palmerston just at this time is easily explained. Plotting as he was a war on behalf of Sardinia against Austria as a means of furthering the cause of Italian unification, he preferred to deal with Palmerston, who had the reputation of supporting liberal movements on the continent, rather than the Conservatives, who were regarded as pro-Austrian and staunchly behind the Vienna Final Act. His crude attempt to break down British unity on foreign policy was wholly unavailing, for Clarendon promptly called on Malmesbury after his return, and filled him in on the information he had picked up in France.

There was still another issue arising at this time between Britain and France which was to accelerate as the months went by to become perhaps the leading, though *sub rosa*, issue during the next administration. In March, at the time war with France seemed a definite possibility, the Conservatives drew up a statement of the relative naval strengths of the two countries, which revealed that Britain had in commission nine line-of-battle ships with 855 guns and aggregate steam power of 5,000, while France had eight such ships with 750 guns, and 6,550 aggregate steam power. The memorandum concluded that the situation 'cannot be considered satisfactory'.[4] It was made even less so the following summer. 'Prince Albert has read me the report of the trial of 68 pounders at 400 yards upon a plated ship wh. appears to settle the question', Malmesbury wrote Derby, '& proves wrought iron plates can repel a cannon Ball at that distance'.[5] If steam-power had arisen in the 1840's to create anxiety in Britain regarding her naval strength, in 1858 the spectre of iron-clad ships was even more disturbing. Still in 1858–9 the Conservatives did not panic. Several years later Pakington recalled: 'You must not infer . . . that we were in /59 so convinced of the importance of iron-cased ships (then wholly untried except as batteries) that we did not contemplate any more wooden ships'.[6] In 1858 the Conservatives simply increased the strength of the Royal Navy, and, at Malmesbury's insistence,[7] stationed a permanent squadron in the Channel to guard against a French sneak attack.

Despite all efforts by Aberdeen and others to break the Franco-American combination, it was still feared in Britain at this time. Malmesbury saw a definite threat in the laying of an Atlantic cable. 'I do not think we shd. commit ourselves to anything', he wrote Derby in September. 'In the first place the cable is more important to the Yankees than to us because it gives them the news of *all Europe* & to us only their own. In the next place we might be (as we have been before) at war with the U.S. & France & a temporary occupation of the Irish Coast by the enemy might be inevitable. It wd. never do to leave them a telegraphic communication'.[8]

Yet, despite the growing hostility between Britain and France, Malmesbury, like Palmerston before him, was quick to utilise French aid wherever and whenever he could in his American diplomacy, and he was again quite successful.

At this time the Conservatives to the delight of diplomatic historians began to summarise the state of Britain's foreign affairs at given intervals in the form of Cabinet papers. One such was drawn up as of 25 February 1858, and provides us with an interesting insight into British thinking at this time: [9]

> Whatever may be the real cause of the change, it must be admitted that our intercourse with the United States is at the present moment on a more satisfactory footing than it has been for many years. The President finds, probably, that the responsibility of power restrains the impulses of his own inclinations, and that although out of office he might advocate an aggressive policy, yet the carrying out of such a policy in office is a task of far more weighty importance. There is much, too, in the internal state of the Union which must make the President anxious not to add to his other difficulties a collision with England. It may not, however, be uncharitable to suppose that, not laying aside forever the schemes of annexation and aggrandisement which were imputed to him before he entered his new office, the President may consider that the surest means of attaining his end will be to disarm, at the outset of his presidential career, the suspicions to which his previous conduct had exposed him.

This analysis of the psychology of the American President was probably drawn up by Lord Derby himself, who had hoped for the election of John C. Fremont in 1856. The suspicion lingered that Buchanan would 'seize on the first favourable opportunity to establish American power over states which once belonged [Central America] or which still belonged [Cuba] to Spain'.

The Central American policy contemplated in this memorandum was based on a deep, underlying suspicion of American intentions in that area of the world. The Derby Government noted a number of alternatives. The United States might possibly reply favourably to the offer of arbitration, but this was evidently not expected. Ouseley, still waiting in Washington, might go to Central America and settle the Bay Islands, Mosquito, and British Honduras questions by treaties with the interested Central American states. This step, the Government decided, would be taken only if America firmly agreed to renounce in perpetuity any abrogation of the Clayton–Bulwer Treaty. There was no point in moving out of Central America, if it meant opening the door for the Americans to move in. Why should Britain not simply abrogate the Clayton–Bulwer Treaty herself? This would mean she could maintain the status quo, and retain the Bay Islands. It was within the realm of possibility, a daring possibility.

A second objective to be undertaken by Ouseley, if he were sent to Central America, would be to induce the Central American states, and possibly Venezuela, to band together in some sort of defence system against filibusters.

This was the thinking of the Derby Government in February 1858. Meanwhile the United States had still not signified its pleasure regarding the alternatives for the solution of Central American affairs posed by the previous government. In an attempt to secure some action, Napier on 17 February requested that the United States reply to the arbitration proposal, and to comment on the Ouseley mission in the event arbitration were unacceptable to her. The American Government still would not commit itself, so Napier, still acting under Clarendon's instructions, advised Cass that Britain would not object to America's abrogation of the Clayton–Bulwer Treaty providing that some alternative canal agreement could be reached at the same time. The United States still made no comment.

Derby and Malmesbury hoped that the United States would abrogate the Clayton–Bulwer Treaty, which would remove the club American politicians so often used to beat the drum against Britain, and leave Britain not only in possession of the Bay Islands, but give her a new freedom of action in Central America. This freedom took on added significance because of the gold strike in the Fraser River area of British Columbia in 1858, which added to the importance of east-west communications via the proposed Central American canal.[10] If the United States abrogated the Clayton–Bulwer Treaty unconditionally, Britain would be free, acting perhaps with France, to make new communications arrangements.

When Napier, acting under his new instructions from Malmesbury, signified to Cass that Britain would accept the unconditional American abrogation of the much-disputed treaty, the United States suddenly displayed a keen interest in Britain's Central American proposals. On 6 April Cass informed Napier the United States would not consider abrogation of the treaty if Britain were left in the undisturbed possession of her Central American holdings. He also belatedly rejected the arbitration offer, but accepted the plan for an Ouseley mission provided the United States were made privy to its precise objectives.

When the news of Cass's views reached the Foreign Office, Malmesbury was much annoyed. Not only had the abrogation plan been rejected, but Napier had more or less committed his Government to the Ouseley mission, which neither Malmesbury nor Derby desired,[11] and which was wholly unacceptable to them if their negotiator were compelled to constantly consult with the United States. 'Napier has made a mess by confidential conversations uncovered by official documents', Malmesbury wrote Derby, '& the Yankees have taken further advantage of it. I will call on you in the afternoon to consider what our *first move* should be'.[12]

The 'first move' agreed upon by Derby and Malmesbury was to do nothing for four long months. The reason for their procrastination seems clear enough. The American Congress showed deep hostility toward the Clayton–Bulwer Treaty, and went so far in May as to recommend its abrogation, which was all that Malmesbury desired at the moment. Any hopes that the Buchanan Administration would act upon the recommendation was dispelled when Cass informed Napier the United States would consider abrogation only after Britain had made suitable arrangements to withdraw from Central America. This candid statement confirmed Derby and Malmesbury in their view that Britain would have to take a strong stand to protect her interests in Central America, and they turned to France for aid.[13] It is clear, however, that Britain still had no firm commitment from France in August, when the decision was made to go ahead with the Ouseley mission.[14]

Malmesbury's instructions to Ouseley of 9 August projected two treaties (or three if an innocuous postal treaty is counted) with Nicaragua, one a commercial treaty which was to embody the military provisions of the pending Cass–Yrissari Treaty between Nicaragua and the United States, and a second to abolish the Mosquito protectorate with compensation to the Indians.[15] A second set of instructions projected a commercial treaty with Costa Rica similar to the one with Nicaragua, a postal treaty, and a treaty by which Costa Rica accepted the provisions of the Mosquito treaty in so far as they involved her interests. These treaties would secure British rights in the Canal area if the United States abrogated the Clayton–Bulwer Treaty, and provide for the passage of British troops across the Isthmus en route to British Columbia.[16] The Foreign Secretary also had in mind a British-sponsored defensive convention among the five Central American Republics as a protection against filibusters, and possible American aggression. Missing at the moment was any plan to abandon the Bay Islands.

It seems clear that Malmesbury hoped for a quick and comprehensive settlement of the Central America issues which would partially satisfy the United States, but would actually vastly strengthen the British position in that area. Without actually prevaricating, he hoped to conceal the wider aspects of Ouseley's mission from the United States until he had achieved a *fait accompli*, and he was therefore insistent that Ouseley and Napier provide some information to the American Government as a matter of courtesy, but not to go into details, or accept advice or assistance from the American Government.[17]

Although the correspondence is not entirely clear on this point, it appears that Malmesbury was quite ready to divulge to the United States the defensive provisions of the Nicaraguan commercial treaty that he had lifted from the Cass–Yrissari agreement because, under the terms of the Clayton–Bulwer Treaty, Britain could claim a right to equality, but he seems to have preferred – at least until he had received a commitment from France – not to have divulged his treaty with Costa Rica, or his five-power project. As it turned out, Ouseley and Napier did not check their stories, and the truth leaked out,[18] so in a despatch of 5 October he instructed Napier to inform Cass of 'all of the objects' of the Nicaraguan Treaty, and one dated 18 November empowered him to tell the Secretary of State that the Costa Rican treaty was meant to guarantee the neutrality of the proposed canal.[19] At the same time he sent along a copy of his projected five-power convention. Significantly, these revelations were made shortly after France in November had indicated it would cooperate with Malmesbury in Central America.[20]

Malmesbury could feel satisfied that Britain would probably retain a strong influence in Central American affairs regardless of what the United States did with regard to the Clayton–Bulwer Treaty. Appropriating part of the Cass–Yrissari Treaty showed a fine diplomatic touch; enlisting French aid seemed to be another canny move. Such spirited British diplomacy in Central America had not been seen since Palmerston's abortive projects of 1848–9.

The threat of filibusters in Nicaragua during the period of the negotiation provided Malmesbury with an opportunity to further strengthen Britain's Central American position by adding a naval threat. '. . . it won't do', he wrote to Derby, 'to have our negotiator with an independent State stopped, & H. M. Envoy driven away by a set of Pirates, who it appears are preparing to descend again on Nicaragua'.[21] On 11 October Malmesbury asked Sir John Pakington to send another ship to Grey Town, or Point Arenas.[22] Pakington complied immediately, but he realised the gravity of the situation which might be created, and he took up the reinforcement problem with his naval advisers. They reported that the United States had the screw frigate *Roanoke* (44), the frigate *Savannah*, the corvette *Plymouth*, and the sloop *Saratoga* on the scene, and decided that the British fleet should receive powerful reinforcement by sending the *Caesar* and the *Diadem*. 'It seems to be a case in which if we show our teeth, we shd. be prepared to bite', Pakington wrote.[23] Once the decision had been reached, Malmesbury hastened to instruct Napier to inform the United States that the purpose of the reinforcements was simply to protect against filibusters. He added: '. . . the French Govt., who contemplate entering into a similar treaty with Nicaragua to that which Sir William Ouseley is instructed to propose, are invited by Her Majesty's Government to send Ships of War for the same purpose'.[24]

Nor did Malmesbury stop even here in his intervention into trans-Atlantic affairs. In Mexico the War of the Reform had broken out, a struggle with strong anti-clerical overtones that attracted the attention of Catholic France and Spain. In September France expressed fears that the United States might use the situation as an excuse for annexation, but Malmesbury assured them that such a development would be good for European trade, and at the same time would probably break up the Union.[25] He advised that neither Britain nor France accept any annexation offers that might come from the Mexican 'hornet's nest'. By October the annexation threat did not come from any of the countries mentioned, but from Spain, which made some hostile demands on bleeding Mexico. Thus began the chain of events which was to lead to the tripartite intervention of 1861.

At the moment Malmesbury welcomed the Mexican situation because it provided him with another opportunity to contest the Monroe Doctrine. He wrote an official proclamation on the subject to Napier in November:[26]

> I have to note to you that your Ldp. appears in that conversation [with Cass] to have given the authority of H. M. Govt. to the so-called 'Monroe Doctrine', a doctrine which successive Governments in this Country have always repudiated & against wh. the very possession & maintenance of our N. American colonies & British Honduras is a standing refutation. H. M. Govt. are using their best efforts with France to prevent a collision between Spain and Mexico, but they cannot admit as a principle that the Mexicans are not free to accept the sovereignty of any other State, altho' that state may not belong to the Western Hemisphere.

With this blast at America's special guardianship of her hemisphere, Malmesbury's spirited diplomacy reached its climax.

Neither Derby nor Malmesbury was a warlike man. The only sounds of shot they enjoyed hearing came from their fowling pieces. Nor was the Conservative Party a warlike party.[27] Why, then, did they seek a confrontation with the United States over the Central American issue? The answer is that they believed the correct tactic in dealing with the Buchanan administration was to be, as Derby put it, 'very civil, very firm, and to go our own way'. The Prime Minister added: 'It is the only way to deal with them, and in spite of all their bluster, they will think twice before they quarrel with us'.[28] The forceful approach seemed to

have justified itself in the Oregon question, and the Canadian
Reciprocity issue, so it was employed again in this attempt to
solve the problems of Central America.

Once again Derby and Malmesbury seemed to have anticipated American reaction correctly. Cass's letter of 8 November
was described by Malmesbury as 'the most civil one ever written
to this country'.[29] The American minister expressed satisfaction
regarding the Ouseley mission, and noted that the only real
points of disagreement between Britain and the United States in
Central America involved the Bay Islands and the boundaries
of Belize. The British Government for the time being had won
the right to solve the Central American issues free from American threats and menace.

Once they had established their freedom of action in Central
America, both Derby and Malmesbury were inclined to be conciliatory. 'Now unwilling as I am to give away anything especially to bullies', the latter wrote, 'I cannot conceal from myself
that the British Govt. have over & over again declared themselves ready to cede the Bay Islands to Honduras. It is almost a
question of honour on our part to accept the solidarite usually
attached to successive Govts. upon such points of national
agreements'.[30] The Prime Minister must have agreed, for several
days later the Foreign Secretary wrote to Napier that Britain
would cede the Bay Islands 'upon terms compatible with the
serenity of the inhabitants', and establish the boundaries
of Belize as soon as Ouseley had solved the Mosquito
question.[31]

Although reports came in that the Americans were 'tamper-
ing' with the French ministers and influencing them against
Anglo-French cooperation in Central America, the Buchanan
Government adopted a conciliatory attitude in public. In his
annual message of 6 December, the President stressed the ties
which bound his country with Britain, and declared that a
solution of the Central American question would remove the
last subject of dispute between them. Malmesbury was much
gratified and ready for a *detente*. 'If we send more ships to Greytown, it will look like bullying the United States instead of
helping Nicaragua', he wrote.[32] Derby agreed, and added: 'You
may depend upon it, if he had meant mischief, his language to
Congress would have been much more in the line of bluster'.[33]

The same day the Prime Minister wrote to Edmund Hammond, the permanent Under Secretary at the Foreign Office, who seems to have been nervous over the spirited diplomacy of his superiors, that it was perfectly natural that the United States should oppose Anglo-French cooperation in Central America, but that she wished to remain on good terms with Britain, especially so long as France remained firm.[34] To prevent the further escalation of the crisis, the Government had decided to send no more ships to the Grey Town area.

Until late December the Derby–Malmesbury diplomacy seemed to be in a most flourishing state. Then everything went wrong. Some of the mortar, if not the keystone itself, fell out of the arch when France and Sardinia began to generate the crisis with Austria that was to bring on war in April 1859. '. . . Lord Derby and I are determined to use every effort to prevent war, which would cost 100,000 lives and desolate the fairest parts of Europe', Malmesbury recorded in early January. 'My whole mind is occupied by that object'.[35]

Despite this redirection of British diplomatic involvement, Lord Derby (at least it sounds like him) took time to summarise the state of Anglo-American affairs at the end of 1858. Relations were not altogether bright, but sufficiently encouraging. He observed:[36]

> . . . we cannot but feel a certain degree of anxiety in regard to our relations with the United States, where the powers of Government are always much more restricted than in other countries, and where it too often happens that, from motives of what may almost be called self-preservation, the Executive Power is obliged to give way to external pressure, and, in many cases, is tempted to raise a popular cry against this country to divert attention from its own position. This may be considered the danger of the present moment. The Executive, being no longer possessed of the confidence of the Legislature, may see its momentary advantage in encouraging animosity in regard to this country. . . . It is very clear that the Government of the United States looks, with little favour, on our attempt to extricate ourselves, without its intervention and on terms of our own choosing, from the entanglements of the Clayton–Bulwer Treaty. . . .

No progress had been made as yet by Ouseley in untangling the Mosquito entanglement, but the main concern of the British Government in this region was the state of affairs in Mexico, where British and other foreigners were being wronged with impunity.

The failures of British diplomacy in the New World during the remainder of the Derby Administration were traced officially to the incapacity of three of its diplomatic servants – Napier in Washington, Ouseley in Central America, and Loftus C. Otway in Mexico, and the rest of the story of this period might be organised around the trials and tribulations of the three.

Lord Napier was the first to go. 'Napier is much too frank and too yielding for the Yankees', Derby wrote, 'and they take advantage of him in every way'.[37] The British diplomat lacked both the strong fibre and wiliness to execute a forward foreign policy in the hurley-burley Washington atmosphere, where a diplomatic storm could unexpectedly blow up and reach fearful intensity while the minister sat helplessly by awaiting instructions. Malmesbury was ready to transfer him to the milder climate of Spain as early as September 1858.[38] Remonstrances from the Foreign Secretary reached Napier with monotonous regularity – in early October for divulging to President Buchanan that Britain was ready to surrender the Bay Islands and other Honduran territory,[39] later the same month for failing to keep Otway in Mexico informed of developments in Washington relating to that country,[40] and in November – an ultimate *faux pas* – for seeming to recognise the Monroe Doctrine in a conversation with Cass.[41]

In December 1858 Richard B. (2nd Baron) Lyons was named to replace Napier. The new peer was welcomed officially the following year by the Americans, who quickly and routinely tested his mettle. 'Lyons seems to be already alarmed at American clamour', Malmesbury wrote disgustedly in June, 'wh. is always the case with our diplomatists'.[42] It was not an auspicious debut for the minister who was to manage British affairs in Washington during the stormy Civil War period.

Ouseley's mission to Central America might be considered rather more successful than his venture to the La Plata in 1845, which had resulted in a quasi-war, but it was almost as barren of accomplishments. In Washington he had been timid and fearful, but once on his mission his spirits improved, and his first accounts led Malmesbury to believe it would be 'easy and rapid'. 'I am only afraid of his stupidity increased by large quantities of brandy & water to wh. he is addicted', the Foreign Secretary confided to Derby.[43]

Illness prevented Ouseley from meeting either the November or the Christmas deadlines established by Malmesbury, who, though disappointed he would not have something to boast about in the Speech from the Throne,[44] was by no means unsympathetic. The Foreign Secretary on 16 December officially appointed Charles Lennox Wyke, the Chargé at Guatemala, as substitute negotiator, if Ouseley felt he should return home.[45] As the weeks went by without bringing news of his progress, Malmesbury on 12 February warned Ouseley that there might be 'changes of feeling' in both the United States and Nicaragua that would undermine the negotiation, if it were too long delayed.

The brief report from Ouseley that reached Malmesbury on 15 February was somewhat perplexing. The despatch noted that the Nicaraguans had wanted to negotiate the Mosquito treaty first, but he had persuaded them to take up the commercial treaty instead.[46] As the Nicaraguans wanted the commercial treaty, and at the moment were indifferent regarding the other, this decision by Ouseley has been regarded as a serious tactical blunder, and Malmesbury himself was inclined to regard it in that light;[47] but, if we recall that the protectorate and troop provisions were in the commercial, not the Mosquito, treaty, Ouseley's anxiety to secure the former is understandable.

The delay irked Malmesbury, and the more because war in Europe was becoming daily more probable. The very day that he recorded his controversial interpretation of Napoleon's motives in entering upon war in his diary,[48] Malmesbury instructed Wyke to negotiate the Belize frontier with Guatemala, and drew up precise instructions which gave Britain the disputed Sarstoon River area. Shortly thereafter he ordered Lyons to inform Cass that this new project was being undertaken. Wyke went about his assigned task with celerity, and politely bribed Guatemala to accept the treaty by promising British aid for a cart road to link their country with Belize. The treaty was signed on 30 April 1859.

Ouseley's treaty of commerce arrived in London on 20 March 1859. It established Britain's right to protect the canal zone, and to have the same rights to send troops across the isthmus as any other power, so in most respects it was an excellent treaty, save for one provision which gave momentary umbrage to the United States.[50] This provision and a few more minor ones caused Malmesbury to return the treaty to Ouseley, who was given orders to impress on Nicaragua that no commercial treaty would be signed until the Mosquito treaty had also reached that stage.

The Nicaraguans did not like the Mosquito treaty for a number of reasons – it provided for buying out the rights of the Mosquito Indians, was somewhat vague as to the sovereignty they acquired over Mosquitia, and finally, at the moment, they preferred that Britain retain her protectorate because of the filibuster threats. Believing that securing an accession treaty from Costa Rica would put pressure on Nicaragua to sign the Mosquito treaty,[51] Ouseley in February went to that country, where he shortly received indignant instructions from Malmesbury to get on with the Mosquito convention. The Nicaraguan Government sent him some counter-proposals, which he quickly despatched to London. On going over these proposals, Malmesbury was ready to accept all the changes except two – abandoning the compensation to be paid by Nicaragua to the Mosquito ruler, and providing for a continued British protectorate until some defence arrangement could be worked out among America, Britain, and Nicaragua. Pending the reorganisation of Nicaraguan defences, Malmesbury was willing to prolong the British protectorate for one year after the signature of the treaty.

Ouseley's failures stood in contrast to Wyke's success. The war broke out in Europe in April, and the United States began to express some uneasiness and dissatisfaction at Britain's lack of progress in Central America, which made Malmesbury the more impatient to wind up the affairs in that vexing area.[52] An Ouseley despatch received on 2 May which contained the counter-proposals, also contained a Nicaraguan objection to including Costa Rica in the treaty system.[53] Another despatch which reached London in June disclosed new Nicaraguan objections to granting mining rights along with the land reserved for the Mosquito Indians, and to the use of 'eminent domain' rather than unconditional sovereignty in the treaty.[54] Clearly no Mosquito treaty was in prospect.

That same month, which marked the end of the Second Derby Administration, the state of Central American affairs was summarised in a Cabinet paper as follows:[55]

> Our negotiations with Central America have not yet resulted in a settlement of the Mosquito question with Nicaragua; and the treaty which Sir William Ouseley concluded with that State on other matters cannot be ratified by Her Majesty in the terms in which it was signed, and has been sent back for amendment. We have succeeded in obtaining by direct negotiations with Guatemala, a settlement of the boundaries of British Honduras, as far as that State is concerned; and thus one point which has been the fruitful source of discussions with the United States had been disposed of. The question respecting the renunciation of British sovereignty over the Bay Islands remains, however, in abeyance, waiting for the opportunity of the conclusion of the Treaties with Nicaragua to resume the negotiation on that matter with the Republic of Honduras.

Thus, the major effort which the Conservatives had launched with such high hopes in the summer of 1858 had achieved few tangible results. What, indeed, did they accomplish? Perhaps the main accomplishment was an intangible one – they had established the right of Britain to settle her Central American affairs free from threats and menace from the United States. The policy of strength, far from offending the United States, seems to have created a much friendlier atmosphere than had existed at the close of the Palmerston administration.[56]

The third of the three more or less discredited diplomats, Loftus C. Otway in Mexico, had been one of Clarendon's appointees, and he had continued the policy of the previous Government of supporting the church-dominated conservative party headed by Zuloaga at Mexico City against the constitutionalist party of Juarez at Vera Cruz. He became particularly friendly with the reactionary General Miramon, and, if a charge lodged against him in the Commons is to be believed, Otway was observed to be 'on the most familiar terms of intimacy with Madame Miramon'.[57] It would seem he carried out all too well the governmental policy of identifying with the Zuloaga cause.

British policy in Mexico was fairly well established. Since the Mexican War they had recognised that state to be within the American sphere of influence, a policy described in one of Otway's letters as 'the traditional desire of England not to thwart the action of the United States in Mexico. . . .'[58] Although Malmesbury actively enlisted the aid of France in Central America, he was strongly against the intervention of that state into Mexican affairs. 'The latter [French domination] would not suit us in the rear of our West India Islands and commanding the Gulf', he wrote to Cowley.[59] In this situation he enlisted French aid to restrain Spain from intervening in Mexico, and tried to encourage the United States to assume the responsibility of protecting foreign commercial interests in that state.

As the war wore on, and the contestants secured funds and supplies *ad libitum* without much regard for legal forms, the outcries of indignant British merchants began to be heard in Britain, and to put pressure on the Derby Government in late 1858. *The Times* carried stories of merchants who were forced to pay a double duty on their goods, the levying of extraordinary taxes, and the collection of forced loans – all this in addition to suspending payment to the holders of Mexican bonds. Some stories were even more serious, involving the execution of British citizens, and – at Tampico – invading the British consulate to arrest one of them.[60] In such circumstances, the British Government was expected to do something.

Napier in Washington was provided with a steady stream of despatches in late 1858, and he at times talked over the Mexican situation with the American Government. It was after a report of one of these conversations that Malmesbury felt obliged to warn him that Britain was not restraining Spanish intervention because she recognised the Monroe Doctrine. On 27 November Malmesbury reported to him an interview with Dallas as follows:[61]

We then entered upon the Mexican question and I assured Mr. Dallas that France and England were doing their utmost to effect an arrangement between Spain & Mexico, and that so anxious was I to prevent complications which might ensue if Spain attacked that Country alone, I had most unwillingly postponed for a time the strong measures which Her M.'s Govt. must finally take to obtain redress from Mexico. . . . Mr. Dallas said that he thought England, Spain, and the United States should consider what was to be done in respect to Mexico which was in a state of anarchy. He observed that France was not interested in that country, and had no right to interfere.

The conversation ended with Malmesbury warning that he could not delay indefinitely satisfaction for the Tampico outrages, and suggesting that an understanding among England, France, Spain, and the United States might possibly restore a 'respectable' Government in Mexico. In December Malmesbury informed Napier that Britain would look with favour upon American arrangements with Mexico to secure payment for the British bondholders.[62]

When the United States failed to enter upon an agreement for the coercion of Mexico, the Derby Government in the Speech from the Throne on 3 February announced that the wrongs and indignities done to British residents in Mexico had reached such a point that the Government had given 'Instructions to the Commander of My Naval Force in those seas to demand, and if necessary to enforce, due reparation'.[63] This intervention was carried out very quietly by Britain the following month at Vera Cruz, whose governor secured an indemnity for one of the ill-used British citizens, promised to repay another from whom sums had been extorted, arranged to set aside a portion of the tariffs to satisfy British claims, and to honour the British flag with a 21 gun salute.[64] This agreement resulted in some small payments being made to the British bondholders.[65] By and large it was a peaceful enough intervention, the most warlike feature of which was the capture and detention of a Mexican ship by the British commander as a means of coercing the Mexican government.[66]

While these steps were taken to secure British interests in Mexico, the Derby Government found itself under increasingly heavy pressure at home. Forced by public opinion to propose an extension of the franchise of 1859, the proposed legislation, though moderate and conservative, caused deep divisions within the Derby Government, and alienated Lord John Russell, whose political career was identified with the liberalisation of the franchise. Russell introduced a hostile resolution against the bill in March 1859, which attracted support from the Palmerston Whigs, the Liberals, and Radicals, and placed the Government in a minority. Instead of resigning, Derby dissolved parliament and held an election. Although the Conservatives made some gains, they were still short of a majority in the Commons. Palmerston then contacted Russell through an intermediary with a proposition that both should agree to serve in the new Cabinet, if Derby were defeated, and, although Russell demurred, their respective followers entered the fray with vigour. The Derby Government was defeated on a no-confidence motion on 11 June 1859.

So Derby left Downing Street, and Malmesbury the Foreign Office. Derby would return to his position again in 1866, but for Malmesbury the seals were relinquished forever. His Anglo-American diplomacy was not the most fruitful of the period – this distinction must be accorded to Lord Aberdeen without contest – but it was by far the most spirited, and showed the best understanding of American psychology. The Republic was young, forceful, and vigorous, and its leaders played the diplomatic game as energetically as its frontiersmen conquered the West. Derby and Malmesbury seem to have understood this, and to have understood also that American threats were usually political and tactical, intended hopefully to secure American interests, not to bring on an actual war. They operated upon the assumption that most American leaders would appreciate vigorous action by British statesmen to protect their own obvious interests, and, by and large, they proved to be correct. Although Derby and Malmesbury solved neither the Canadian Reciprocity, nor the Central American problem, in both cases they prepared the ground, and made solution rather easy for their successors.

When Lord Palmerston returned to office in 1859, he formed the strongest government since the Aberdeen Coalition of 1852, including not only the Whigs and Liberals, but the survivors of the defunct Peelite section, such as Gladstone, Herbert, and Newcastle. It is quite certain he would have preferred to have Lord Clarendon at the Foreign Office,[67] but despite his popularity and strength in the country, Palmerston thought it wise to grant Russell's request for that position. When Russell paid his courtesy call on Malmesbury on 18 June, he expressed anxiety regarding the defences of the country, and a determination to keep up the navy. The outgoing secretary, knowing that Palmerston's return had been hailed with delight in France because he favoured the unification of Italy, wondered at this concern, which indicates that he was now out of touch with Palmerston's views. Though all seemed to be sweetness and light in Anglo-French relations, at no time in his long career of checking real or imaginary French designs was Palmerston more consistently suspicious of France than during these years.

Although Palmerston helped France engineer a truce in the Italian War, and in 1860 sent that veteran Radical, Richard Cobden, to France to negotiate a long overdue commercial treaty between the two nations, the Prime Minister's mind was by no means at rest. Early in 1860 he wrote to Russell: 'There seems good Reason for thinking that Napoleon has great schemes in his Head for which he is trying to get the Concurrence & Co-operation of Russia, and that the dismemberment of the Turkish Empire is the object he next aims at, afterwards the Rhine and perhaps Belgium, but all in a most friendly manner & spirit toward England'.[68]

Palmerston was convinced that France was trying to surpass Britain in ironclad ships, and that her naval building had an obviously hostile purpose, so he launched a stepping-up of the shipbuilding programme, and made proposals for the fortification of strategic sites in Britain in case of invasion. The pacifist Cobden's bitterness knew no bounds. '. . . the most inexcusable act of any Government or prime minister of my time', he wrote, 'was the project of fortifications & the speech of Ld. Palmerston in the midst of my negotiations of a Commercial Treaty'.[69] Later Cobden wrote a protesting letter to the Prime Minister, who replied in a classic statement of his diplomatic and preparedness philosophy.[70] Cobden disgustedly concluded that Britain was in the hands of old men who did not change with the times.

There was some truth in Cobden's observation. Convinced that republics in the hands of unpredictable mass emotions were warlike and dangerous, Palmerston lacked the insight into the true nature of American diplomacy possessed by Derby and Malmesbury, as well as the trustfulness in human rationality displayed by Lord Aberdeen; but the Prime Minister was simply uneasy in his relations with America, not hostile to her, and this uneasiness since 1850 had been expressed in a desire to stay out of trans-Atlantic disputes as much as possible. Lord John Russell during these years finally gave up his contest with Palmerston, and in foreign affairs was content to learn from him, and follow his leadership. Malmesbury was quick to note how different was the situation between Prime Minister and Foreign Secretary now than it had been when Russell held the former position, and Palmerston was his subordinate.[71]

Whether it was so intended or not, the American attitude seemed to change with the administrations, almost as if they desired to put Palmerston and Russell to the test. In July 1859 Lord Lyons assured President Buchanan that it was Russell's desire to treat with the United States in the most open and friendly spirit, to which the President replied with a complaint regarding Britain's lack of progress in disposing of the Mosquito and Bay Islands questions, the only outstanding matters of dispute between the two nations. If they had not been solved by December, he warned he would have to take up the situation in his annual message.[72] Though not strictly speaking an ultimatum, it was obvious that lack of progress would result in some sort of Anglo-American crisis at the end of the year. To this Russell replied he was very willing to settle these disputes – 'But there is a little place called Europe, which has given us a good deal of trouble of late & I am not ready with any definite alteration of the views of Lord Malmesbury. I will be as civil as I can to the Americans who come here'.[73] This was his private reaction.

Russell's official reaction, written a week later, showed considerable progress toward meeting the American demand for action. Malmesbury shortly after leaving the Foreign Office had pronounced Ouseley unsatisfactory in the Government service,[74] and Russell quickly came around to this point of view. In a despatch dated 4 August Russell told Lyons that he would try to meet the deadline by sending a fresh mission to Central America, and by 15 August he had selected Charles Lennox Wyke to head the mission, and had drawn up his instructions, which were a considerable modification of those composed by Malmesbury. The American tactic of veiled threat had obviously worked.

Perhaps the main change by Russell was to leave Costa Rica, a friend of Britain, wholly out of the negotiation, and to give priority to the solution of the Bay Islands dispute, which Malmesbury had intended to leave for last.[75] The instructions sent to Wyke regarding the Bay Islands ordered him to transfer them and the Mosquito territory in Honduras to that state, to make 'reasonable arrangements' for the whites and Indians involved in the transfer, and to establish a mixed commission to settle land claims of British subjects. This was a considerable modification of the Clarendon–Herran agreement of 1856, which made the Bay Islands a free territory with their own municipal government. The 'reasonable arrangements' for the whites included provisions for the undisturbed use of their property, freedom of religion, and freedom to emigrate if they desired to do so. Russell explained that he had removed all reasonable objections which might be advanced by Honduras, and that, if British overtures were met in a friendly spirit, the negotiation should be over within two or three weeks. If the Honduran legislature were not in session, they should convoke it to consider the subject immediately.[76]

This note of urgency in Russell's instructions indicates how seriously he regarded the December deadline. The selection of the Bay Islands as the first of the problems to be considered is also significant. The British terms were so generous that Honduras was almost certain to accept them with alacrity, which meant that, regardless of how the more difficult Nicaraguan negotiation progressed, President Buchanan would be at least partly satisfied by December.

After paying a courtesy call on Guatemala, which was to be asked to help facilitate the negotiations with Honduras and Nicaragua, and negotiating the Bay Islands treaty, Wyke was ordered to go to Nicaragua to complete the work undertaken by Ouseley. Ouseley's only accomplishment there had been the conclusion of an innocuous postal treaty. The instruction given by Russell with regard to the commercial and Mosquito treaties, save for the major concession of excluding Costa Rica from the arrangement, were similar to those drawn up by Malmesbury and modified after he received the counter-proposals. On only two points was Wyke to be adamant – compensation had to be given to the Mosquito Indians, and Britain would not continue her protection of the area beyond three months after the treaties were ratified. The latter provision, which seems to have been adopted with a view to mollifying further the Americans, was a modification of the year's protection after the signing of the treaty suggested by Malmesbury, but, as Russell pointed out, time would elapse between the signing and the ratification of the treaty, so the nine months reduction of time would actually be considerably less. Wyke was ordered to pursue a hard line after making his concessions, Britain expected the treaties to be signed and ratified promptly – the alternative was the immediate severing of all connections with the country.[77]

In other communications of the same date, Russell permitted Wyke to use the British naval forces in the area to protect Central America against filibusters during the term of his mission, providing he did not land British marines, and ordered him to report the results of his negotiations to Lyons in Washington so that there would be a minimum delay in informing that country of them.[78] Unlike Malmesbury, Russell was perfectly willing to carry out the negotiations under the watchful eye of the State Department.

The same day Russell broke the sad news to Ouseley that his services were no longer required. The chief counts against him were failure to report his negotiations adequately, and the lack of progress in the negotiations.[79] Ouseley replied to these charges in a despatch, which pointed out that it had taken two years for the United States to obtain a treaty from Nicaragua,[80] and a private letter which presented his defence in more detail. In some respects his case, as in his La Plata difficulty, seems fairly sound, but in others, not so much so.[81]

Russell's comprehensive arrangements displayed a certain good will toward the United States which did not seem to be entirely reciprocated. Shortly after he had sent a copy of the Guatemala treaty to America, but before it had been received, Lyons sent him a report of another interview with 'Old Buck'.

The President charged Britain with appropriating the territory north of the Sarstoon River and neglecting the Mosquito and Bay Islands issues, which was followed by a repetition of the December deadline.[82] And, despite Buchanan's assertion that the solution of these Central American problems would exhaust outstanding differences between Britain and the United States, a quite unrelated crisis appeared in the autumn.

The unpredictable American general, William S. Harney, ostensibly acting on his own initiative, on 27 July sent Captain George E. Pickett (later of Gettysburg fame) to occupy San Juan island (near Vancouver and the Fraser River gold fields) which had been disputed between Britain and the United States since the Oregon Settlement. Troops were landed, annexation proclaimed, and the protests of Governor James Douglas were ignored. Owing to communications difficulties, the news of this illegal act did not break in Britain until mid-September. British reaction is illustrated by a letter from the pro-American, Lord Lyndhurst, to Lord Brougham: 'What will Ld. John say as to the seizure of San Juan? The Americans in that quarter greatly outnumbering us wd. like a war as they wd. in that case hope to make themselves master of the gold fields on the Fraser River. They are not bad hands at blowing up a breeze where they conceive their interests are concerned'.[83] To many it appeared that the United States had intentionally created a crisis to serve one or another of its purposes.

The information received in Britain did not support the supposition that the United States planned a war.[84] Furthermore, Britain had the *Tribune, Plumper, Satellite,* and *Ganges* on the scene to take possession of the harbour, and prevent the landing of more American troops on San Juan, so there was no immediate danger of her being driven from the area. Instead of taking strong action, Lord John Russell sought the opinion of the Duke of Somerset, the First Lord of the Admiralty, as to the value of San Juan. The Duke replied that the Admiralty had investigated the situation in 1858, and had concluded that the island itself was unimportant to Britain, but that the channel south of the 49th parallel must be kept open to the vessels of both countries. He suggested that Britain relinquish her claim to San Juan in return for the right of navigation.[85]

The solution of the difficulty followed the classic pattern when the countries involved wish to avoid war. Russell asked for explanations, the United States disavowed Harney's action, and sent copies of his instructions, as well as the new instructions given to General Winfield Scott, who had been sent to relieve him, to London; then both nations waited while Scott and Douglas agreed to a compromise which provided for the joint occupation of the island.[86] Neither the United States nor Britain, despite Somerset's advice, modified its claims to the island at this time.

Meanwhile Wyke had proceeded to Guatemala in October, and had induced that nation to intercede with Honduras and Nicaragua on behalf of his projects;[87] then he went on to Honduras with whom he concluded a treaty on 28 November. This document ceded the Bay Islands to Honduras with the provisions that they would be neutralised and retained by her without rights of cession to another state, and provided also that their inhabitants would continue to enjoy their property and their religion. The provisions ceding a section of the Mosquito territory to Honduras represented a personal triumph for Wyke as the Hondurans agreed to grant $5,000 a year for ten years to promote the social welfare of the Mosquito Indians. This was followed by the establishment of a commission to adjust outstanding claims.[88] As the Honduran legislature was not in session, the President took it upon himself to ratify the treaty.[89] Thus ended an episode in British diplomatic history that one observer describes as an 'extremely discreditable one'.[90]

The United States certainly could not complain that Britain failed to keep them informed in this instance. Lord Lyons reported Cass's 'extreme pleasure' on learning of the treaty in a letter to Russell dated 26 December, whereas Wyke's despatch to London on the subject did not reach home until 2 January!

Superficially it might appear that Wyke had exceeded his instructions in wringing the $5,000 grant to the Indians from Honduras, which was obtained only after a 'severe struggle'.[91] In all probability Russell had ordered him to press strongly for such a grant so that a similar one might be obtained from Nicaragua. It was probably omitted from his instructions lest Wyke fail to secure it, and these documents later become public property. He could not come away without a treaty, grant or no grant.

The indefatigable Wyke with both the Guatemalan and Honduran treaties to his credit arrived in Nicaragua in late December. The treaty with that nation, he later wrote, caused him six weeks of anxiety and incessant labour, and he finally had to warn the Nicaraguans that he was presenting Britain's final offer.[92] The postal treaty had already been signed by Ouseley, so there was no difficulty there, nor was there much argument about the commercial treaty, which gave Britain equal rights with the United States to protect the transit route, and placed her commerce on a 'most favoured nation' basis.[93] The Mosquito treaty gave Nicaragua sovereignty over the area, but set aside a reservation for the Mosquito Indians where they had rights of self-government not inconsistent with Nicaraguan sovereignty. Their 'social improvement' – an acceptable substitute for their land title, which Nicaragua would not recognise – was provided for by a $5,000 yearly grant for ten years. Grey Town was made a free port under the sovereignty of Nicaragua, but it was agreed that its duties and other charges on shipping would be sufficient only to maintain its facilities. The Indian grants of limited areas made since 1 January 1848 were recognised, and other clauses set up machinery for the settlement of claims.[94] The commercial treaty was signed on 11 February 1860; the Mosquito treaty on 28 January 1860.

In his negotiations with Nicaragua Wyke had the greatest difficulty in securing acceptance of the Grey Town provisions, which represented a rather curious restriction of Nicaraguan sovereignty over the town; and he had to fight for the Mosquito arrangements; but he emerged from the struggle as Britain's premier negotiator. He had secured a favourable boundary from Guatemala, a generous grant for the Indians from Honduras, and suitable Grey Town arrangements from Nicaragua. The Bay Islands treaty was ratified by the two countries on 18 April 1860; the Nicaraguan treaties, on 2 August 1860, and so ended a passage in British diplomatic history equalled in its tediousness only by some obscure aspects of the Eastern Question.

10
The Mexican Coup and the Last Great Crisis

The solution of the lingering problems of Central America did not exhaust the Latin American issues bequeathed to the Palmerston administration by the Conservatives. It is true that Malmesbury had succeeded in securing a convention to settle British claims, but the anarchy in Mexico continued, and it was quite obvious that any satisfactory settlement must await the coming of peace.

While still out of office, Palmerston in a letter to Clarendon once again affirmed his conviction that it would be in the British interest for the United States to annex Mexico,[1] a policy which, of course, Malmesbury had adopted. He also approved Malmesbury's intervention at Vera Cruz, although it had been directed against the Constitutionalists, the least guilty of the two parties in so far as ill treatment of British subjects was concerned. '. . . as we cannot send an army to invade the Country', he wrote at the time, 'we seem to have no other Choice than either to coerce Vera Cruz or to do nothing.'[2]

The most pressing Mexican problem Palmerston and Russell faced upon returning to office involved the unsatisfactory state of British representation there. In a belated valedictory letter of 30 June Malmesbury described Loftus C. Otway as unsatisfactory in the Government service, adding that Otway was 'always quarrelling with his own people & dissatisfied with the position in wh. he was placed by Clarendon only 18 months ago'.[3] The very same day, either as a result of Malmesbury's censure of Otway, or in anticipation of a parliamentary attack shortly to be made upon him, Russell recalled the British minister. It was just in the nick of time. On 8 July a member of the Commons reviewed Otway's activities in Mexico, including his partisanship of the Miramon cause and relations with Mira-

mon's wife, but the most damning charge brought against him
was one of callous indifference toward the well-being of British
subjects. This had become so painfully obvious that the American minister in Mexico, shocked at Otway's indifference, had
called upon him to exercise his powers on behalf of his fellow
countrymen.[4]

When Otway received the notice of his recall, he believed
that it heralded a major change in British policy towards
Mexico, as Britain followed the United States in switching to
the support of Juarez and Constitutionalists, which would make
him *non grata* because of his close ties to their opponents.[5]
When he found that recall had been merely preliminary to
being cashiered from the service, he wrote a lengthy defence
of his conduct in the hope of being reinstated.[6]

To a limited extent the recall of Otway did, indeed, herald
a change of British Mexican policy for his interim replacement
was George B. Mathew, a Conservative and friend of Malmesbury, and a partisan of Juarez and the Constitutionalists even
though British policy still officially recognised the Mexico City
government.

About the time he took over in the autumn of 1859, Russell
received a curious, indirect, American approach for cooperation in Mexican affairs. The American journalist and
politician, Duff Green, had been given a letter of introduction
to Richard Cobden by President Buchanan, and Cobden, who
was strictly a nominal supporter of the Government,[7] recommended him to Russell. Shortly before his return to the United
States he penned a lengthy letter to the Foreign Secretary,
stressing the traditional ties between Britain and America, for-
swearing all political designs of the United States upon Mexico,
and calling upon Britain to unite with her in recognising the
Juarez Government.[8] It was difficult to determine from the contents of the letter just how much official authorisation it had
from Buchanan.

Why Russell did not take the hint and transfer recognition
from the Miramon Government to that of Juarez seems fairly
clear. British objectives in Mexico, as later defined by Mathew,
were of modest dimensions – to aid in the establishment of
peace, to secure in practice the religious liberties provided for
in the Mexican constitution, and to secure low duties on British

exports to that country;[9] but a number of considerations helped determine how those objectives might be best secured.

As one recent writer has pointed out, France and Spain to a considerable extent followed the British lead in Mexico.[10] For Britain, the latter was an embarrassment, and an obstacle to the achievement of the religious liberty that Russell sought – to some extent, perhaps, to please his Protestant supporters, for Russell was as keen a politician as the period produced. France was an entirely different matter. Since the Oregon crisis in 1845, Britain had managed on more than one occasion to secure French support in her diplomatic wrangles with the United States, a support that was convenient, if not decisive, and which relieved Britain from the nightmare of a two-front war against the Franco-American alliance. The gains made in this area could not be lightly thrown away by suddenly deserting France on the Mexican issue. Furthermore, it was most convenient for Britain to cooperate with France in trans-Atlantic affairs, for the more France was involved in that area of the world, the less likely she was to forward her alleged plots in Europe. Furthermore, during 1859–61 British concern, if not panic, over the naval race also dictated that she should keep this slender, Mexican tie with France. So at this moment she was unwilling to offend France and Spain by suddenly switching to Juarez.

The new British chargé, however, could hardly be said to have acted the part of a friend to the Miramon Government. As Mathew viewed the civil war, it was a struggle between the 'Constitutionalists' and the 'Church Party', the last of whom regarded all British citizens as 'foreigners and hereticks', and thus nothing constructive could be expected from them.[11] The origins of the war he traced to the corruptions of a prominent smuggler, who provided funds for the Church Party to pronounce against the Government.[12]

Mathew was a man of considerable insight and ability, self-confident, if not wholly lacking in modesty. In his first private letter to Russell, dated 20 October 1859, he assured the Foreign Secretary that, despite the recent decline in British prestige in Mexico – 'I have reason to believe that I could at once make terms of amity & amnesty between the parties . . . but such is the state of the country, that it would be no permanent peace. . . .' [13] Russell decided, shortly after receiving this assurance, to give his minister a chance.

Russell's decision to intervene for peace in Mexico was made shortly after President Buchanan, in December, had asked Congress to consider sending troops into Mexico, and after the signing in the same month of the McLane–Ocampo Treaty, which granted broad powers to America to protect Mexico. The correspondence does not reveal how these events influenced Russell's change to a more activist policy in Mexico, but it is clear that his decision was simply an alternative peace measure dictated by public pressure to protect the interests of British citizens.[14] Its timing nevertheless made it seem like a policy in competition with that of the United States.

Mathew was instructed to call for an armistice, a general amnesty, the election of a new national assembly, and the establishment of religious and civil liberties. France was asked to cooperate in this peace effort, which would be entirely free of force or coercion, and the United States was to be invited to share in it, if the Senate rejected the McLane–Ocampo Treaty. Spain was ignored.[15]

It was a fruitless gesture. Despite his boast, Mathew was unable to secure its acceptance by either side. 'I much fear that the main points at issue, the church property, and religious toleration', he wrote in May, 'forbid the hope of any voluntary peace, or of other close than a party triumph'.[16] In this same letter Mathew subscribed to the Palmerston thesis that Britain should not fear an extension of American territory into Mexico, which would benefit British commerce, and he urged that Britain take no steps in conjunction with France and Spain, who were too deeply committed to the Church Party. With the overwhelming majority of Mexicans against them, the outlook of the Church Party seemed hopeless.

While Spain pressed for an activist policy in Mexico, and France consulted Britain, the last awaited the fate of the McLane–Ocampo Treaty in the Senate. Once it had been rejected, Britain asked the United States to join her and her two partners in seeking a cease-fire. The American reply declining the offer indicated her opposition to the joint intervention of the European powers in Mexican affairs, but she recognized the right of France to intervene, even by force, to secure justice for her citizens. Yielding to the American point of view, as well as the course of events in Mexico, Russell ordered Mathew to withdraw from Mexico City and suspend relations with the Church Party. He did not in August take the next step and recognise Juarez, but this dissociation of Britain from the Church Party would certainly have been expected to aid the Constitutionalist leader. In Mathew's opinion – '. . . the recognition of European powers & especially of England has been the chief cause of hitherto prolonging the power of the church party'.[17] The French rightly viewed this, and a subsequent British suggestion to call for a truce, as an attempt to undermine the Church Party.[18]

In November Russell considered the Mexican situation important enough to provide some private instructions to Mathew. Noting that they had been quite right in attempting to secure a cease fire, he continued:[19]

> We & the French have assured President Buchanan that we have no thoughts of intervening by force in Mexico. Then what is to be done? The U.S. will not act with European powers to settle the question. Then let them settle it themselves. The present state of robbery & carnage in a country flowing with silver can hardly be allowed to go on. Let the Americans interfere by force if they will, & put up President Juarez if they like and let our merchants have freedom of trade and passage. Do not promote or oppose this consummation at present. Such are my private thoughts perhaps soon to be public opinions.

From this letter it is obvious that Russell was quite willing to recognise the Constitutionalists, but his twin fears of offending France, on the one hand, and the United States on the other, dictated an inactive policy.

The course of events in Mexico rushed by Russell, if not his minister. Two atrocities of late 1860 bore heavily on Britain. The Constitutionalist General Delgollado took $1,000,000 worth of specie into protective custody, 40% of which was British, and another claim against Mexico came into existence. Even worse from a diplomatic, and an economic standpoint, was the raid in November by General Marquez of the Church

Party on the British Legation in Mexico City, which was looted of $660,000. Russell was particularly incensed by the latter outrage.[20]

As Mathew had predicted, the Church Party had few supporters in the nation and by December the Constitutionalists had achieved a military victory. From the tone of his letters, it is clear that Mathew gave active assistance to the Constitutionalists during this end phase of the struggle. 'I must not deny to your Lordship, that the change has been greatly my doing', he wrote, 'when I found by the rejection of Delgollado's peace proposals and by Sr. Pacheco's views on religious toleration that conciliatory arrangements were impossible, and when the outrages we had received from the Miramon Govt. and their evident determination to continue in the same hostile course – had put neutrality out of the question'.[21] This cool avowal of his activities in support of Juarez, despite Russell's instructions not to 'promote or oppose', brought no censure from the Home Government. Russell continued to have the greatest confidence in him, the more so, perhaps, because his minister had chosen the winning side.

When Juarez returned in triumph to Mexico City on 11 January 1861 all that remained in so far as Britain was concerned was a claims agreement after which the Constitutionalists would be formally recognised. The Juarez Government proved tractable, save in the matter of the Marquez robbery, which had been the work of their late opponents; but they eventually accepted all of the British conditions, and on 26 February 1861 Britain formally recognised Juarez. Later Mathew explained that he could not press on Juarez the claim for the Marquez robbery as strongly as that in which Delgollado was involved, 'but I established the *principle* that the nation was responsible for *both* sums ... and I received the repeated assurances of the Minister of his readiness to enter into any arrangements in his power with the Bondholders' agent'.[22]

Mathew's seemingly successful term of office was now rapidly drawing to an end, for a permanent British representative, Sir Charles Wyke, was shortly to replace him. Although Mathew rather liked the Constitutionalists, he was by no means convinced of their ability to run Mexico efficiently. Their leaders were 'a poor, helpless, tho' *well meaning* set', he assured

Russell.[23] He would have preferred that the United States intervene at this point and take over the customs houses – indeed, he even suggested that Russell issue a formal declaration calling on her to do so; but he suspected that the United States would prefer to see Mexico break up into small states, and become another Central America. Still he was quite satisfied with the results of his own activities. The anarchy in Mexico had been put down, British lives and property were safe again, and 'the prestige of the English name stands as high as it ever did'.[24]

On his return to London, Mathew was offered the post of chargé to Guatemala, a poor return, he thought, for his services. Upon reconsideration Russell evidently agreed with him, for a month later he had raised the offer to that of Minister Plenipotentiary to the Republics of Central America, which Mathew gratefully accepted.[25]

Sir Charles Lennox Wyke, still wearing the laurels he had gained in Central America, arrived in Mexico on 30 April 1861, some two weeks after the firing on Fort Sumter had altered the diplomatic picture in Mexico by withdrawing its self-appointed guardian. At this point, the story is traced so minutely and effectively in a recent study that there is no reason here to provide more than an outline of how the situation in Mexico degenerated to the point that outside intervention was invited by the British minister.[26]

Britain had a fairly large stake in the claims against Mexico – $18 million in claims down to early 1861,[27] plus British-held bonds to a value between £30–40 million.[28] It was Wyke's unenviable task to try to collect the former, and interest on the latter from a neophyte government which was desperately short of funds, and which was too inexperienced to use its powers effectively. In May Wyke spent much of his time trying to secure recognition of the Marquez claim; on 3 June payments to all creditors, with certain exceptions were suspended for one year by presidential decree; on 17 July the Congress, which had stripped Juarez of much of his power, suspended all payments, even those provided for under various conventions. Under these circumstances, in late September, the Chairman of the Bondholders wrote Russell that only foreign intervention could save Mexico from destruction, and her creditors from ruin. Was Britain under such circumstances forced to intervene? As we have seen earlier, Palmerston in the past had recognised such a governmental obligation, but Lord Aberdeen had denied it.

Parallel to the claims story runs that of the break-down of law and order in Mexico during the period January–August 1861. The stable condition of Mexico described by Mathew just before his departure was not long-lived, if it ever really existed. Once their regulars had been beaten, the supporters of the Church Party took to guerrilla warfare, which was carried out so successfully that the Marquez forces actually staged a hit-and-run attack on Mexico City in June. The situation gave rise to more claims, more atrocity stories in which the British were sometimes victims. One might ask the question – did these circumstances force Britain to intervene? Did Palmerston feel called upon to give force to his *obiter dictum*, as Aberdeen had called it, regarding Britain's obligation to protect the financial claims of its citizens, and the *civis Romanus sum* doctrine that he had often upheld?

Certainly there was pressure on the Government from the mercantile interest to intervene, which had been strong even in the time of Malmesbury, and Palmerston had ample precedents to justify coercion. Still, it seems likely that another factor weighed heavily with him, a motive that must be assumed because it is not documented, but which might actually have played the major role in the intervention scheme of 1861.

There can be no question but that Lord Palmerston was worried in 1861, and that he was shrewd and capable enough to work out an intricate, even bizarre scheme to further British security. The latter statement is borne out by the curious development of British domestic politics during 1860–61 which found the conservative Palmerston making *sub rosa* deals with Derby through his old friend Malmesbury to frustrate the Radicals, who were supposed to be his supporters.[29] On one occasion they scuttled a Reform Bill, dear both to the Radicals and Lord John Russell; on another Palmerston worked with the Conservatives to defeat a proposal offered by his Cabinet colleague, William E. Gladstone. Relations between the Government and Opposition leaders were so warm and intimate that

Lord Derby gave Palmerston almost *carte blanche* for his conduct of foreign affairs.[30]

During the first half of 1861 Palmerston's main interest was the naval race with France, and his quest for security. Although the Derby Administration had constructed some ironclads, they were thinly armoured at both ends. 'I see in my Mind's eye', Palmerston wrote to Somerset, 'the Warrior and the Black Prince, with their pasteboard ends knocked to slivers; the underwater compartments filled with water, everything above the waterline smashed to fragments.'[31] He, therefore, sought £2 million from Parliament for the plating of some wooden ships, and a like amount to construct fortifications in Britain to protect certain vital points in case of a French invasion.

Securing such additions to the budget involved a running battle with his Chancellor of the Exchequer, the economy-minded William E. Gladstone, who was deeply chagrined at having his financial plans upset. In a long letter to him in July Palmerston elaborated on the theme: 'Peace & good understanding between England & France are most likely to be permanent when France has no naval superiority over England'.[32] Of the highest importance was his general review of the naval situation – that Britain's navy would be qualitatively inferior to that of France by the summer of 1862, and that it would actually be numerically inferior in ironclads by May, 1863! So many technological developments were taking place both in guns and armouring that the situation was fraught with the deepest and most alarming uncertainties.

What he expected France to do is not entirely clear, but he thought he saw French machinations in many places. 'The project you mention of giving Belgium to France and Hungary to Leopold', he wrote Russell in January, 'would certainly accomplish Two objects highly advantageous to England & Europe. It would give a great additional military & naval Power to France whose present weakness in these respects everybody now laments, and it would entirely break down the power of Austria. . . . It is the sort of Plan that Bright & Cobden would probably very much approve.'[33]

In June Palmerston wrote to Sidney Herbert: 'I have just got your Ireland Information which I have sent on to John Russell. It confirms with more detail what we knew generally

before as to the French Proceedings in Ireland, and it corrobo-
rates the conviction which every reasoning man ought to
entertain that our Friend the Emperor is only waiting till he has
succeeded in being strongest at sea (which it is our Business to
prevent) to launch his Thunders and satiate his long pent up and
craftily concealed enmity against England'.[34] The same month
he wrote to Russell: 'I read a Despatch yesterday giving an
account of French intrigues in the Island of Sardinia to induce
the people to vote for annexation to France. I have always been
struck with the equivocation of Cavour's denials of any intention to cede that Island to France'.[35] Another letter to Somerset
the same month noted that Napoleon was carefully preparing a
war of revenge against Britain to make up for past humiliations,
and noted: '. . . in the meantime Russia is building iron ships
which might be united with those of France in any dispute we
might have with France'.[36]

French gestures of friendship were heavily discounted. In
July Palmerston had a conversation with the French Ambassador, the Comte de Flahaut, who observed '. . . it is of great importance that England & France should act as closely in Concert
as possible, so that the Washington people may see that there is
no Chance of dividing the Two great European Powers, and
that when any disagreeable step towards America is to be taken
. . . he, Flahaut, would suggest that France should take the
most prominent Part, as the best means of undeceiving the
Yanks as to any false expectations they may have formed'.[37]
Not long after this highly cordial interview, Palmerston wrote
his lengthy letter to Gladstone warning about the growth of the
French navy, then in August he called Russell's attention to the
fact that the French were undertaking 'very extensive works at
Dunkirk, wh. when completed will make that Port a Place of
Assembly for a Naval force almost as capacious as Cherbourg'.[38]

Late in August Palmerston wrote to Sir George Lewis: 'I
have no fear of any blow up this year in Europe',[39] which might
on the surface indicate that the Prime Minister's suspicions of
France were temporarily laid to rest. Nothing could be further
from the truth. There would be no 'blow up' because the French
would not achieve qualitative superiority at sea until the summer
of 1862, and actual superiority – the period of ultimate danger –
in May 1863.

In evaluating Palmerston's assessment of French intentions, it must be recalled that the Battle of the Nile, Trafalgar, and Waterloo were for him not mere names, but personal recollections, and even sharper in his mind were his own humiliations of France, especially his diplomatic triumph in the Eastern Question in 1840–41. Lord John Russell, who could also recall these British victories, and French defeats, seems to have accepted Palmerston's line of reasoning without much question.[40]

It was in the minds of these ageing statesmen, ripe of years, but still extraordinarily keen, that the Mexican intervention was planned and carried out. Save for Somerset at the Admiralty, the other members of the Cabinet were not even consulted about it. In October Somerset suggested that the other members of the Cabinet might take it 'amiss' if they were totally ignored, so Palmerston decided to bring the group together.[41] 'Nominally, we were summoned in order to decide the Mexican question', Sir George Lewis wrote to Clarendon, 'but practically the question was already decided. . . .'[42] This exclusion of other Cabinet officers from their secrets might be interpreted merely as an act of Palmerstonian arbitrariness,[43] or, just as likely, it may have arisen from a desire to confide in as few people as possible.

The detailed story of the complex negotiations leading up to the Convention Relative to Combined Operations Against Mexico, signed on 31 October 1861, and ratified the following 15 November can be found elsewhere.[44] Certain points involved in those negotiations would seem to call for special emphasis. Britain obviously wanted to sign and execute this intervention with as little adverse effect as possible upon Anglo-American relationships. Although Russell wrote Lyons with a flourish – 'Our Mexican policy would have been ill taken in the palmy days of the Republic. But it must now be accepted',[45] it is clear that he and Palmerston tried as much as possible to take the sting out of it. Russell had a lengthy conversation with the American Minister, Charles Francis Adams, on 25 September and assured him that any agreement reached with Spain would exclude interference into the internal affairs of Mexico.[46] Palmerston and he also insisted that – one, the United States should be invited to join in the expedition, and two, that the allies should disclaim any intention of interference in Mexican internal affairs. Although France, and to a lesser extent, Spain, opposed this circumscribing of the scope of the intervention, the British ministers were successful in inserting them in the treaty. Article II pledged the allies not to seek territory or special advantage in Mexico, or to prejudice the right of the Mexican nation freely to constitute its own form of government; and Article IV provided for sending a copy of the convention to the United States along with a request for her to accede to it.

The convention, then, seemed to point to a military occupation of the forts and ports along the Mexican coast, after which the occupying powers would demand and receive satisfaction of their claims. But did Palmerston and Russell expect it to end there? It is hard to believe that they did. They had known as far back as 1856 that Napoleon toyed with the idea of setting a foreign prince on the Mexican throne, and, even if they were not informed of his decision of 9 September to install Maximilian there, they must have suspected it when the French ambassador sounded them out on the subject in October. Both Russell and Palmerston expressed doubt that such a plan could succeed, but they did not entirely discourage the idea, providing that Britain were not expected to further it.[47]

Whether or not Palmerston and Russell at this point could foresee the future – the retirement of Britain and Spain from the intervention in 1862, leaving France to bear the burdens and the onus of violating the Monroe Doctrine, it is impossible to say. But what became obvious to a minor diplomatic official could hardly have escaped their attention at one time or another. George B. Mathew wrote from Central America:[48]

If he [Napoleon III] persists in *making a President* by the aid of a large force – within two years the Yankees will follow his example with greater local popularity, from the Northern provinces. From whatever hostile source the prompting came to him, it is impossible not to admire the political sagacity of a plan, whose effect withdrew French attention from European affairs, laid the root of ill will between France and the United States, and destroyed the prestige of one of whom hitherto it had been thought *nil molitur inepte*.

Perhaps it was merely coincidence that France would have her attention diverted from Europe during the summer of 1862,

when Palmerston believed the British navy would be qualitatively inferior to that of France. Perhaps the old Aberdeen plan
to separate France and the United States diplomatically, as a
means of enhancing British security, has no relationship to the
events in Mexico in 1861-2. Yet, as one reviews the unfolding
of this story, he is likely to imagine he sees the two ageing
makers of British foreign policy, after signing the convention,
lifting their sherry glasses in a toast to human folly in general,
and that of Napoleon III in particular.[49]

Meanwhile Palmerston and Russell had anticipated the outbreak of hostilities in the United States, and had established a
policy toward the conflict before the firing on Fort Sumter.
While President Buchanan, the former *bete noir* of Britain,
helplessly watched the division of his nation into opposing
camps, some suggestions were made that Britain should try to
mediate the quarrel. 'I quite agree with Lord John Russell and
Lord Lyons', Palmerston wrote in December 1860. 'Nothing
would be more inadvisable than for us to interfere in the Dispute, if it should break out, between any of the States of the
union, and the federal government. . . .'[50] Lord John Russell
held similar language in a letter to Thomas Baring, a family
always interested in American affairs, the same month. 'Lord
Palmerston & I think it would be unsafe for us to mediate in
American affairs', he wrote, 'unless we were called upon by both
parties to do so – & even then we should be unwilling'.[51]

Both of the statesmen viewed this struggle, as they viewed
other diplomatic events, strictly within the context of the safety
and good of their own country, an attitude for which some
politicians in the North, hoping for strong partisanship, could
never forgive them. Thus, the same month Palmerston warned
Lord Somerset: 'Then again it seems pretty certain that some
serious differences will be established between the *dis*-united
States of North America, and there is no saying what attitude
we may have to assume, not for the purpose of interfering in
their quarrels, but to hold our own & to protect our Fellow
subjects and their interests from being too unceremoniously
dealt with by the contending parties'.[52]

Gladstone later wrote that Palmerston desired the severance

of the United States so that America would cease to be so dangerous to Britain,[53] and it is quite likely that Palmerston expressed some such opinion on occasion. As we have seen, the Duke of Argyll once recorded such a sentiment, and it is occasionally encountered elsewhere.[54] For Palmerston the United States had become an unpredictable interloper into the diplomatic scene, one which annoyed him for many reasons, not the least of which was that he knew so little about her.[55] Long experience had taught him how to piece together the jig-saw puzzles of European diplomacy, but if the picture were enlarged to include America, he experienced difficulties. There is no reason to disbelieve the sentiment so often encountered in his letters that what he wanted most from the United States was for her to let Britain alone diplomatically, and confine their relations to trade and occasional meaningless exchanges of prominent visitors.

If Palmerston's main concern in 1861 vis-a-vis France was the enlargement of her navy, his principle interest in the American war was Canadian defence, and even to this area his attention turned slowly. He wrote to Russell in February: 'Lyon's account of Seward's language strongly confirms the Soundness of your Proposal that a British Regt. shd. be sent to Vancouver's Island, and it ought to be accompanied by some artillery; Armstrong guns if practicable'.[56] Reports from the same source regarding the language of the same prominent American caused him to write a longer letter on the same subject in May. Seward would create some serious difficulty between Britain and the United States, and the defenceless nature of Canada would encourage him to do this, so he proposed to send there three regiments instead of the one agreed upon by the Cabinet, which 'might be a useful hint to Seward and Lincoln and their associates' even though they could not defend Canada against an American invasion. They might, however, provide the foundations upon which a militia and volunteer force might be built up by the Canadians themselves. He urged that the reinforcements be sent during the summer before the cold weather made sending them difficult, if not impossible.[57] Newcastle countered with a suggestion that British naval forces in the area be augmented, and Palmerston sent his letter to the Duke of Somerset with his personal approval. 'Seward, who is a vapour-

ing, blustering, ignorant Man', he continued, 'may drive us into
a quarrel without intending it, or he may find his Southern
neighbours too hard a morsel for his teeth, and he may try to
make up for ill success against the South by picking a quarrel
with . . . a less strong and less prepared neighbour in the North.
If he sees we are on our guard, he will have sense enough to
respect us'.[58] This spurt of interest in American affairs inspired
two letters to Sidney Herbert in which he recommended the
three regiments be dispatched with haste, and that they be composed mostly of British and Scots, not Irish.[59] Thereafter, Palmerston lapsed into a familiar groove, and wrote Russell about
French designs on Sardinia.

American reaction to British decisions regarding the diplomatic position and rights of the seceded states, usually heated,
periodically forced American affairs on Palmerston's attention.
On 23 June noting that 'the Yankees will be violent & threatening in Proportion to our increasing local strength', he recommended to Somerset that two more frigates be sent out to the
North American station.[60] As it turned out, Admiral Milne believed that he already had on hand sufficient strength to cope
with 'anything the Americans could bring against him', so
Palmerston's fears of naval unpreparedness were quieted, if not
completely obliterated during the summer of 1861 in so far as
America was concerned.[61]

It was quite otherwise in the matter of Canadian defence.
Although 3,000 troops were sent to Canada, there was much
truth in Disraeli's caustic comments in the Commons in July
that such a small number of men could not cope with an American invasion of Canada, and sending them merely would convince the United States that Britain was hostile to her.[62] No one
was more keenly aware of the defenceless state of Canada than
Palmerston who in a letter of 9 July recommended that before
winter set in 'Ten Thousand Troops of the Line with propor-
tionable artillery should be sent there.[63] Russell agreed with him,
and a battle ensued within the Cabinet.

The coalition he had formed in 1859 had brought into the
Cabinet several powerful former Peelites, such as Sydney Herbert, the Secretary of State for War, the Duke of Newcaste at the
Colonies, and especially, William E. Gladstone at the Exchequer. All three had at one time inbibed the pacifistic ration-

alism of Lord Aberdeen, and the last of the three had made it his own outlook on foreign affairs. Then in the most vigorous period of his career, and widely regarded as a Prime Minister of the future, Gladstone did not hesitate to take up the cudgels with Palmerston on behalf of economy, and to try to undermine all of his preparedness schemes. Many Cabinet members, not only the former Peelites, were susceptible to Gladstone's skilful presentations, and Palmerston was forced to plead for support on occasion. After outlining his preparedness case a few months before in a letter to Somerset, Palmerston concluded: 'These & many other circumstances ought to make us deaf to the voice of that charmer Gladstone, charm he ever so wisely. . . .'[64] Of course, Palmerston, if he wished, could go ahead with his plans despite Cabinet opposition, but, rather than do so, he preferred to carry out his diplomacy in conjunction with Russell and one or two others without consulting his colleagues in formal session.

In the matter of dispatching more troops to Canada, Palmerston decided to seek Cabinet support, and his worst fears were rapidly realised. The theme he used is found in a letter to Sir George Lewis – 'There is in the Northern States a Party, not without influence, who look to a rupture with England as a ride off for any failure in the South, and they reckon greatly upon what they think is the defenceless state of Canada. They rather court than shun a quarrel with England, though they wish to avoid one with England and France United; and hitherto, luckily, France has gone with us'.[65] Palmerston further argued that the troops had to reach Halifax before winter if they were to go on to Quebec, for the only railway connection between the two cities went through the United States, and it was impossible at that time of year to make the trip on foot. So he tried to have up to 10,000 troops sent in relays on the *Great Eastern*, a very large ship, before the summer was over. That 'Charmer Gladstone' and others advanced all sorts of obstacles to Palmerston's plan, emphasising especially that the Canadian provinces could not house so many troops, and the Prime Minister and Russell reluctantly gave in, much to the former's regret.[66]

Palmerston believed that the earlier dispatch of troops, though small in numbers, had had 'a wholesome effect upon the Tone & Temper of Lincoln and Seward',[67] and, convinced (like Derby and Malmesbury) that successful diplomacy with the

United States could be carried on only from a position of
strength, this failure to reinforce Canada in the summer of 1861
seemed to pierce a hole in his American policy, and to invite an
American-made diplomatic crisis. The Prime Minister's letters
of early November were especially apprehensive of the future.

As it turned out, the course of events proved that Palmerston
had been correct in his forecast. An American-made crisis
materialised, and Canada was defenceless, or at most weakly
defended.[68]

A goodly number of interesting and interpretive accounts of
the origins and evolution of the *Trent* Crisis have appeared
from time to time,[69] and the story is so well known that it should
suffice to note at this point that the crisis arose on 8 November
1861, when Captain Charles Wilkes of the U.S.S. *San Jacinto*
stopped the British mail packet on the high seas, and removed
two Southern envoys from it.

Contrary to the opinions expressed by some authorities, the
crisis occurred during a moment of profound peace in Britain.
Despite Palmerston's fear of France, the two nations had
triumphantly concluded their China intervention in 1860, and
had solved the Syria–Lebanon problem to their mutual satisfaction in 1861. At the time of the *Trent* crisis France was embark-
ing on her Mexican adventure, which seemed likely to occupy
her attention for an indefinite period. Europe as a whole was
more quiet than at any time since before the Crimean War.
Cavour had died in June 1861, after uniting almost all of Italy;
the Russian Tsar was deep in his reform programme; the
German unification wars were still in the future. From the Volga
to the Pyrenees there was scarcely a cloud on the horizon.

During the crisis itself the European powers, according to
Gladstone, all supported the British case.[70] When Russell sent
his demands that America release the prisoners and apologise
for the incident, he was able to tell Lyons, in a private letter,
that M. de Thouvenel was sending out a despatch in which
France gave moral support to Britain,[71] and on 6 December
Palmerston himself admitted that the course taken by the French
was very satisfactory both because it was in the interest of
France to support the British case, and because of Napoleon's
hostile feelings toward the Federal Government.[72] In a letter of
9 December to Russell, Palmerston noted that 'Russia is over-

flowing with Friendship for England, in return for which she hopes & expects that England will prevent the French Emperor from creating disturbances in Poland'.[73] Palmerston's eye was never off Europe, but at the moment there was little there to attract his gaze.

Calm had settled over the broad Empire. Viscount Canning's moderate and conciliatory measures had removed the scars of the Sepoy Rebellion in India, and in 1861 the first steps were being taken to give the Indians some small voice in running the government. Australia and New Zealand had had their own requests for self-government more than satisfied during the previous decade; so had Canada. The guerrilla warfare of the Maoris on the North Island of New Zealand in 1860 was nothing new, or of much more than local interest. Burma since her chastisement in 1852 had been peaceful, and since the Dutch and British had agreed to part company in the Transvaal and Orange Free State during 1852–4, the conflict there had come to an end. The Colonial Office in 1861 could survey the whole imperial scene and scarcely find a Moslem Nawab, Hindu Rajah, Malay Prince or Zulu Chief in rebellion.

So there was nothing in Britain's diplomatic or imperial relations in 1861 to deter her from crossing swords with the United States had she chosen to do so. At home the opposition was distinctly minimal. 'The feeling here is very quiet and very decided', Russell could write. 'There is no party about it; all are unanimous'.[74] Lord Clarendon gave Russell his support for a strong policy based on the assumption that the United States simply would not respond well to kindly treatment.[75] The Conservative Pakington told Clarendon, who told Russell, that 'the American difficulty was far too grave to be made a marker for party warfare'.[76] Lord Derby did not contact Palmerston directly – there was hardly any need to do so after the arrangement he had made the year before – but his support was apparently assured to Palmerston through Russell.[77] Like Clarendon – and even more so – Derby was convinced that Britain must speak softly in her dealings with America, and carry a very large stick.[78]

The only opposition was carried on by Richard Cobden and John Bright. The former wrote Gladstone a plea not to strike America in her hour of weakness, and Gladstone replied stiffly.[79]

Bright called for peace in a speech at Rochdale. Both sent letters to President Lincoln, which may have had more effect on his policy than their activities did upon Palmerston.[80] The fact was that they were powerless to sway public opinion either in the Commons, or outside of it. Cobden was the first to admit the powerlessness of their position.[81]

All of these facts – the calm in Europe, the support of France and Russia, the lack of imperial concerns, and the virtual unanimity of opinion behind the Government at home – suggest that Lord Palmerston in 1861 was virtually free to handle the *Trent* crisis as he saw fit. Had he believed British security demanded a war, and the splitting of the Union, he certainly could have started one. One does not have to postulate a fancied British dependence on Northern wheat, or the decadence of the British aristocracy,[82] to discover why he acted as he did.

There is no reason to believe that Palmerston would have refrained from resorting to war as an extension of his diplomacy if two conditions had been present – first, that the war was necessary to sustain Britain's international position, and vital interests; and two, that Britain had a good chance of winning it.

Although the United States in the recent past had shown some tendency to increase her own international stature by pursuing hard-line policies toward Britain, all the reports of usually reliable sources received during the past twenty years indicated that America never seriously sought a war with Britain. Nor did she seem to harbour (as France was thought to do) a desire to ruin Britain. Rather she had played a legitimate, if often annoying, game of bluff at the expense of the Mother Country to achieve what from her point of view were vital interests. The only undying hatred that British statesmen found in the United States was among the Irish, and their influence was necessarily limited. By this time it was generally believed in Britain that she had a strong interest in preserving peaceful and friendly relations with America.

Just how Palmerston evaluated Britain's chances of winning a war against the United States at this time is not entirely clear.[83] He apparently believed that Britain could fight America successfully (save in Canada) if she were not simultaneously attacked by another major power, but the growth of American strength injected some uncertainty into the situation. Such a contest would not be a mere repetition of the war of 1812, but a major war.

Under these circumstances, the idea of starting a war over the *Trent* affair never seems to have crossed Palmerston's mind. But Britain had her international honour and prestige to uphold, and she was forced by circumstances to react strongly. The question was – how strongly? Palmerston frankly mistrusted both Seward and Lincoln, and was not sure how to handle them. Russell, on the other hand, while also distrusting Seward, was probably the first British statesman to realise Lincoln was a great and responsible person.[84]

Palmerston's initial reaction was surprisingly mild. He wrote to Russell on 29 November suggesting that Britain should ask for an apology and the release of the prisoners, the alternative being the recall of Lord Lyons from Washington and the ending of British arms shipments to the North.[85] How different was this from his reaction in 1841, when he threatened a war of retaliation and vengeance over the McLeod affair! Even this mild programme was based on the assumption that Washington was seeking a rupture.

The Cabinet held meetings on both 29 and 30 November, and agreed that the United States should be told that the seizure of prisoners was a violation of British rights and international law, a hope should be expressed that the act would be disavowed, and that Britain expected the prisoners to be restored to British protection. The alternative being a breaking of diplomatic relations.[86] As Palmerston described the thinking of the Cabinet as of 29 November, there was no mention of an apology, or of cutting off war supplies to the North.

These views were subsequently embodied in a short despatch that was given to the Queen on 30 November. The biographer of the Prince Consort tells how this excellent, high-minded man, suffering his last illness, revised the 'meagre' draft and added such mollifying phrases as 'unwilling to believe' America intended an insult, and 'glad to believe' she would 'spontaneously offer' redress in the form of liberating the passengers, and offering an apology.[87] Palmerston thought his suggestions were excellent, and the tone of the final draft, which was drawn up by the Cabinet,[88] showed some of Prince Albert's benign influence.

Even though the wording had been softened, the official draft still demanded the return of the prisoners to British protection, and a 'suitable apology', which could have meant an abject American surrender unless softened by private instructions as to the manner in which the demands were to be presented. Russell was the author of these vital instructions; whether he was their sole author is still not clear. Lord Lyons was to 'prepare' Seward for the despatch before reading it to him.[89] After the reading he could tell him informally that Britain would be 'rather easy' about the apology – all that was wanted was a return of the prisoners and an explanation. If Seward asked what would follow an American refusal of the demands, Lyons was to state that he desired 'to abstain from anything like menace'.

The absolutely vital change that was made through these private instructions was the transmutation of the term 'apology', with its unpleasant connotations to a proud country, to a mere 'explanation'. This permitted Seward, if he were seeking a way of maintaining the peace, and were alert to the nuances of diplomatic language, to escape from his dilemma gracefully. Palmerston does not seem to have expected him to give a straight answer; Russell, on the other hand, was more hopeful.

As it turned out, Seward proved to be a much more canny practitioner of Anglo-American diplomacy than they had anticipated. 'He understood,' Lyons later reported, 'H. M. Govt. to leave it open to the Govt. of Washington to present the case in the form which would be most acceptable to the American people. . . .'[90] By justifying his return of the prisoners on the traditional American position that impressment was illegal, Seward concocted an explanation that took the sting out of American compliance with British demands. And so the crisis ended.

Looking back upon Anglo-American diplomacy during the two decades before the American Civil War, certainly the outstanding fact of the whole period was the emergence of the United States as a strong economic, military, and naval power, who was Britain's chief maritime competitor. The central problem facing British foreign policy makers of the era was how to solve the issues, some of long-standing, others of recent origins, between Britain and America so that they could live comfortably with the expansive republic.

Britain never created any grand diplomatic strategy which she followed faithfully from crisis to crisis. Although some authorities conclude that a strategy for containing American expansion actually existed, and was evident in such areas as Texas, Mexico, Central America, the Caribbean and Hawaii,[91] this master plan seems to have been *ex post facto* in its origins to explain British reactions to specific situations, some of which had little to do with containing American expansion.

A grand strategy might have been suggested to British diplomats by the sectional conflicts within the United States. A division of the United States would not only have sharply reduced the power of the country, but would have provided infinite future opportunities for Britain to play off one American state against the other. Although one occasionally finds references in the private correspondence to the diplomatic advantages of such a split, there is not the slightest evidence that Britain at any time tried overtly or covertly to promote it. The only occasions on which she tried to influence American domestic affairs involved attempts to assert the rights of free British Negroes who fell afoul of the slave laws in ports of the South.

In the area of diplomatic tactics, the threat of outright war came to be in disfavour, and was abandoned. Palmerston used it in 1841 in the McLeod crisis for the last time. Aberdeen came close to it when the Oregon crisis entered a menacing stalemate, and Lord John Russell skirted its outposts in the *Trent* crisis; neither, however, would issue an ultimatum the alternative to which was war. As a matter of fact, it became increasingly difficult for a British Foreign Secretary to use it credibly as the years went by. War with the United States had always been highly unpopular with the British people as a whole, and as strong, new economic bonds were formed between the two countries in the 1850's, the sentiment for peace became a fixed attitude of the British Parliament.

On the other hand, the threat of British naval action was a tactic Britain saw fit to employ on a number of occasions. Aberdeen's use of it during the Oregon crisis seems to have made a considerable impression in diplomatic circles. Clarendon resorted to the naval threat in 1854 to arrest the deterioration of

Anglo-American relations during the Crimean War period, and did so again in 1855, and 1856. Malmesbury used the same tactic to strengthen Britain's hand in her Central American negotiations in 1858. Still, it should be stressed that an action by the British Navy would not have necessarily meant full scale war, for no country ever employed the quasi-war tactic more skilfully and congenially than Britain in the nineteenth century. How effective it was in actually influencing American policy is left for specialists in that field to determine. But the fact that Britain resorted to the naval threat so often would indicate a belief that it was a useful extension of her conventional diplomacy.

The most ingenious diplomatic tactic developed by Britain during the period was enlisting America's traditional friend, France, against her two-time war partner. Aberdeen used this tactic in Texas simply to establish its feasibility, not to protect Texas, and his policy bore more fruit in late 1845, when France adopted a friendly attitude toward Britain during the Oregon crisis. Even though he wrecked the Anglo-French *entente* for a time, Palmerston nevertheless possessed an uncanny ability to enlist French aid when he wanted it. Malmesbury, the close friend of Napoleon III, utilised the latter's dislike of the Monroe Doctrine to secure some French diplomatic support in his various contests with the United States. Time and again France could be counted on to aid in thwarting the United States in the Caribbean, Hawaii, or elsewhere. However, in view of the bitter sectional domestic politics then existing in the United States, it would probably be an exaggeration to state that Anglo-French opposition kept America out of those areas.

The extra dividend paid by this French policy was that in enlisting France against the United States, Britain reduced the possibility of their co-operating against her in a future war. Lord Aberdeen especially emphasised this. Knowing that this policy existed in British thinking, one might conclude that the Convention of 1861 represented the culmination of this policy even though proof of it is lacking.

Two tactics often employed by the Americans during this era – frightening the British minister in Washington, and creating a diplomatic crisis whenever Britain seemed deeply involved elsewhere – were only rarely used by British Foreign Secretaries, who usually maintained at least an outward show of cordiality toward American ministers in London. Palmerston, of course, frightened Andrew Stevenson in 1841, and he departed from Britain in high dudgeon. Malmesbury, in 1852, intentionally 'blew up a breeze' over the fisheries question in order to secure reciprocity for the Canadians, and the tactic worked very well indeed.

Anglo-American negotiations were often informal, and even disorderly, each side trying to make the other appear unreasonable, raising legalistic objections, and employing veiled threats. As the negotiators worked within the same ethical tradition, they were confident that their opponents would keep their promises provided those promises were made in unambiguous language, but phrasing such agreements was often difficult. It was made the more so on those occasions when no meeting of minds was possible, and the agreement concluded was intentionally ambiguous. The signing of ambiguous agreements, however, was one of the finest evidences of a mutual desire to keep the peace.

The disorderly diplomacy of this period was not without solid accomplishments. On the British side, credit for the lasting Maine Boundary agreement should go to Lord Ashburton, and secondarily to Lord Aberdeen. The Oregon Boundary was the accomplishment of the latter, who drew up the final items himself. These were the most important products of the era.

The Claims Convention of 1853 should be credited to Lord Malmesbury, who also played a leading role in the settlement of the fisheries and reciprocity questions, which were not so permanent, but were highly important at the time. The last two, however, were monuments to the skill of Lord Elgin, whose excellent grasp of American psychology permitted him to achieve a settlement at a time when Anglo-American relations were in retrograde motion.

The chief ambiguous agreements of the period were not only interesting, but important. The Cruising Convention of 1842 was a political instrument, which enabled the British statesmen to claim America had pledged herself to act against the slave trade, and the Americans to aver that Britain had given up her so-called right of visit. The Clayton–Bulwer Treaty of 1850 was merely a paper dam against the further deterioration of Anglo-American relations. Britain did not even try to interpret its meaning until 1853, and the United States did not counter with its own view of it until the following year. One would have hardly expected such a strangely-born treaty to have possessed such longevity.

The same willingness to say something strikingly ambiguous but nevertheless productive of mutual harmony was evident in Ashburton's handling of the *Caroline* and *Creole* issues. In some respects the treaties noted above and the notes covering these incidents show Anglo-American diplomacy at its best. Britain tried to use this same tactic in 1853 in the Vienna Note, which was designed to paper over the differences between Turkey and Russia, but those nations lacked the maturity, goodwill, wisdom, or whatever one might term it, to seize upon this device to cool the war fever.

On two occasions especially, Anglo-American diplomacy broke down completely. Palmerston unwisely adopted a too-advanced position in the McLeod crisis, and there was little that Aberdeen could do but wait hopefully for an American court to solve the diplomatic problem he had created. Diplomacy also failed to give satisfaction to Britain in the menacing Hollins Affair of 1854. In this situation Britain simply let the problem continue until it died a natural death.

British diplomacy in dealing with the United States often had a leisurely extempore air about it that sometimes offended Americans, who regarded the problems at issue as of the highest importance, and of deep concern. Part of this British attitude stemmed from the fact that she had so many international and imperial problems that the issues between the United States and herself tended to be overlooked among them. Part also of it might be explained by the conviction of British statesmen that the United States really would not resort to war to achieve her ends. As time went by, however, there was an increasing fear in Downing Street that the Americans in conducting their rough-and-ready diplomacy might create a situation from which neither country could withdraw gracefully, and an unsought war would result.

Fortunately, this hypothetical situation never arrived, and the Anglo-American diplomacy of this period was able to cope with the problems that arose. So all of its practitioners on both sides of the Atlantic can be deemed to have been more or less successful. Still, Lord Aberdeen, who was contemptuous of diplomatic molehills and courageous in its mountains, tends to stand out from the crowd as the most unusual of the diplomats. He perhaps deserved to live in a better, or at least more rational, world. How much more fruitful the period would have been, and how much more progress toward Anglo-American friendship could have been made if the Americans had taken their cue from him and followed a less abrasive course after 1842, are interesting topics for speculation among all those who value those rare moments in history when his type of rational and conciliatory diplomacy holds sway.

Notes

The following abbreviations are used to identify the various manuscript sources cited in the notes:

AUCK	Auckland Papers	*EP*	Ellenborough Papers*
AP	Aberdeen Papers	*F.O.*	Foreign Office Papers*
BP	Brougham Papers[1]	*GP*	Gladstone Papers
BRP	Bright Papers	*GRAN*	Granville Papers*
CLAR	Clarendon Papers[2]	*NEWP*	Newcastle Papers[5]
COB	Cobden Papers	*PAMP*	Palmerston Papers
COP	Colonial Office	*PP*	Peel Papers
	Papers*	*RIPP*	Ripon Papers
CP	Colchester Papers*	*RUSP*	Russell Papers*
DERP	Derby Papers[3]	*WP*	Wellington Papers*
DISP	Disraeli Papers[4]		

The unmarked papers are located at the British Museum; those marked with an asterisk, at the Public Record Office. The locations of the others are as follows: 1. University College London; 2. the Bodleian Library, Oxford; 3. presently in the custody of Professor Robert Blake of Queen's College, Oxford; 4. Hughenden Manor, Bucks.; 5. Nottingham University; 6. Apsley House, London.

1 THE DIPLOMACY OF MENACE

1. There was (and even continues to be) a reluctance on the part of Americans to acknowledge the splendid contributions of Lord Castlereagh to Anglo-American rapprochement, and to exaggerate those of George Canning, long a favourite of historians. In his excellent work on early American diplomacy Bradford Perkins adopts a more favourable attitude toward Castlereagh, and concludes that: 'Far more than anyone

A.P.B.D.—8

at Washington he [Castlereagh] can claim credit for the postwar amelioration of spirit.' See: Bradford Perkins, *Castlereagh and Adams; England and the United States, 1812–1823* (Berkeley: University of California Press, 1964) pp. 196–200. Perkins also observes that Lord Grenville was probably the earliest British statesman to pursue the soft-line. The present writer recently presented the claims of the Robinson family to recognition as friends of the Anglo-American connection. Wilbur Devereux Jones, *Prosperity Robinson* (London: Macmillan, 1967) pp. 73–87.

2. A. C. Benson and Viscount Esher (eds.), *The Letters of Queen Victoria* (New York: Longmans, Green and Co., 1907) I, 325 Palmerston to Victoria, 1 Feb. 1841.

3. Ashley's summary of Palmerston's thinking was undoubtedly accurate. '. . . to give up to-day to the Americans, who are an encroaching people, a point deemed of small importance, is certain to lead to our being asked to give up another point of importance tomorrow, and being thus eventually brought to give up something of great importance, or to fight because we decline to give it. . . . If it is still said "Don't let us fight," war with the Americans is indeed avoided; but other nations, who have watched our conduct with them, will imitate their conduct to us'. Evelyn Ashley, *The Life and Correspondence of Viscount Palmerston* (London: Richard Bentley and Son, 1879) I, 424.

4. Kenneth Bourne, *Britain and the Balance of Power in North America, 1815–1908*, (Berkeley: University of California Press, 1967) p. 83, and Jasper Ridley, *Lord Palmerston* (New York: E. P. Dutton & Co. Inc., 1971) pp. 261–73.

5. Hon. Mrs. Hardcastle, *Life of John, Lord Campbell* (Jersey City: Frederick D. Linn & Co., 1881) II, 180.

6. See: Bourne, *Britain and the Balance of Power*, pp. 84–6.

7. See: Alastair Watt, 'The Case of Alexander McLeod,' *Canadian Historical Review*, XII (June 1931).

8. But Ridley's view that the Tories, who claimed Castlereagh, Robinson, and Aberdeen in their ranks, were more hostile toward the United States than the Whigs seems quite unwarranted. See: Ridley, *Palmerston*, p. 272.

9. This description is rather amusing in view of Stevenson's parting blast, and his anti-British activities upon his return to the United States.

10. Ashley, Palmerston, I, 408, Palmerston to Fox, 9 Feb. 1841.

11. Ibid., p. 407, Palmerston to Temple, 9 Feb. 1841.

12. Ridley presents an interesting discussion of Palmerston's consistency on this issue. See: Ridley, *Palmerston*, p. 365.

13. Henry Reeve, *The Greville Memoirs* (London: Longmans, Green, & Co., 1875) I, 334–5, *Diary*, 12 Mar. 1841.

14. *Hansard*, 3rd ser., LVI, 1386–7.

15. B. & E., *Victoria*, I, 327, Russell to Victoria, 6 Mar. 1841.

16. *Hansard*, 3rd ser., LVII, 1498.

17. Watt, 'Alexander McLeod,' 145–167.

18. *Hansard*, 1st ser., XXIV, 633–44.

19. Alexander Baring (Lord Ashburton) in 1813 bluntly declared that the sole cause of the War of 1812 was the British Orders in Council, whose earlier withdrawal would have prevented the conflict. Ibid, XXIV, 619. As his banking house maintained American credit abroad during the war, his views on this subject were usually discounted when he addressed the Commons.

20. *RIPP,* BM 40877, Goulburn to Ripon, 30 Oct. 1847.

21. Reeve, *Greville,* I, 334. *Diary,* 12 Mar. 1841.

22. B. & E., *Victoria,* I, 409, Melbourne to Victoria, 12 Sep. 1841.

23. Another reason why many British statesmen distrusted Americans stemmed from the espousal of the American cause by Radicals and Whig-Radicals. Sir James Macintosh, for example, once told Parliament that America was 'spreading her pacific conquests, and blessing with her rule a wider extent of territory than absolute monarchy ever cursed'. *Hansard,* 2nd ser., VII, 641.

24. *AUCK,* BM 34459, Lansdowne to Auckland, 25 Sep. 1817.

25. Reeve, *Greville,* I, 257. *Diary,* 21 Dec. 1829.

26 See: Bourne, *Britain and the Balance of Power,* p. 120. Bourne interprets certain of Lord Ashburton's remarks as indicating a certain hostility toward the United States. The present writer regards Lord Ashburton as a consistent friend of the United States even after he left his bank in 1830.

27. See: Edward Stanley, *Journal of a Tour in America, 1824–1825* (London: Privately printed, 1930). This is particularly interesting because Stanley as Prime Minister took a deep interest in American policy.

28. Ralph W. Hidy, *The House of Baring in American Trade and Finance* (Cambridge: Harvard University Press, 1949) p. 309. This is a splendid study of the financial operations of the Barings.

29. *AP,* BM 43063, Ashburton to Croker, [?] Jan. 1843.

30. Charles S. Parker, *Sir Robert Peel* (London: John Murray, 1899) II, 492–3, Graham to Peel, 1 Aug. 1841.

31. E. Jones Parry, *The Correspondence of Lord Aberdeen and Princess Lieven 1832–1854* (London: Royal Historical Society, 1938) pp. 189–90, Aberdeen to Lieven, 21 Dec. 1841.

32. Bourne, *Britain and the Balance of Power,* p. 93.

33. It was not reduced in strength until early 1843. *COP,* 43/102, Stephen to Addington, 10 Feb. 1843; Stephen to Sir John Barrow, 18 Feb. 1843.

34. B. & E., *Victoria,* I, 446, Peel to Victoria, 28 Oct. 1841.

35. Watt, 'Alexander McLeod,' pp. 145–67. Bourne, *Britain and the Balance of Power,* p. 94.

36. See: Bourne, *Britain and the Balance of Power,* pp. 93–4, and especially footnotes 2, p. 94. Bourne shows that Fox was under the impression that the naval commanders would begin hostilities as soon as he informed them that he was leaving Washington, and that the British administrator of United Canada and the American Government were under a similar impression.

37. B. & E., *Victoria,* I, 446, Peel to Victoria, 28 Oct. 1841.

38. The British Government made some formal representations to compensate McLeod for his suffering, but they did not press the matter. They turned him down flat when he applied to Britain for compensation, and resisted a request from the Canadian Assembly on the same subject later. COP, 43/100, Stephen to Addington, 1 June 1842; *COP*, 43/105, Stephen to Addington, 9 June 1845.

39. Paul Revere Frothingham, *Edward Everett* (Boston: Houghton Mifflin Co., 1925) p. 188.

2 THE DIPLOMACY OF RATIONALITY

1. *Hansard*, 3rd ser., LXVII, 1164–1218.

2. Ibid., p. 1165.

3. Palmerston would have rejected any Mitchell map as real evidence. He pointed out that if one drew a line on a Mitchell map from the sources of the Connecticut to the upper end of the Bay of Chaleurs, it would run entirely north of the St. John, but, if a similar line were run on a correct map, it would run south of that river. *Hansard*, 3rd ser., LXVII, 1179.

4. Ashley was undoubtedly correctly describing Palmerston's tactics when he wrote: 'Never give up a pin's head that you ought to keep and think you can keep; and even if you think that in the last extremity you will not be able to keep it, make as many difficulties as you can about resigning it, and manifest a doubt as to whether you should not sooner go to war than resign it.' Ashley, *Palmerston*, I, 424.

5. Peel believed that Palmerston's method would have delayed the settlement for five years. *Hansard*, 3rd ser., LXVII, 1247–9. Palmerston, however, operated on the assumption that the United States as a whole was not interested in the Maine Boundary question. 'The great mass of the Union do not care two straws about it . . .,' he wrote. Bourne, *Britain and the Balance of Power*, p. 85, Palmerston to Lansdowne, 25 Apr. 1840.

6. *Hansard*, 3rd ser., LXIV, 1242.

7. *PP*, BM 40497, Ripon's Minute on World Trade, Nov. [?] 1841.

8. Ibid., Peel's Memorandum, 'England and America,' Dec. [?] 1841.

9. Peel and Ripon seem to have had on hand about the same statistics that one finds in Arthur D. Gayer, et al, *The Growth and Fluctuation of the British Economy, 1790–1850.* (Oxford: Clarendon Press, 1953). It appears that during the 1821–41 period Britain's overseas customers (from the best to poorest) were in this order: Northern Europe, Southern Europe, the United States, British North America and the British West Indies, the Asian nations, and South and Central America. During this period the United States purchased only 72% and 93% as much as Northern and Southern Europe, but British North American and British West Indian, Asian and Central and South American purchases were only 76%, 75%, and 69% of the purchases made by the United States. British exports, then, were widely distributed, and she was not overly dependent upon any single area; on the other hand, American purchases would obviously be sorely missed.

10. By the second quarter of the 19th Century, British exports to the United States were more important to her than to America. See: H. C. Allen, *The Anglo-American Relationship Since 1783* (London: Adam and Charles Black, 1959) pp. 68–9. The same, however, cannot be said of the British money market.

11. *Hansard*, 3rd series, LXII, 578–9.

12. Peel, Ripon, and Goulburn had been members of the British equivalent of the 'War Hawks' during the 1808–14 period. Jones, *Robinson*, pp. 29–31.

13. Frothingham, *Everett*, p. 237, Webster to Everett, 28 Dec. 1841.

14. *AP*, BM 43189, Aberdeen to Clarendon, 5 Nov. 1854.

15. Parker, *Peel*, II, 498.

16. *AP*, BM 43123, Ashburton to Aberdeen, 5 Sep. 1841.

17. Ibid., Aberdeen to Fox, 3 Jan. 1842. 'If Mr. Webster should retain office, I think we are likely to see an end to our differences'.

18. Ibid., Ashburton to Aberdeen, 22 Dec. 1841. '. . . it may be feared', wrote Ashburton, 'that the various conflicting interests . . . may break up the present administration there upon whose dispositions you mainly rely'.

19. *AP*, BM 43189, Aberdeen to Clarendon, 5 Nov. 1854.

20. *AP*, BM 43123, Ashburton to Aberdeen, 28 Dec. 1841.

21. Ashley noted that the selection of Ashburton to negotiate indicated that Britain was ready to 'purchase agreement by concession'. Ashley, *Palmerston*, p. 423.

22. Aberdeen wrote in 1844: 'We are terribly hampered by this Slave Trade the questions about which meet us in every quarter & estrange us from our best friends. France, the U. States, Spain, Portugal, Brazil all furnish matter for angry discussion every day. Never have a people made such a sacrifice as we have done to attain our object, & the payment of money is the least part of it'. *AP*, BM 43064, Aberdeen to Peel, 8 Oct. 1844.

23. Maps showing this Award, as well as the other proposed lines, are available in most texts on American diplomacy. The Netherlands Award was quite favourable to British claims.

24. See: *AP*, BM 43123, Vaughan to Palmerston, 4 Jul. 1833; Palmerston to Bankhead, 30 Oct. 1835.

25. Ibid., Wellington's Memorandum, 8 Feb. 1842.

26. See: Frank Thistlethwaite, *The Anglo-American Connection in the Early Nineteenth Century* (Philadelphia: University of Pennsylvania Press, 1959) p. 23.

27. As might be expected when the British negotiator, upon his arrival, was hailed by a prominent American as a member of his family. *AP*, BM 43123, Albert Gallatin to Ashburton, 21 Apr. 1842.

28. Aberdeen to Everett, 20 Dec. 1841. *Executive Documents*, 27th Cong., 3rd ser., vol. 422, pp. 7–10.

29. *AP*, BM 43123, Ashburton to Aberdeen, 29 June 1842.

30. Ibid., Aberdeen to Ashburton, 3 June 1842.

31. Ibid., Ashburton to Aberdeen, 13 July 1842, and enclosure. The expunged paragraph read: '. . . and should the traffic in slaves continue notwithstanding the efforts made for its suppression, the contracting parties will hereafter confer together as to the most effectual means of attaining an object so earnestly desired'.

32. *AP*, BM 43123, Ashburton to Aberdeen, 28 Jul. 1842.

33. Ibid., 9 Aug. 1842.

34. Ibid., 3 June 1842.

35. Ibid., Webster to Ashburton, 1 Aug. 1842; Ashburton to Webster, 6 Aug. 1842. Hunter Miller, ed., *Treaties and Other International Acts of the United States of America* (Washington: 1931–1948) IV, 461–8.

36. *AP*, BM 43123, Aberdeen to Ashburton, 18 Jul. 1842.

37. Aberdeen later paraphrased the 'tenor' of Ashburton's instructions as follows: 'It would prove to him that although the Govt. lamented the necessity, they fully justified the act itself. . . .' AP, BM 43063, Aberdeen to Peel, 18 Jan. 1844.

38. *AP*, BM 43123, Ashburton to Aberdeen, 28 Jul. 1842; 13 Aug. 1842.

39. Samuel Flagg Bemis calls it 'not exactly an apology'; Julius W. Pratt, a 'quasi-apology'. See: Samuel F. Bemis, *A Short History of American Foreign Policy and Diplomacy* (New York: Henry Holt and Co., 1959) p. 146, and Julius W. Pratt, *A History of United States Foreign Policy* (Englewood Cliffs: Prentice-Hall, 1965) p. 103. Aberdeen called it 'apologetick language', but Peel referred to it as 'his apology'. *AP*, BM 43063, Aberdeen to Peel, 18 Jan. 1844; Peel to Aberdeen, 27 Jan. 1844.

40. *AP*, BM 43123, Aberdeen to Ashburton, 3 June 1842.

41. Ibid., Wheaton to Webster, 15 Feb. 1842, Cass to Webster, 12 Mar. 1842, and Hamilton to Tyler, 29 Apr. 1842.

42. Ibid., Wellington's Memorandum, 8 Feb. 1842. Ibid., BM 43072, Stanley's Notes on Aberdeen's Papers regarding the Maine Boundary, undated.

43. Ibid., Aberdeen to Sir James Kempt, Sir Howard Douglas, Lord Seaton, and Sir George Murray, 24 Feb. 1842, and their replies dated 1, 7, 9, and 6 Mar. 1842.

44. See: Thomas Le Duc, 'The Maine Frontier and the Northeastern Boundary Controversy'. *American Historical Review*, LIII (Oct. 1947) p. 32. This writer would seem to have been correct in assuming Britain's interest in this controversy was Canadian defence, but she sought the highlands near Quebec rather than any particular road.

45. *AP*, BM 43123, Ashburton to Aberdeen, 26 Apr. 1842.

46. Ibid., Ashburton to Aberdeen, 12 May 1842.

47. 'I must first observe', Aberdeen wrote, 'that I do not quite understand why you feel yourself so much crippled by the modification of your original Instructions. By these the Award of the King of the Netherlands was made our Ultimatum, and to this . . . I am still disposed to adhere'. Ibid., Aberdeen to Ashburton, 16 May 1842.

48. Ibid., Webster to Everett, 25 Apr. 1842. Everett to Aberdeen, 14 May 1842. Everett later sent Aberdeen two other letters from Webster, which stressed the importance of ceding the 'Narrow Strip'. Webster

thus could contact Aberdeen and influence him throughout the negotiation.

49. *AP*, BM 43123, Aberdeen to Ashburton, 2 Jul. 1842.

50. Ibid., Aberdeen to Ashburton, 18 June 1842.

51. This seems to be a fair interpretation of Ashburton's statement: 'The money I wrote about went to compensate Sparks & to send him, on my first arrival, to the Governors of Maine & Massachusetts. My informant thinks that without this stimulant Maine would never have yielded. . . .' Ibid., Ashburton to Aberdeen, 9 Aug. 1842.

52. See: Lawrence Martin and Samuel Flagg Bemis, 'Franklin's Red-Line Map was a Mitchell'. *New England Quarterly*, x (1937) pp. 105–11.

53. *AP*, BM 43123, Ashburton to Aberdeen, 14 June 1842.

54. Ibid., Aberdeen to Ashburton, 2 Jul. 1842.

55. See: Wilbur Devereux Jones, 'The Origins and passage of Lord Aberdeen's Act.' *Hispanic American Historical Review*, XLII (Nov. 1962) p. 518.

56. *AP*, BM 43123, Ashburton to Aberdeen, 14 June 1842.

57. Ibid., Ashburton to Aberdeen, 29 June 1842.

58. Ibid., Gratton to Aberdeen, 31 Dec. 1842.

59. Ibid., Ashburton to Aberdeen, 13 Jul. 1842.

60. Ibid., T. C. Gratton to Aberdeen, 30 Jul. 1842.

61. 'Webster', Ashburton wrote, 'yields & promises everything, but when it comes to execution is so weak & timid and irresolute that he is frightened by everybody, and at last does nothing.' Ibid., Ashburton to Aberdeen, 13 Jul. 1842.

62. Ibid., Ashburton to Aberdeen, 9 Aug. 1842. See also: Richard N. Current, 'Webster's Propaganda and the Ashburton Treaty'. *The Mississippi Valley Historical Review*, XXXIV (Sep. 1947) p. 200. Perhaps Webster's tempering of American public opinion was noted and appreciated by Ashburton.

63. *AP*, BM 43123, Aberdeen to Ashburton, 26 Sep. 1842.

3 THE CRISIS OF CONFIDENCE

1. See: Bemis, *American Foreign Policy*, p. 155, who calls it a 'British diplomatic victory'. This interpretation is based on 'recent investigations into historical cartography' (p. 154), which seemingly validate American territorial claims in Maine. At the time, however, Ashburton believed that the cartographical evidence favoured those of Britain.

2. See: Frederick Merk, 'British Party Politics and the Oregon Treaty'. *The American Historical Review*, XXXVII (July 1932) and Frederick Merk, *The Oregon Question* (Cambridge: Belknap Press, 1967 p. 281. The charge that Lord Aberdeen feared to proceed with the Oregon negotiations because of Palmerston's hostility seems to be wholly unfounded.

3. *AP*, BM 43063, Ashburton to Croker, Jan. [?] 1844.

4. 'I am not certain that, failing to obtain the whole line of the St.

John', Aberdeen wrote, 'it might not have been preferable, for the sake of the impression to be produced, to have adhered without alteration to the Award of the King of the Netherlands in all its parts.' *AP*, BM 43123, Aberdeen to Ashburton, 26 Sep. 1842.

5. Ibid., Ashburton to Aberdeen, 29 Sep, 24, 27 Oct. 1842, and Aberdeen to Ashburton, 26 Oct. 1842.

6. 'I did all I could to persuade Lord Ashburton that unusual and extravagant reward for the Treaty would be injurious to him, to us, and to the country', Peel wrote, 'to the country as showing misplaced exultation on account of our differences, or rather, some of our differences with the United States having been terminated.' Louis J. Jennings, ed., *The Correspondence and Diaries of the Late Right Honourable John Wilson Croker* (New York: Charles Scribner's Sons, 1884) II, 193, Peel to Croker, 23 Feb. 1843. It should be added that Peel was one of the more miserly Prime Ministers in distributing peerages.

7. *AP*, BM 43123, Aberdeen to Ashburton, 26 Oct. 1842.

8. Ibid., Aberdeen to Ashburton, 26 Sep. 1842.

9. Ibid., Ashburton to Aberdeen, 6 Jan. 1843.

10. *Croker*, II, 191, Aberdeen to Croker, 25 Feb. 1843.

11. *The Times* (London) 16 Mar. 1843.

12. *Croker*, II, 191, Aberdeen to Croker, 25 Feb. 1843.

13. *The Times* (London) 26 Jan. 1843.

14. Ibid., 28 Mar. 1843.

15. Ibid., 8 Mar. 1843.

16 Allen, *Anglo-American Relationship*, p. 76.

17. See: Ashley, *Palmerston*, I, 423. Palmerston to Minto, date not shown.

18. See: Merk, *Oregon Question*, p. 258.

19. *Hansard*, 3rd ser., LXVII, 1217.

20. Ibid., pp. 1246–9. Peel told the House that the Faden Map, received from the French Foreign Office, a map found in Bewes Journal of 1783, and the so-called Oswald Map all substantiated the American territorial claims in Maine. Regarding the famous Red-Line Map, Peel declared that Webster was under no obligation whatsoever to show it to Ashburton, and besides there was no way of proving that it was the map referred to by Franklin in his letter. While Peel agreed that maps might be evidence of the intentions of the signers of the treaty, 'the treaty must be executed according to the words contained in it'. Offers of maps continued to be made to the British Government in 1843. See: *COP*, 43/102, Hope to Palser, 6 Mar. 1843: Hope to Addington, 24 Mar. 1843.

21. Frederick Merk, 'The Oregon Question in the Webster–Ashburton Negotiations.' *Mississippi Valley Historical Review*, XLIII (Dec. 1956) reprinted in Merk, *Oregon*, pp. 189–215.

22. *AP*, BM 43123, Ashburton to Aberdeen, 6, Jan. 1843.

23. Ibid., Ashburton to Aberdeen, 1 and 23 Jan. 1843.

24. 'Webster does not look as if he would outlive our treaty', Ashburton wrote, 'and I would not answer for myself if the work were to last

long, but I am much more comfortable since Preble is gone back to Maine'. Ibid., Ashburton to Aberdeen, 28 July 1842.

25. Everett made such a good impression that Lord Stanley, later Prime Minister, projected abortive plans with him to import free American Negroes into the British West Indies as labour, and to establish a joint British-American protectorate of Liberia. See: *AP*, BM 43072, Stanley to Everett, 8 Nov. 1842; Stanley to Aberdeen, 4 Apr. 1844. Before Everett left England, Aberdeen and Stanley granted his request to permit American fishermen into the Bay of Fundy, as an 'amicable concession'. Frothingham, *Everett*, p. 251.

26. The British despatches can be found in many places. Those quoted herein are taken from: *Correspondence Relating to the Oregon Territory Subsequent to the Treaty of Washington of August, 1842* (London: T. R. Harrison). (Hereafter cited as *Oregon Correspondence*.) Aberdeen to Fox, 18 Oct. 1842; Fox to Webster, 15 Nov. 1842; Webster to Fox, 25 Nov. 1842.

27. *AP*, BM 43123, Ashburton to Aberdeen, 1 Jan. 1843.

28. Ibid., Ashburton to Aberdeen, 6 Jan. 1843.

29. *RIPP*, BM 40864, Peel to Ripon, 24 Apr. 1843.

30. *Oregon Correspondence*, Aberdeen to Fox, 18 Aug. 1843; Fox to Aberdeen, 12 Sep. 1843.

31. See: Sir Arthur Gordon, *The Earl of Aberdeen* (New York: Harper & Bros., 1893) pp. 154–6. It is unfortunate that Gordon, who had family tradition as well as Aberdeen's private papers to aid him, did not write a longer work.

32. *AP*, BM 43123, Ashburton to Aberdeen, 6 Jan. 1843.

33. See: Justin H. Smith, *The Annexation of Texas* (Barnes & Noble, Inc., 1941) pp. 382–406. The present writer's interpretation is found in more detail in: Wilbur Devereux Jones, *Lord Aberdeen and the Americas* (Athens: University of Georgia Press, 1958) pp. 31–7.

34. *PP*, BM 40454, Peel to Aberdeen, 26 May 1844.

35. *AP*, BM 43123, Aberdeen to Pakenham, 7 Oct. 1843.

36. Ibid. Everett to Aberdeen, 1 and 30 Nov. 1843.

37. 'As you have always said . . . that you thought the question could be settled without much difficulty', Everett wrote, 'I have naturally inferred, though you have never said so, that you would finally agree to that basis; viz., the 49th degree for the mainland & you to have the Island'. *AP*, BM 43123, Everett to Aberdeen, 26 Jan. 1846. Unfortunately, Everett did not say when he reached that conclusion, and Aberdeen and he conferred informally so often that it is impossible to date it. See: Frothingham, *Everett*, pp. 196 and 205, Everett to Brooks, 17 May and 19 Dec. 1842.

38. *AP*, BM 43123, Aberdeen to Pakenham, 4 Mar. 1844.

39. Richard W. Van Alstyne, *American Diplomacy in Action* (London: London University Press, 1944) p. 497.

40. Bourne, *Britain and the Balance of Power*, pp. 125–8.

41. *PP*. BM 40454, Peel to Aberdeen, 21 Aug. 1844.

42. Gordon, *Aberdeen*, pp. 156–7.

43. Jones, *Lord Aberdeen*, pp. 40–55.

44. *AP*, BM 43064, Aberdeen to Peel, 25 Sep. 1844.

45. Ibid., Aberdeen to Peel, 21 Oct. 1844. Aberdeen wrote that the importance of the Oregon issue was 'insignificant', but that public clamour made it difficult for either country 'to act with moderation, or even common sense'.

46. Ibid., Peel to Aberdeen, 23 Feb. 1845.

47. *The Times* (London), 28 Mar. 1845.

46. *PP*, BM 40454, Aberdeen to Peel, 31 Dec. 1844. The emergence of steamers at this time tended to make the Channel a less dependable barrier than it had been in the past.

49. *AP*, BM 43064, Aberdeen to Peel, 29 Mar. 1845.

50. It had come up twice in 1843, on 24 Feb. and 10 Aug. in response to Tyler's charge that Britain was delaying the settlement, and on 5 Feb. 1844 when reports that Americans were fortifying the Oregon frontier were received. Both the questions and answers were brief and uninformative. There had been no Oregon debate, or even extended discussion prior to 4 Apr. 1845.

51. *Hansard*, 3rd ser., LXXIX, 178–93. Palmerston spoke only briefly during the debate, and then merely to answer an attack made upon him by Ashburton in the Lords.

52. Ibid., pp. 193–9.

53. Ibid., pp. 115–20.

54. Ibid., pp. 120–3.

55. *AP*, BM 43123, Aberdeen to Pakenham, 2 Apr. 1845.

56. Ibid., Aberdeen to Pakenham, 18 Apr. 1845.

57. See: Bourne, *Britain and the Balance of Power*, pp. 144–6.

58. *AP*, BM 43064, Aberdeen to Peel, 18 Sep. 1845.

59. Ibid., Peel to Aberdeen, 20 Sep. 1845.

60. Ibid., Aberdeen to Peel, 23 Sep. 1845. Scholars who lay all the blame for the Mexican War at the door of the United States should consider this bit of evidence, and also another statement by Aberdeen: 'War has not yet been declared by Mexico, and they would no doubt if necessary, regulate their mode of proceeding in this respect to render our course more easy'. Ibid., Aberdeen to Peel, 25 Sep. 1845. The British believed Mexico was convinced she must declare war on the United States to protect her national honour.

61. Ibid., Peel to Aberdeen, 24 Sep. 1845.

62. Ibid., Aberdeen to Peel, 25 Sep. 1845.

63. *PP*, BM 40455, Peel to Aberdeen, 17 Oct. 1845.

64. *AP*, BM 43065, Aberdeen to Peel, 21 Oct. 1845.

65. Ibid., Aberdeen to Peel, 27 Nov. 1845.

66. *AP*, BM 43123, Aberdeen to Pakenham, 3 Oct. 1845.

67. *AP*, BM 43065, Peel to Aberdeen, 2 October 1845; Aberdeen to Peel, 3 Oct. 1845.

68. Ibid., Peel to Aberdeen, 22 Nov. 1845.

69. Ibid., Peel to Aberdeen, 2 Oct. 1845.

70. *Oregon Correspondence*, Aberdeen to Pakenham, 28 Nov. 1845.

This despatch was obviously written with a view toward possible publication, and intended to convince both domestic and world opinion of the conciliatory nature of the British position.

71. *AP*, BM 43123, Aberdeen to Pakenham, 3 Dec. 1845.

72. *AP*, BM 43064, Peel to Aberdeen, 11 Feb. 1845.

73. *The Times* (London), 5 Dec. 1845.

74. On the other hand, the *National* backed American claims; the *Courrier Francais* denied that either country had title to Oregon. Ibid., 4 Dec. 1845.

75. See: Merk, *Oregon Question*, pp. 309–36. This source presents some valuable facts regarding the effects of the repeal of the Corn Laws in America, but his theory that Aberdeen prepared Britain for a 'treaty of renunciation' detracts from the value of his research.

76. The writer has covered this crisis in several places. See Wilbur Devereux Jones, *Lord Derby and Victorian Conservatism* (Oxford: Basil Blackwell, 1956) pp. 105–15; *Prosperity Robinson*, pp. 265–8, and *History of the Peelites* (Columbus: Ohio State University Press, 1971) pp. 8–15. Suffice it to say, British domestic politics at this time were unbelievably complex.

77. *AP*, BM 43065, Aberdeen to Peel, 25 Dec. 1845. Some years later, however, he wrote: 'The Oregon question was more difficult and dangerous than the NE Boundary'. *AP*, BM 43189, Aberdeen to Clarendon, 5 Nov. 1854. When his Christmas letter was written, Aberdeen obviously did not anticipate the American negative to his November initiative.

78. *AP*, BM 43065, Aberdeen to Peel, 29 Dec. 1845.

79. *The Times* (London), 29 Dec. 1845.

80. *AP*, BM 43123, Aberdeen to Pakenham, 3 Feb. 1846.

81. Extract from McLane's despatch of 3 Feb. 1846 *in*: Ibid., McLane to Aberdeen, 17 Mar. 1846.

82. *GP*, BM 44363, Gladstone to Cathcart, 2 Mar. 1846.

83. See: Bourne, *Britain and the Balance of Power*, pp. 155–69.

84. *RUSP*, PRO 30/22–5C, Wood to Russell, 18 Sep. 1846.

85. *AP*, BM 43065, Peel to Aberdeen, 26 Dec. 1845. *WP*, Gladstone to Wellington, 24 Dec. 1845; Wellington to Gladstone, 25 Dec. 1845.

86. *RIPP*, BM 40874, Ripon to Hardinge, 24 Dec. 1845.

87. Ibid., BM 40875, Ripon to Hardinge, 7 Feb. 1845.

88. 'We are sending out many ships of War to the American coast', Lyndhurst wrote Brougham. 'I am far from convinced that we shall be able to escape war. I shall feel the inconce. as Soph's property is there'. *BP*, Lyndhurst to Brougham, Wednesday 4 Feb. 1846 (?).

89. *WP*, Sir John H. Pelly to Wellington and Gladstone, 24 Apr. 1846. *GP*, BM 44364, Colonial Office to Pelly, 28 Apr. 1946.

90. *EP*, PRO 30/12–14, Napier to Ellenborough, 9 Feb. 1846.

91. *EP*, PRO 30/9–6 (1), Sandon to Colchester, 15 Feb. 1846.

92. *CP*, PRO 30/9–3 (1), Ellenborough to Colchester, 5 Oct. 1847.

93. *EP*, PRO 30/12–21, Ellenborough to Napier, 3 Jun 1846. There is a part of a letter in the Ellenborough collection (PRO 30/12–14) which may be the one referred to in Ellenborough's letter of 3 June. The con-

queror of the Sind, perhaps the most quarrelsome and unpleasant public figure in contemporary British life, was an inveterate enemy of the American Republic. In the fragment mentioned above he boasted of a stratagem whereby his force bayonetted 300 Kentucky riflemen with a loss of about 70 of his command.

94. *AP*, BM 43123, Aberdeen to Pakenham, 18 May 1846.

95. See: J. W. Pratt, 'James K. Polk and John Bull', *Canadian Historical Review*, xxiv (1943), and Pratt, *United States Foreign Policy*, pp. 108–13. Pratt regards the despatch as a major factor in the solution of the question. Frederick Merk (*Oregon Question*, pp. 342–6) stresses that threats had been made before, and minimises the effect of this one. Bourne (*Britain and the Balance of Power*, p. 161) attaches some weight to Polk's willingness, as far back as 23 December, to submit a British proposal to the Senate, and does not believe too much emphasis should be placed on the threat. Professor J. Chal Vinson, collaborating with the present writer, backed the Pratt position in: 'British Preparedness and the Oregon Settlement', *The Pacific Historical Review*, xxii (Nov. 1953).

96. *CLAR*, c. 44, Crampton to Clarendon, 10 Sep. 1855.

97, *AP*, BM 43123, McLane to Aberdeen, 17 Mar. 1846.

98. That Aberdeen would resort to a threat of force was made the more credible because of his adoption of a Palmerstonian policy in Brazil.

99. See: Bemis, *American Diplomacy*, p. 155.

100. *The Times* (London), 15 May 1845.

101. Ibid., 1 Dec. 1845.

102. Ibid., 12 December 1845.

103. *AP*, BM 43123, McLane to Aberdeen, 31 Jul. 1846.

104. Ibid., McLane to Aberdeen, 6 June 1846; Aberdeen to McLane, 8 June 1846.

105. Ibid., Aberdeen to McLane, 27 June 1846. 'I should be very sorry to leave office without all our pending questions being settled, at least as far as possible,' he wrote.

106. Ibid., Aberdeen to Everett, 1 Jul. 1846. *Vergil*, 6, 143. The Golden Bough – 'One plucked, another fills its room. And burgeons with like precious bloom'.

4 The Diplomacy of the Mexican War Period

1. See: *RUSP*, PRO 30/22–5A, Palmerston to Russell, 2 Feb. 1846. In this letter he was wholly conciliatory, and absolutely opposed to doing anything that might embarrass the Government in its negotiations with America. His emphasis on Pacific harbours, partly resulting from Britain's acquisition of Hong Kong and anticipation of an expanding China trade, was shared by others. Lord Ellenborough at the Admiralty discussed at some length this situation in a letter to Aberdeen, in which he sought one of the Sandwich Islands – 'a Malta in the centre of the Pacific', he called it – or two islands, perhaps Pagopago in Samoa, and

another near the Mexican coast. He looked with longing at San Francisco harbour, which was not only the finest harbour in the area, but one
which was easily defended. Ellenborough was apparently unaware that
Mexico had offered California to Aberdeen not too many months before
this letter was written. *EP*, PRO 30/12–34, Ellenborough to Aberdeen,
16 May 1846.

2. Marked on Pakenham's despatch #106, 13 Aug. 1846 concerning
the Oregon compromise was a terse comment: 'It wd. have been strange
if the Americans had not been pleased with an arrangement which gives
them everything which they ever really wanted'. *PAMP*, BM 48575,
Pakenham to Palmerston, 13 Aug. 1846.

3. *RUSP*, PRO 30/22–5C, Charles Wood to Russell, 18 Sep. 1846.

4. Palmerston thought it in order to send a copy of the Spanish Marriages Papers to the American Secretary of State. Pakenham discussed
Buchanan's reaction to the crisis: 'Mr. Buchanan seems to be of opinion
that the Montpensier marriage is at variance with the Treaty of Utrecht.
He views with anything but regret the interruption of the cordial understanding between England and France'. *PAMP* BM 48575, Palmerston
to Pakenham, no. 19, 18 Nov. 1846; Pakenham to Palmerston, no. 138,
13 Dec. 1846.

5. Lord Stanley wrote that Wellington's defence projects had been 'so
vast, that they discouraged Peel from even beginning them. *EP*, PRO
30/12–21, Stanley to Ellenborough, 16 Sep. 1847.

6. *RUSP*, PRO 30/22–5, Wellington's Defence Memorandum, 8 Dec.
1846; ibid. PRO 30/12–6B, Wellington's Defence Memorandum, 8 Feb.
1847.

7. Ibid. PRO 30/22–5C, Palmerston to Russell, 6 Nov. 1846.

8. Ibid. PRO 30/22–6C, Palmerston's Defence Memorandum, 10 Apr.
1847.

9. Ibid., PRO 30/22–6H, Palmerston's Defence Memorandum, 31
Dec. 1847.

10. Ibid. PRO 30/22–5C, Auckland to Russell, 7 Oct. 1846.

11. Ibid., PRO 30/22–6B, Wellington's Defence Memorandum, 8
Feb 1847.

12. Ibid. PRO 30/22–5C, Minto to Russell, 10 Sep. 1846.

13. Ibid. PRO 30/22–6E, Auckland to Russell, 20 Aug 1847.

14. *PAMP*, BM 48575, no. 25. Palmerston to Pakenham, 29 Dec.
1846; no. 16, 31 Mar. 1847; no. 49. Pakenham to Palmerston, 28 Apr.
1847.

15. Ibid., unnumbered, H. U. A. to Pakenham, 3 Mar. 1847; unnumbered, Pakenham to Palmerston, 29 Mar. 1847.

16. *RUSP*, PRO 30/22–5C, Auckland to Russell, 7 Oct. 1846.

17. Ibid., PRO 30/22–6B, Wellington's Defence Memorandum, 8 Feb.
1847.

18. Ibid., PRO 30/22–6H, Auckland to Captain Houston Stewart,
14 Nov. 1847.

19. Ibid., PRO 30/22–7A, Palmerston to Russell, 18 Jan. 1847.

20. There were 69 traditional Peelites after the election of 1847.

Although Russell was not absolutely dependent upon their support, he sought and received it on most divisions.

21. *RUSP*, PRO 30/22–7A, Palmerston to Russell, 30 Jan. 1848.

22. See: R. W. Van Alstyne, 'The Central American Policy of Lord Palmerston, 1846–1848.' *Hispanic-American Historical Review,* XVI (1936). This authority asserts that Palmerston was interested in America as a granary, and as a naval power which could embarrass Britain in wartime, and that he had no intention of antagonising this country during this period. All of these statements, up to a point, would appear to be accurate.

23. *RUSP*, PRO 30/22–6H, Palmerston to Russell, 20 Dec. 1847.

24. Lord Aberdeen had tendered his good offices before quitting his post, and Palmerston felt that he was bound to take notice of the project. The greatest care, however, was taken to avoid embarrassing the United States. *RUSP*, PRO 30/22–5B, Palmerston to Russell, 9 Aug. 1846. *PAMP*, BM 48575, Palmerston to Pakenham, no. 10. 18 Aug. 1846.

25. *PAMP*, BM 48575, Palmerston to Pakenham, no. 16. 31 Oct. 1846.

26. Ibid., Palmerston to Pakenham, no. 20. 18 Nov. 1846; ibid., Pakenham to Palmerston, n. 139. 13 Dec 1846.

27. Even in cases when the property owner had some claims to British citizenship. Ibid., Palmerston to Crampton, no. 12, 4 Oct. 1847.

28. This included quartering American soldiers, and taking over houses. Ibid., Palmerston to Crampton, no. 8, 25 February 1848; ibid., Crampton to Palmerston, no. 16, 9 Feb. 1848.

29. Transmitted in this fashion were a pecuniary offer by the United States to Mexico, and the recall of the American agent, Nicholas P. Trist. Ibid., Pakenham to Palmerston, no. 46, 29 Mar. 1847; ibid., Crampton to Palmerston, no. 49, 16 Nov. 1847.

30. Ibid., Palmerston to Crampton, no. 16, 18 Nov. 1847.

31. Ibid., Palmerston to Pakenham, no. 30, 19 April 1847.

32. Ibid., Palmerston to Pakenham, no. 2, 20 Jan. 1847. His protest arrived just before the excitement in America over the Wilmot Proviso, and Buchanan told Pakenham that any attempt by the Federal Government to seriously interfere in the South would cause the 'dissolution of the Union'. Pakenham did not believe this, but Palmerston evidently did, for he instructed Pakenham to drop the matter. Ibid., Pakenham to Palmerston, no. 38, 29 Mar. 1847; Palmerston to Pakenham, no. 27, 19 Apr. 1847.

33. Ibid., note on Pakenham to Palmerston, no. 125, 29 Oct. 1846.

34. Gayer, *Growth and Fluctuation*, p. 314 and p. 341; Allen, *Anglo-American Relationship*, p. 60 and p. 76.

35. Alfred LeRoy Burt, *The British Empire and Commonwealth* (Boston: D. C. Heath & Co., 1956) p. 266.

36. 'I think you undervalue the strength of the party which not choosing openly to support the separatn. of the Colonies is yet prepared to push reductn. of expenditure to an extent which wd. involve it', Lord Grey wrote with reference especially to the Peelites. *RUSP*, PRO 30/22–8A, Grey to Russell, 23 Aug. 1849.

37. *PAMP*, BM 48575, Pakenham to Aberdeen, no. 92, 13 Jul. 1846.

38. Ibid., Pakenham to Palmerston, no. 108, 13 Aug. 1846.

39. Pakenham described him as 'not popular' with any American party, but able to conduct affairs in an agreeable manner. *PAMP*, BM 48575, Pakenham to Palmerston, no. 114, 13 Sep. 1846.

40. *RUSP*, PRO 30/22–6E, Bancroft to Russell, 23 Aug. 1847.

41. Ibid., Labouchere to Russell, 13 Sep. 1847.

42. Wood to Russell, 23 Aug. 1847.

43. *PAMP*, BM 48575, Bancroft to Palmerston, 3 Nov. 1847.

44. Ibid., Palmerston to Bancroft, 17 Nov. 1847.

45. *RUSP*, PRO 30/22–7A, Labouchere to Russell, 14 Jan. 1848.

46. Ibid., PRO 30/22–7E, Palmerston to Russell, 30 Jan. 1848.

47. Labouchere for a time hoped to secure a reciprocal opening of the coasting trade between the United States, and Canada and the West Indies, but he feared that the United States would demand the opening of the British coasting trade itself. Ibid., PRO 30/22–7C. Labouchere to Russell, 17 Sep. 1848. Why Britain did not open the coasting trade – which Labouchere considered 'valueless' to the United States – is not clear. She was to do so in 1854.

48. *RUSP*, PRO 30/22–8A, Labouchere to Russell, 29 Sep. 1849.

49. *F.O.* 5–501, Crampton to Palmerston, n. 90, 21 Oct. 1849.

50. *RUSP*, PRO 30/22–7E, Bancroft to Russell, 29 Jan. 1849.

51. *PAMP*, BM 48575, Palmerston to Crampton, no. 21, 10 Dec. 1847.

52. For example: 'Whenever the government, impelled by popular interest, took any steps towards carrying out the expansionist dreams, it encountered the direct opposition of Great Britain in each field; and diplomatic dealings which resulted were not confined to Spain or the petty Central American republics, but bore the character of a duel with a determined and persistent adversary and rival.' Theodore C. Smith, 'Parties and Slavery, 1850–1859'. *The American Nation: A History*, vol. 18 (1906) p. 81.

53. '. . . the British government became fearful that the Americans meant to seize the isthmus, and, by monopolising the transisthmian routes, to strike a blow at British commerce. As a result . . . British interest in Central America now greatly increased.' Mary W. Williams, *Anglo-American Isthmian Diplomacy* (Washington: American Historical Assn., 1916) p. 322.

54. Kenneth Bourne, 'The Clayton–Bulwer Treaty and the Decline of British Opposition to the Territorial Expansion of the United States, 1857–1860.' *Journal of Modern History*, XXXIII (Sep. 1961).

55. R. W. Van Alstyne, 'The Central American Policy of Lord Palmerston, 1846–1848', *Hispanic American Historical Review*, XVI (1936); and R. W. Van Alstyne, 'British Diplomacy and the Clayton–Bulwer Treaty, 1850–1860'. *Journal of Modern History*, XI (June 1939).

56 Joseph B. Lockey, 'A Neglected Aspect of Isthmian Diplomacy'. *American Historical Review*, XLI (Jan. 1936) p. 299.

57. Robert A. Naylor, 'The British Role in Central America Prior to

the Clayton–Bulwer Treaty of 1850'. *Hispanic American Historical Review*, XL, no. 3 (Aug. 1960).

58. Ibid.

59. Mark J. Van Aken, 'British Policy Considerations in Central America Before 1850'. *Hispanic American Historical Review*, XLII, no. 1 (Feb. 1962).

60. Williams, *Isthmian Diplomacy*, pp. 40–3.

61. *PP*, BM 40498, Stanley to Peel, 9 Jan. 1842.

62. Williams, *Isthmian Diplomacy*, pp. 43–4.

63. Lockey, 'Neglected Aspect', pp. 299–300.

64. He wrote: 'Our protectorate of Mosquito rests on usage; and if it should be formally resigned . . . it would be necessary to stipulate for some terms for those Indians, from the State of Nicaragua. I apprehend however that the great difficulty would be not on account of the Indians, but a certain number of English, or rather Scotch adventurers, who have obtained for a gallon of brandy, large grants of land from a drunken savage whom we have thought fit to call a King. I looked into this subject five and twenty years ago, and I never could discover on what pretext we made San Juan . . . a part of Mosquito Territory. . . .' *AP*, BM 43189, Aberdeen to Clarendon, 5 Nov. 1854. Twenty-five years before Aberdeen was Foreign Secretary in Wellington's Government, long before the events described above, and, if he had not 'looked into this subject' since that time, he hardly could have taken much interest in the residency of 1844.

65. *RUSP*, PRO 30/22–33, J. Bowstead to Russell, 26 Oct. 1850. Bowstead described the Shepherds as Jamaican merchants who supplied the Mosquito King with the 'necessaries & luxuries of life', which were paid for by the grants of land in question.

66. *CLAR*, c. 246, Correspondence Respecting the Mosquito Territory. Palmerston to Chatfield, Walker and O'Leary, 30 Jan. 1847.

67. Williams, *Isthmian Diplomacy*, pp. 46–7.

68. Commercial Tariffs and Regulations. *Spanish American Republics* by John Macgregor. Presented to Parliament, 1 Feb. 1847.

69. Macgregor noted that the claims of the Mosquito kings stretched from Cape Honduras south to a landing point near Escudo de Veragua, but also that the southern area was in dispute with Granada and other states. Palmerston's boundaries, then, were not based on the extreme claims. See: Macgregor, *Spanish American Republics*, p. 41. The approximate maximum claims of the Mosquito ruler, based on the letters of British agents in the area, are shown in the map on p. 67.

70. Ibid., p. 146.

71. *CLAR*, c. 246, Palmerston to Chatfield, Walker and O'Leary, 30 June 1847.

72. *PAMP*, BM 48575, Pakenham to Palmerston, no. 43, 3 Apr. 1847.

73. Ibid., Pakenham to Palmerston, nos. 55, 56, 28 Apr. 1847.

74. *CLAR*, c. 246, Chatfield to Palmerston, 7 Mar. 1848. 'The suggestion which I made last year, on the advantage of securing a hold on this

coast, in anticipation of coming events, having met with your Lordship's approval . . .'.

75. Ibid., Mosquito Council of State to Government of Nicaragua, 25 Oct. 1847.

76. Ibid., Sir Charles Grey to Palmerston, 23 Mar. 1848.

77. *RUSP*, PRO 30/22–7A, Grey to Russell, 10 Feb. 1848.

78. Ibid., PRO 30/22–7B. Grey to Russell, 6 Mar 1848.

79. *PAMP*, BM 48575, Crampton to Palmerston, no. 60, 28 Nov. 1847.

80. Ibid., Palmerston to Russell, 20 Dec. 1847.

81. Ibid., Russell's note on the above letter.

82. Ibid., Grey to Palmerston, 21 Dec. 1847.

83. Ibid., Palmerston to Crampton, 31 Dec. 1847.

84. Ibid., Crampton to Palmerston, no. 19, 9 Feb. 1848.

85. Ibid., Palmerston to Crampton, no. 13, 24 Mar. 1848.

86. Ibid., Crampton to Palmerston, no. 53, 30 Apr. 1848.

87. Williams, *Isthmian Diplomacy*, pp. 51–67.

88. *PAMP*, BM 48575, Palmerston to Crampton, 27 Apr. 1848.

89. Van Alstyne, *Policy of Lord Palmerston*, p. 351.

90. *RUSP*, PRO 30/22–7D, Palmerston to Russell, 20 Dec. 1848.

91. See: *EP*, PRO 30/12–34, Ellenborough to Aberdeen, 16 May 1848, discussed in note 1 of this Chapter.

92. Williams, *Isthmian Diplomacy*, pp. 73–82.

93. During July–September 1849 Palmerston was involved in another phase of the Eastern Question, and in the latter month he was laying plans for his Brazilian intervention. Neither of these, or the two combined, was sufficiently demanding to have forced Palmerston to change his Central American policy.

94. *RUSP*, PRO 30/22–8A, Palmerston to Russell, 16 Sep. 1849.

95. Palmerston's note on *F.O.* 5–501, Crampton to Palmerston, no. 85. 1 Oct. 1849.

96. So named for Sir Charles Grey, the Governor of Jamaica. Despite the compliment, the Governor opposed the assumption of responsibility for Mosquitia. '. . . the Mosquito Kingdom itself is utterly helpless', he wrote, 'and has not a man in it who at present deserves to be called a soldier.' *CLAR*, c. 246, Grey to Palmerston, 5 Apr. 1848.

97. *PAMP*, BM 48575, Lawrence to Palmerston, 8 Nov. 1849.

98. Ibid., Palmerston to Lawrence, 13 Nov. 1849. The stricken paragraph noted that a connection between Britain and the Central American states 'for many reasons' would not be productive of advantage to either party.

99. Ibid., Palmerston to Lawrence, 13 Nov. 1849. (Second letter of this date.)

5 THE CLAYTON–BULWER FORMULA

1. Van Alstyne, *Clayton–Bulwer Treaty*, p. 149.

2. 'It has also given me great satisfaction', Bulwer wrote Peel, 'to see the general praise bestowed on Lord Aberdeen's calm and conciliatory

statesmanship, which has been the more creditable and more efficient from the preparations which have [been] made for the contingency of war during the constant exertion to preserve peace.' *PP*, BM 40596, Bulwer to Peel, 18 Jul. 1846. This was his interpretation of the diplomacy of the Oregon question.

3. 'Bulwer . . .,' Russell wrote, 'need not go till we receive accounts from Petersburg'. *RUSP*, PRO 30/22–8B, Russell to Baring, 15 Oct. 1849.

4. Ibid., Lord Elgin to Russell, 10 Dec. 1849. According to Elgin, the Canadian farmers believed that annexation to the United States would add 25% in value to their incomes.

5. Ibid., PRO 30/22–8A, Palmerston to Russell, 18 Sep. 1849.

6. Ibid., PRO 30/22–8B, Russell to Baring, 15 Oct. 1849.

7. Ibid., PRO 30/22–8A. Labouchere to Russell 29 Sep. 1849.

8. Ibid., PRO 30/22–8B. Palmerston to Russell, 11 Oct. 1849.

9. Ibid., Bulwer to Russell, 11 Nov. 1849.

10. Ibid., Russell to Lord Elgin, 9 Jan. 1850. That Elgin should have written his warnings about Canada to Russell, rather than Lord Grey, indicates a sense of urgency. Russell's reply was exceedingly unsympathetic: 'Sir Henry Bulwer has full instructions to make many proposals to the United States. But the Canadian politicians should recollect that they, only a few years ago, when I was Secretary of State, were calling out for protection against United States corn. They should also bear in mind that they obtain British manufactures at a moderate duty, that they have not to pay for Army, Navy, Ordnance or General Government and that the real obstacle to their improvement lies in their own want of energy and their foolish factions. However I hope now that the seat of Government has left Montreal, Canada will make rapid progress to prosperity'.

11. *F.O.* 5–501., Crampton to Palmerston, no. 85, 1 Oct. 1849.

12. *RUSP*, PRO 30/22–8B, Grey to Russell, 16 Nov. 1849.

13. *F.O.* 5–511, Bulwer to Palmerston, no. 10, 6 Jan. 1850.

14. In a quotation that has a certain ring of authenticity to it, Squier was supposed to have told the British in Nicaragua that they 'had better be off, unless they wish to become Yankees'. *F.O.* 5–501, Chatfield to Bulwer, 15 Sep. 1849.

15. David Waddell, 'Great Britain and the Bay Islands, 1821–61'. *The Historical Journal*, II (1959) pp. 64–5.

16. *F.O.* 5–511, Bulwer to Palmerston, 6 Jan. 1850 and enclosures.

17. See: Williams, *Isthmian Diplomacy*, pp. 91–103.

18. A story was picked up later by Crampton that Clayton 'had heavy pecuniary interest in the Canal and Transit Route Co., and is open to a charge of having been in such a hurry to get that Treaty which was to protect that interest through the Senate that he neglected to take proper precautions for completely evicting us out of Central America'. Stories of this type were readily believed in Britain at this time. *CLAR*, c. 63, Crampton to Clarendon, 27 Jan. 1856.

19. Ibid., c. 24, Bulwer to Clarendon, 24 Jan. 1854.

20. Bemis, *American Foreign Policy*, p. 164.

21. Williams, *Isthmian Diplomacy*, p. 323.

22. Richard W. Leopold, *The Growth of American Foreign Policy* (New York: Alfred A. Knopf, 1964) pp. 50–1.

23. Bourne, 'Clayton–Bulwer', p. 287.

24. Van Alstyne, 'Clayton–Bulwer', p. 128.

25. *RUSP*, PRO 30/22–9C, Palmerston to Russell, 15 Mar. 1851.

26. Waddell, 'Bay Islands', pp. 65–6.

27. *RUSP*, PRO 30/22–8B, Palmerston to Russell, 5 Mar. 1850.

28. *CLAR*, c. 24, Bulwer to Clarendon, 24 Jan. 1854.

29. *GRAN*, PRO 30/29–215, Granville to Crampton, no. 14, 23 Jan. 1852.

30. Williams, *Isthmian Diplomacy*, pp. 110–19.

31. The old fear of the Franco-American alliance appears in one of Graham's letters during this crisis. 'At the beginning France may back Spain and England', he wrote, 'but let us once be committed in a naval War with America, no Government which is likely to exist in Paris . . . could resist the impulse of taking in the end an active part against us. . . .' *AP*, BM 43190, Graham to Aberdeen, 11 Sep. 1851.

32. *GRAN*, PRO 30/29–29A, Clarendon to Granville, 8 Jan. 1852.

33. 'Ld. John is uneasy about France', Graham wrote Aberdeen, 'and is turning his attention to preparing means of defence against a sudden attack.' *AP*, BM 43190, Graham to Aberdeen, 11 Dec. 1851. Though still technically a Peelite, Graham was an ex-Whig and friend of Lord John Russell, and his information as to the Prime Minister's views can probably be trusted.

34. See: *RUSP*, PRO 30/22–9E, 'Memorandum on the Strengths of the British and French Fleets', 22 Mar. 1851. This memorandum showed that France was ahead of Britain only in steam frigates, 35–29. In other categories of ships Britain had a marked preponderance.

35. Ibid., PRO 30/22–9G, Printed extracts from a Report of the Secretary of War of the United States on the exploration of the Minnesota Territory by Brevet Captain Pope. The comments are marked with 'R's', and in all probability were made by Russell.

36. See: *GRAN*, PRO 30/129–215, Granville to Crampton, no. 8 and no. 9, 21 Jan. 1852. The Hudson's Bay Company with good reason charged American officials in Oregon with breaching the Oregon Treaty by interfering with their trade.

37. This incident involved some American 'adventurers' who allegedly set forth on an expedition against the Sandwich Islands late in 1851. Webster sent out orders to prevent such filibusters. GRAN, PRO 30/29–215, Doyle to Palmerston, no. 102, 5 Dec. 1851.

38. Ibid., PRO 30/29–29A, Clarendon to Granville, 8 Jan. 1852.

39. *GRAN*, PRO 30/29–215, Crampton to Palmerston, no. 80, 29 Dec. 1851.

40. Ibid., Crampton to Granville, no. 1, 4 Jan. 1852.

41. Ibid., Granville to Crampton, no. 6, 16 Jan. 1852, and enclosures.

42. Ibid., Granville to Crampton, no. 14 and no. 15, 23 Jan. 1862.

43. Ibid., Crampton to Granville, no. 13, 25 Jan. 1852.

44. Ibid., Granville to Crampton, no. 22, 20 Feb. 1852.
45. Ibid., Crampton to Granville, no. 16, 25 Jan. 1852.
46. Ibid., Granville to Crampton, no. 24, 20 Feb. 1852.

6 THE DERBY–MALMESBURY POLICY

1. *Hansard*, 3rd ser., CXIX, 893–4.
2. 'The New and Old Ministers', *The Quarterly Review*, XC (Mar. 1852) pp. 567–92.
3. Earl of Malmesbury, *Memoirs of an Ex-Minister* (London: Longmans, Green and Co., 1884) I, 307–9. Napoleon to Malmesbury, 24 Feb. 1852; Malmesbury to Napoleon, 26 Feb. 1852.
4. Ibid., pp. 317–19.
5. Ibid., p. 320.
6. Ibid., p. 359. *Diary*, 24 Oct. 1852.
7. Ibid., p. 362. *Diary*, 3 Nov. 1852.
8. *Croker*, II, 439–40. Derby to Croker, 22 Dec. 1851.
9. Malmesbury, *Memoirs*, I, 354. Derby to Malmesbury, 3 Oct. 1852.
10. Ibid., pp. 355–7. Malmesbury to Derby, 8 Oct. 1852.
11. Ibid., II, 412.
12. *Hansard*, 3rd ser., CXX, 1282–3.
13. Malmesbury, *Memoirs*, I, 358–9. *Diary*, 19 Oct. 1852.
14. *Hansard*, 3rd ser., CXXIII, 26.
15. *Sessional Papers*, LX, 1856 (Coms.)
16. Ibid., Malmesbury to Crampton, no. 11, 6 Apr. 1852 and no. 114, 8 Apr. 1852.
17. Ibid., Malmesbury to Crampton, no. 117, 23 Apr. 1852, and no. 118, 23 Apr. 1852.
18. Ibid., Malmesbury to Crampton, no. 125, 18 June 1852.
19. The curious mixture of lack of interest in American affairs, and the readiness to criticise concessions to the United States is evident from one of Graham's letters to Aberdeen. 'What are the real merits of our case with respect to the Mosquito shore?' he asked. 'I conclude that a question of boundary enters into the dispute . . . they beat us always at Washington by hardihood of Claim'. *AP*, BM 43190, Graham to Aberdeen, 20 Dec. 1851.
20. *Sessional Papers*, LX, 1856 (Coms.) Malmesbury to Crampton, no. 128, 16 Jul. 1852.
21. Ibid., Crampton to Malmesbury, 23 Aug. 1852.
22. Mary Williams, however, scored Webster for not securing for Nicaragua the settlement she 'had been led to expect'. Williams, *Isthmian Diplomacy*, p. 137.
23. Ibid., p. 140.
24. Waddell, 'Bay Islands', pp. 66–8.
25. Malmesbury, *Memoirs*, I, 321. Malmesbury to Cowley, 16 Mar. 1852. See also: *Hansard*, 3rd ser., CXX, 16.
26. Malmesbury, *Memoirs*, I, 322–3. Malmesbury to Crampton, 26 Mar. 1852.

27. *DERP*, 144/1, Malmesbury to Derby, 19 May 1853.

28. Ibid., 179/2, Derby to Pakington, 14 Apr. 1852.

29. Britain had periodically sounded out the United States regarding reciprocity, and, when Bulwer failed to secure satisfaction, Francis Hincks had visited Washington in 1851 on a similar mission.

30. 'Our Fisheries have been the very nurseries of our Navy', Webster declared in 1852. 'If our flag-ships have conquered the enemy on the sea, the fisheries are at the bottom of it'. *New York Times*, 26 Jul. 1852. This consideration was probably the chief 'imperial interest' in the situation.

31. When the crisis developed, Webster noted that America would never permit her vessels to be adjudicated upon 'in the petty tribunals of the Provinces'. Ibid., 26 Jul. 1852.

32. Ibid., 3 Aug. 1852. Among the *Derby Papers* there is a curious 'private proposal from parties at Washington' to settle the reciprocity problem. This plan called for a commission to run the boundary from Lake Superior to the Pacific, a reciprocity treaty, and a national railroad on or near the 49th parallel from Lake Superior to Vancouver Island. *DERP*, 40/1, 'Private Proposal from Parties at Washington to Settle the Question of Reciprocity'. It is difficult to place this proposal into the diplomatic situation of the time. The western areas of Canada were practically unsettled during this era.

33. *The Times* (London), 2 Sep. 1852, quoting an article from the American *Journal of Commerce*.

34. *DERP*, 144/1, Malmesbury to Derby, 5 Aug. 1852.

35. *The Times* (London), 2 Sep. 1852, quoting an article from the American *Journal of Commerce*.

36. *Hansard*, 3rd ser., CXXIII, 24–5.

37. *DISP*, Pakington 107, Pakington to Disraeli, 12 Aug. 1852.

38. *New York Times*, 20 Jul. 1852.

39. *DISP*, Pakington 107, Pakington to Disraeli, 13 Aug. 1852.

40. When American reaction came in, Newcastle wrote: 'I think the Fishery dispute looks ugly – not so much as threatening immediate war as muddling our relations with America, for we shall have to eat dirt'. *NEWP*, 11892, Newcastle to Bonham, 10 Aug. 1852.

41. *The Times* (London), 11 Aug. 1852.

42. *DERP*, Malmesbury 144/1, Malmesbury to Derby, 5 Aug, 1852.

43. *DISP*, Malmesbury 99, Malmesbury to Disraeli, (12? Aug.) 1852.

44. Malmesbury, *Memoirs*, I, 343–4. Disraeli to Malmesbury, 13 Aug. 1852.

45. *DERP*, Malmesbury 144/1, Malmesbury to Derby, 13 Aug. 1852.

46. Malmesbury, *Memoirs*, I, 343, *Diary*, 11 Aug. 1852.

47. *DERP*, Malmesbury 144/1, Malmesbury to Derby, 2 Sep. 1852.

48. Sir Edward Bulwer had recommended a newspaper agent to Malmesbury, whose duty was to secure journalistic support for Conservative foreign policy. *DISP*, Malmesbury 99, Malmesbury to Disraeli, 15 Aug. 1852.

49. *DERP*, 144/1, Malmesbury to Derby, 9 Sep. 1852.

50. Ibid., Malmesbury to Derby, 8 Sep. 1852.

234 *The American Problem in British Diplomacy*

51. Ibid., Malmesbury to Derby, 9 Sep. 1852.

52. Ibid., Malmesbury to Derby, 12 Sep. 1852.

53. Malmesbury, *Memoirs*, I, 348. Derby to Malmesbury, 15 Sep. 1852.

54. When, in April, Derby approved an increased force in the fishing area, he observed: '. . . a portion at all events of expense should be borne, & it appears would be borne, by the Local Legislatures'. *DERP*, 179/2, Derby to Pakington, 14 Apr. 1852.

55. See: *The Times* (London), 27 Sep. 1852, quoting the *New York Herald*.

56. *DERP*, 144/1, Malmesbury to Derby, 3 Oct. 1852.

57. Malmesbury, *Memoirs*, I, 354–5. Derby to Malmesbury, 3 Oct, 1852.

58. See: C. P. Stacey, 'The Myth of the Unguarded Frontier, 1815–1871'. *American Historical Review*, LVI, 1–18 (1950). Stacey stressed that the building of fortifications on both sides of the frontier did not cease until the Treaty of Washington in 1871. Bourne in his work (*Britain and Balance of Power*, pp. viii–ix) acknowledges his debt to Stacey.

59. *DERP*, 144/1, Malmesbury to Derby, 31 Oct. [1852].

60. Frothingham, *Everett*, pp. 333–9. Malmesbury had previously sounded out the United States regarding an Anglo-French-American remonstrance to Santo Domingo also without success. *DERP*, 144/1, Malmesbury to Derby, 13 Aug. 1852.

61. *Hansard*, 3rd ser., CXXIII, 18.

62. Ibid., p. 585.

63. Shortly thereafter Britain sent a minister to the new Urquiza Government, but, as Buenos Ayres refused to join the state, he was in an embarrassing position. '. . . he is utterly useless unless at Buenos Ayres', Clarendon observed. 'His position on bd. a British vessel in the port was absurd, & it is not much better now at Monte Video to wh. place he has retreated.' *AP*, BM 43188, Clarendon to Aberdeen, 3 Aug. 1853. Later in the year he rejected blockade as a means of coercing Buenos Ayres. Ibid., Clarendon to Aberdeen, 7 Nov. 1853.

7 THE ABERDEEN–CLARENDON PERIOD

1. *GP*, BM 44089, Aberdeen to Gladstone, 4 Oct. 1855.

2. John Morley, *The Life of Richard Cobden* (London: Macmillan, 1908) p. 411.

3. *AP*, BM 43188, Clarendon to Aberdeen, 25 Mar. 1853.

4. Ibid., Aberdeen to Clarendon, 12 Feb. 1854.

5. Malmesbury, *Memoirs*, I, 421. *Diary*, 3 Jan. 1854.

6. *BP*, 10250, Aberdeen to Brougham, 19 Aug. 1855.

7. It is interesting to note that Alexander McLeod was still seeking indemnification at this time, and again unsuccessfully. *COP*, 43–115 (Canada), Peel to McLeod, 31 Mar. 1853.

8. *Sessional Papers*, XL, 1856 (Coms.), Russell to Crampton, no. 141, 19 Jan. 1853.

9. Ibid., Crampton to Russell, no. 150, 13 Feb. 1853.

10. Ibid., Crampton to Russell, 21 Feb. 1853.

11. *NEWP* (North America), Elgin to Newcastle, 28 Jan. 1853.

12. Ibid., Newcastle to Elgin, 1 Apr. 1853. The former provided the following statistics regarding the number of British soldiers stationed in Canada: 1792 (3068), 1803 (1741), 1822 (3157), and 1830 (3236).

13. Ibid., Newcastle to Elgin, 18 Feb. 1853.

14. *NEWP* (Newfoundland), Newcastle to Russell, 14 Jan. 1853.

15. Ibid. (North America), Hincks to Crampton, 27 Dec. 1852; *Hansard*, 3rd ser., CXXVI.

16. Ibid., Newcastle to Elgin, 28 Jan. 1852.

17. Ibid., Elgin to Newcastle, 18 Feb. 1852.

18. Ibid., Elgin to Newcastle, 17 Mar. 1853.

19. *AP*, BM 43188, Reeve to Clarendon, Mar.(?) 1853. Later in the year Marcy told Crampton frankly that if the existing government of these islands collapsed, America would be 'disposed to receive them'. *F.O.* 5–567, Crampton to Clarendon, no. 181, 20 Nov. 1853.

20. *COP*, 43–116 (Newfoundland), Merivale to Addington, 6 Aug. 1853.

21. 'I have no reason to think that any definite plan has been formed or pre-concerted in the United States for revolutionising Australia', Crampton wrote. 'There can be no doubt, however, that a revolution in Australia ... would be highly acceptable to the great mass of the American people. . . .' *F.O.* 5–567, Crampton to Clarendon, no. 175, 3 Oct. 1853. Reports from Australia sometimes mentioned the effect of the American example there. See *NEWP* (New South Wales), Bishop of Melbourne to Pakington (?), 5 Oct. 1852; Ibid. (Van Diemen's Land), Sir William Denison to Pakington, 2 Nov. 1852.

22. *Sessional Papers*, XL, 1856 (Coms.), Crampton to Clarendon, no. 157, 21 Mar. 1853.

23. Ibid., Clarendon to Crampton, no. 161, 29 Apr. 1853.

24. Ibid., Clarendon to Crampton, no. 163, 27 May, 1853.

25. Ibid., Crampton to Clarendon, no. 168, 13 June, 1853.

26. Ibid., Clarendon to Crampton, no. 171, 22 Jul. 1853.

27. *COP*, 43–150 (Canada), Newcastle to Elgin, 28 Mar. 1853.

28. *The Times* (London), 4 Aug. 1853.

29. Ibid., 27 Jul. 1853.

30. *F.O.* 5–567, Crampton to Clarendon, 3 Oct. 1853.

31. *The Times* (London), 31 Aug. 1853. Although Mary Williams and some other American historians have scored *The Times* for anti-Americanism, it consistently printed the American side of Anglo-American disputes in reprints of articles from American sources.

32. *GRAN*, PRO 30/29–29A, Clarendon to Granville, 28 Mar. 1853.

33. *The Times* (London), 8 Jul. 1853.

34. *AP*, BM 43188, Clarendon to Aberdeen, 28 Jan. 1854.

35. *CLAR*, c. 24, Crampton to Clarendon, 15 Jan. 1854.

36. Ibid., Crampton to Clarendon, 15 Mar. 1854.

37. *NEWP* (North America), Elgin to Newcastle, 21 Dec. 1853.

38. 'I attach as much importance to the respect entertained for you in the United States', Newcastle wrote, 'as I do to the regard and affection of those over whom you have been Viceroy for so long a time'. Ibid., Newcastle to Elgin, 23 Jan. 1854.

39. *F.O.* 5–589, Clarendon to Elgin, Secret no. 1, 4 May 1854.

40. *CLAR*, c. 24, Crampton to Clarendon, 29 May, 1854; *F.O.* 5–589, Elgin to Clarendon, 12 June 1854.

41. *F.O.* 5–589, Elgin to Marcy, 12 Aug. 1854.

42. After returning to Canada, Elgin wrote: 'I am purposely taking low ground in introducing the advantages of the Treaty to the knowledge of the Colonials. . . . . the more the colonists grumble the more chance there is of the Americans being satisfied with their bargain and ratifying it. On the other hand, American grumble helps us here.' *CLAR*, c. 24, Elgin to Clarendon, 17 June 1854.

43. See: Orville John McDiarmid, *Commercial Policy in the Canadian Economy* (Cambridge: Harvard University Press, 1946) p. 88.

44. During 1850–5 there was a fairly steady increase in British exports to the United States of apparel up to a value of £1,333,660 in 1855; exports of books, copper, and cotton manufactures fluctuated between £2–3 million in value; hardware exports averaged around £500,000; iron and rough steel exports increased notably up to a £6 million value in 1854; linen exports had a value between £1–2 million and woollens by piece and yard between £2–3 million. *Sessional Papers*, LX, 1856 (Coms.) The whole value of the British exports to the United States in 1842 had been only £3·5 million, and, following recovery from that depression year, the value had increased to £7·1 million in 1845.

45. American exports to Britain consisted mainly of beef, wheat, tobacco, and cotton. The first three were not much affected by the war, but there was some increase in the fourth, as well as in oil, seed cake and pork. The sharpest war-related increases were in American exports of maize, turpentine oil, and resin. On the other hand, the American economy seems to have suffered somewhat due to the tightening of the British money market during the war years.

46. Crampton reported the purchase as follows: 'The gist of the matter seems to be that St. Anna, wanting to proclaim himself Emperor, and feeling it necessary to disarm American opposition to that step, has determined to throw to the United States a slice of his territory in order to stop their mouths, and to get a sum of money which will enable him to set up as Despot over the remainder.' *CLAR*, c. 24, Crampton to Clarendon, 6 Feb. 1854.

47. Ibid., Crampton to Clarendon, 6 Feb. 1854.

48. Ibid., Crampton to Clarendon, 3 Apr. 1854.

49. *AP*, BM 43356, Buchanan to Clarendon, 6 Jan. 1854.

50. *CLAR*, c. 24, Bulwer to Clarendon, 24 Jan. 1854.

51. Ibid., Crampton to Clarendon, 15, 23 Jan., 20 Feb. 1854.

52. 'Marcy much pleased with our policy twds. neutrals', he wrote. *AP*, BM 43189, Clarendon to Aberdeen, 25 Apr. 1854.

53. *AP*, BM 43356, Clarendon to Buchanan, 2 May 1854.

54. *CLAR*, c. 25, Crampton to Clarendon, 17 Jul. 1854.
55. *AP*, BM 43189, Clarendon to Aberdeen, 14 May 1854.
56. Malmesbury, *Memoirs*, I, 438, *Diary*, 30 Jul. 1854.
57. Ibid., p. 440, Derby to Malmesbury, 2 Oct. 1854.
58. Ibid., p. 441, *Diary*, 25 Oct. 1854.
59. American and French whalers had turned pigs and cattle loose in the Falkland Islands, hoping to secure a continuing supply of meat. Britain had title to these islands from Spain, and settled them in 1833. In May 1853 the British Government warned against whalers taking spoil on these islands, and an American captain was caught and tried for pig-taking in August. See: *New York Times*, 23 May 1854; CLAR, c. 25, Crampton to Clarendon, 10 Jul. 1854.
60. *CLAR*, c. 25, Crampton to Clarendon, 10 Jul. 1854.
61. Ibid., Crampton to Clarendon, 10 Sep. 1854.
62. Williams, *Isthmian Diplomacy*, p. 180.
63. *CLAR*, c. 25, Crampton to Clarendon, 10 Sep. 1854.
64. *AP*, BM 43189, Clarendon to Aberdeen, 25 Sep. 1854.
65. Clarendon had toyed with the idea of using coercion against Venezuela on behalf of British bondholders, but Aberdeen vetoed the suggestion. 'I fully believe that the Venezuelan authorities may have behaved very ill', Aberdeen replied. 'But have we ever recognised the principle that our Govt. is bound to enforce the claims of Bondholders? .... Heretofore we have not done this, but have confined ourselves to good offices. . . . I know that Lord Palmerston on one occasion . . . laid down a different doctrine; but it was obiter dictum, and I know it was not admitted by the best judges'. Ibid., Clarendon to Aberdeen, 15 Mar. 1854; Aberdeen to Clarendon, 16 Mar. 1854.
66. *AP*, BM 43189, Aberdeen to Clarendon, 25 Sep. 1854.
67. On 26 Oct. 1854 *The Times* reported that the '*Curacao*, 31, screw frigate' would 'proceed either to the Crimea, or to the West India and North America station'. The *Formidable* was reported on 6 November to be loading shot and shell so as to be ready for active service at the shortest notice. On 13 November the former departed not for America, but for the Black Sea.
68. *AP*, BM 43189, Clarendon to Aberdeen, 24 Oct. 1854.
69. Ibid., Aberdeen to Clarendon, 24 Oct. 1854.
70. Ibid., Clarendon to Aberdeen, 5 Nov. 1854.
71. Ibid., Aberdeen to Clarendon, 5 Nov. 1854.
72. R. W. Van Alstyne, 'Anglo-American Relations, 1853–1857', *American Historical Review*, XLII (1936–1937) pp. 491–2.
73. *AP*, BM 43189, Clarendon to Aberdeen, 6 Nov. 1854.
74. *CLAR*, c. 44, Crampton to Clarendon, 10 Sep. 1855.
75. Ibid., c. 25, Crampton to Clarendon, 27 Nov. 1854.
76. Ibid., Crampton to Clarendon, 27 Nov. 1854.
77. Ibid., Crampton to Clarendon, 30 Dec. 1854.
78. Malmesbury, *Memoirs*, II, 10, *Diary*, 22 Feb. 1854.

8 THE PALMERSTON–CLARENDON PERIOD

1. *AP*, BM 43197, Aberdeen to Newcastle, 27 Nov. 1856.

2. Malmesbury, *Memoirs*, II, 5, *Diary*, 30 Jan. 1855.

3. 'The Govt. are making over again the mistakes of Pitt', Malmesbury wrote to Disraeli, 'by sending recruiting Sergeants to the embodied Militia instead of letting the officers recruit out of their own crews. The Garrisons are all drunks & I shd. not wonder to hear of the Dockyard at Portsmouth being burnt down. I am told that our paper army exceeds the real one by 20,000. . . . These two islands cannot furnish males to carry on a European war, & this fact brings the nature & uses of our Colonial Empire to a test. Not one of our so-called territorial possessions abroad are as yet available to furnish a single soldier. . . .' *DISP*, Malmesbury 99, Malmesbury to Disraeli, 4 Nov. 1854.

4. *CLAR*, c. 25, Crampton to Clarendon, 4 Dec. 1854.

5. See: R. W. van Alsyne, 'John F. Crampton, Conspirator or Dupe?' *American Historical Review*, XLI (Apr. 1936).

6. *Hansard*, 3rd ser., CXXXVI, 255, 283–4.

7. Ibid., pp. 519–610.

8. *GRAN*, PRO 30/29–29A, Argyll to Granville, 9 Jan. 1855.

9. *CLAR*, c. 43, Crampton to Clarendon, 4 Feb. 1855; 6 Mar. 1855.

10. Ibid., Crampton to Clarendon, 23 Apr. 1855.

11. Ibid., c. 263, 'Papers Relative to Recruiting in the United States.' Excerpt from the *New York Herald*.

12. Ibid., c. 25, Crampton to Clarendon, 24 Oct. 1854.

13. Ibid., c. 44, Crampton to Clarendon, 29 Oct. 1855.

14. Ibid., c. 43, Crampton to Clarendon, 18 June 1855.

15. Ibid., c. 44, Crampton to Clarendon, 10 Sep. 1855.

16. Ibid., Crampton to Clarendon, 24 Sep. 1855.

17. 'You may be sure', Aberdeen wrote, 'that Russia will do her best to stimulate the U. States against us, and thus to create a diversion in her favour'. *AP*, BM 43189, Aberdeen to Clarendon, 25 Sep. 1854.

18. *CLAR*, c. 43, Crampton to Clarendon, 15 Jan. 1855.

19. *F.O.* 5–641, Crampton to Clarendon, no. 50, 3 Mar. 1856.

20. *CLAR*, c. 43, Crampton to Clarendon, 1 May 1855.

21. Ibid., Crampton to Clarendon, 18 June 1855.

22. Ibid., Crampton to Clarendon, 10 Jul. 1855.

23. *Hansard*, 3rd ser., CXXXVIII, 973–1010.

24. Malmesbury, *Memoirs*, II, 29–30, *Diary*, 7 Jul. 1855. Russell's move was widely interpreted as an attempt by him to replace Palmerston as premier.

25. Malmesbury, *Memoirs*, II, 30, *Diary*, 12 Jul. 1855.

26. *Hansard*, 3rd ser., CXXXIX, 966.

27. *CLAR*, c. 43, Crampton to Clarendon, 7 Aug. 1855.

28. *Hansard*, 3rd ser., CXXXIX, 1660–1. As a matter of interest, the British had established a recruiting station in international waters at Heligoland, and had stationed some ships on the Weser and Elbe rivers

to convey Germans, who wished to 'emigrate', to their recruiting station.

29. Williams, *Isthmian Diplomacy*, pp. 197–8.

30. *CLAR*, c. 44, Marcy to Crampton, 5 Sep. 1855.

31. Ibid., Crampton to Clarendon, 10 Sep. 1855.

32. Ibid., c. 65, Lumley to Clarendon, 11 Nov. 1856.

33. Crampton wrote to Clarendon that Stroble had first sought a bribe from the British in return for his silence. He also charged that Stroble had actually accepted bribes from Russia to implicate British officials, and that he was guilty of a large number of other crimes and misdemeanors.

34. *CLAR*, c. 65, Lumley to Clarendon, 11 Nov. 1856.

35. *The Times* (London), 13 Oct. 1855.

36. Crampton called the reinforcement 'a medicine which I find instantly began to operate', and noted it caused the mercantile interest to put pressure on the American Government to maintain the peace. *CLAR*, c. 44, Crampton to Clarendon, 29 Oct. 1855.

37. 'I hope Pam is not doing foolish things *about America*', Argyll wrote. 'I am one of those who do not care much about the fate of Cuba – at least I do not think it worth a war with America. . . . Sending a great fleet will only have the appearance of a threat agst. the Union and irritate them to madness'. *GRAN*, PRO 30/22–29A, Argyll to Granville, 27 Oct. 1855. Yet this was written after the ships noted above had been sent.

38. See: Bourne, *Britain and the Balance of Power*, pp. 185–8. Bourne relates the dispatch of the fleet to a number of incidents in the New World, and concludes that Britain and France in 1855 frustrated all American efforts to secure naval bases in Cuba, Santo Domingo, and Hawaii.

39. *CLAR*, c. 44, Crampton to Clarendon, 15 Oct. 1855.

40. *F.O.* 5–641, Crampton to Clarendon, 4 Mar. 1856.

41. *CLAR*, c. 44, Crampton to Clarendon, 3 Dec. 1855.

42. Ibid., c. 65, Lumley to Clarendon, 17 Nov. 1856.

43. Ibid., c. 63, Crampton to Clarendon, 27 Jan. 1856.

44. Ibid., Crampton to Clarendon, 27 Jan. 1856.

45. '. . . we cannot with honour', Derby wrote to Disraeli, 'or even with regard to party interests, constitute ourselves a peace Opposition, merely because we have a War Ministry, and I will never consent to weaken an Administration to which I am opposed, by increasing their difficulties in carrying the country through what has become an inevitable war. . . . If the Conservative party cannot be kept together on other grounds, it is time it should fall to pieces. . . .' *DISP*, Derby to Disraeli, 25 Oct. 1855.

46. *Hansard*, 3rd ser., CXL, 34–6.

47. *F.O.* 5–641, Crampton to Clarendon, no. 52, 3 Mar. 1856; Ibid., 5–642, Crampton to Clarendon, 31 Mar. 1856. But later Walker's minister to Washington was received.

48. Ibid., 5–640, Crampton to Clarendon, no. 8, 4 Jan. 1856; Crampton to Clarendon, no. 12, 28 Jan. 1856.

49. Crampton advised Rowcroft to defend himself in court, but not to claim that he had acted under orders from the Government! '. . . there

240 *The American Problem in British Diplomacy*

is not the slightest shadow of a doubt', Rowcroft replied, 'of my being able to prove . . . that such interference as I had in the matter was an "official duty resulting from official communication."' Ibid., 5–642, Crampton to Rowcroft, 12 Mar. 1856; Rowcroft to Crampton, 21 Mar. 1856.

50. The suggestion came from Granville. Clarendon replied: 'What would Elgin do? I fear he has committed himself by some speeches against that wayward country'. *GRAN*, PRO 30/29–29A, Clarendon to Granville, 30 Mar. 1856. But the possibility of an Elgin mission was still being toyed with in June.

51. *New York Times*, 12 May, 1856.

52. *Hansard*, 3rd ser., CXLII, 1509.

53. See: Bourne, *Britain and the Balance of Power*, pp. 193–7.

54. *CLAR*, c. 64, Crampton to Clarendon, 19 May, 1856.

55. See: Malmesbury, *Memoirs*, II, 47, *Diary*, 5 June 1856.

56. *AP*, BM 43255, Dallas to Aberdeen, 11 June 1856.

57. Ibid., Aberdeen to Dallas, [11] June 1856.

58. *Hansard*, 3rd ser., CXLII, 1089–90.

59. Ibid., pp. 1403–4.

60. Ibid., p. 1406.

61. See: Bourne, *Britain and the Balance of Power*, pp. 195–9.

62. *Hansard*, 3rd ser., CXLII, 1404.

63. A Gladstone letter to Aberdeen shows that Aberdeen approved the attack, and that it was partly concerted between the Conservatives and Peelites. 'The American question', he wrote, 'has taught me a lesson which I do not feel that I ought to have to learn again. It is this: that it is utterly vain to trust to the coincidence of *ex tempore* decisions separately formed for the purpose of controuling Parliament'. *GP*, BM 44089, Gladstone to Aberdeen, 8 Dec. 1856.

64. *Hansard*, 3rd ser., CXLII, 1509.

65. *GRAN*, PRO 30/29–29A, Clarendon to Granville, 5 Jul. 1856.

66. This is evident from a letter of the Postmaster General, the Duke of Argyll, who had warmly opposed a hard line towards America early in June. 'It really looks like a civil war in the United States', he wrote. 'How I do wish that Union to be split! It wd. be such a blessing to mankind to have some opposite "nationalities" balancing each other over there and keeping in some check their overbearing impudence – all very rash speaking, but I am a little bilious today & it is hot & close as thunder'. Ibid., Argyll to Granville, 25 June 1856.

67. Williams, *Isthmian Diplomacy*, pp. 221–3.

68. *CLAR*, c. 65, Bulwer to Clarendon, 31 May 1856.

69. Williams, *Isthmian Diplomacy*, pp. 220–1.

70. *CLAR*, c. 64, Lumley to Clarendon, 24 June 1856.

71. *GRAN*, PRO 30/22–29A, Argyll to Granville, 25 June 1856.

72. Edward M. Archibald, British Consul in New York, reported an extraordinary interview with Buchanan late in August. The confident candidate said he had devoted his whole life to improving Anglo-American relations, there was more love for 'Old England' in America

than in any other country, and Britain had nothing to fear from America. The Bay Islands, however, would have to be restored to Honduras. *CLAR*, c. 65, Archibald to Clarendon, 29 Aug. 1856.

73. Waddell, 'Bay Islands', p. 71.

74. Ibid.

75. *CLAR*, c. 64, Bulwer to Clarendon, 26 June 1856.

76. *AP*, BM 43189, Clarendon to Aberdeen, 8 Sep. 1856.

77. An excellent Peelite assessment of Palmerston's conduct of foreign affairs is found in one of Graham's letters at this time. 'We have outraged Russia', he wrote, 'we have insulted Prussia, have nearly ruined Austria, and still threaten her hold of her Italian Dominions. The independence of Turkey is a bubble; and if Palmerston breaks with Louis Napoleon, he cannot rely much on the friendship of [Alvarez?] and Buchanan. But "Civis Romanus sum. . . ." ' *NEWP*, 12542, Graham to Newcastle, 8 Nov. 1856.

78. *GRAN*, PRO 30/22–29A, Argyll to Granville, 25 June 1856.

79. Lumley's distrust of the United States Government seems to have been deeper than that of any other official, and his private letters certainly did nothing to establish confidence between Washington and London. He was particularly resentful of the pro-American newspapers in Britain, which he identified as the *Morning Star*, and *Morning Advertiser* of London, the *European Times* of Liverpool, and the *Manchester Guardian*. He alleged they spoke for the United States, and had been involved in the attempt to overthrow Palmerston, not to mention their continuing policy of stirring up dissension between Britain and France. *CLAR*, c. 65, Lumley to Clarendon, 17 Nov. 1856. Clarendon was so impressed by Lumley's report that he sounded out John T. Delane of *The Times* regarding the possibility of bribing American newspapers. Delane replied that such an attempt would be dangerous because the American press was corrupt and unsteady. Ibid., Delane to Clarendon, 2 Dec. 1856.

80. A curious note in Clarendon's papers, signed 'John Bull', advised him to send a peer to America, adding: 'They like my Lord'. *CLAR*, c. 44, John Bull to Clarendon, [?], 1855.

81. Ibid., c. 65, Napier to Clarendon, 24 Dec. 1856.

82. Ibid., Dallas to Clarendon, 24 Jan., 23 Feb., and 3 Mar. 1857.

83. Ibid., Buchanan to Clarendon, 22 Mar. 1857.

84. *PAMP*, BM 48575, Palmerston to Crampton, no. 3, 30 June 1847; Crampton to Palmerston, no. 20, 29 Jul. 1847.

85. *AP*, BM, 43118, Aberdeen to Clarendon, 1 May 1853.

86. *NEWP* (Hong Kong), Bowring to Newcastle, 6 May 1854.

87. *COB*, BM 43669, Bowring to Cobden, 20 Feb. 1855.

88. *CLAR*, c. 81, Napier to Clarendon, 8 Apr. 1857.

89. Napier to Clarendon, 31 Mar. 1857.

90. Ibid., Napier to Clarendon, 12 May 1857.

91. 'The cession went off with the Treaty', Malmesbury explained later, 'because the Congress wd. not sanction an Anti-Slavery clause wh.

Palmerston insisted on appending to the transfer of Ruatan.' *DERP*, 144/2, Malmesbury to Derby, 2 Dec. 1858.

92. *CLAR*, c. 81, Napier to Clarendon, 25 June 1857.

93. For a summary of the complex developments relating to the Central American situation and the United States in the latter part of 1857 see Williams, *Isthmian Diplomacy*, pp. 231–41.

94. Palmerston to Clarendon, 31 Dec. 1857 in Kenneth Bourne, *The Foreign Policy of Victorian England, 1830–1902* (Oxford: Clarendon Press, 1970) pp. 334–6.

9   THE END OF THE MOSQUITO CONTROVERSY

1. *PAMP*, BM 48582, Palmerston to Lord Ernest Bruce, 20 Nov. 1860.

2. Malmesbury, *Memoirs*, II, 105, *Diary*, 13 Mar. 1858.

3. Ibid., p. 140. Malmesbury to Cowley, 26 Oct. 1858.

4. *DERP*, 141/10, Memorandum: State of the Royal Navy, Mar. 1858.

5. Ibid., 144/2, Malmesbury to Derby, 22 Aug. 1858.

6. *DISP*, Pakington 107, Pakington to Disraeli, 7 Apr. 1862.

7. Malmesbury had in his possession a French 1857 plan for the invasion of Britain. Malmesbury, *Memoirs*, II, 140–1, Malmesbury to Cowley, 26 Oct. 1858. Believing that Napoleon III was determined to maintain a state of war readiness against Britain, Malmesbury recommended the stationing of six sail-of-the-line in the Channel at all times. *DERP*, 144/2, Malmesbury to Derby, 3 Aug. 1858.

8. *DERP*, 144/2, Malmesbury to Derby, 10 Sep. 1858.

9. Ibid., Memorandum: State of Foreign Relations at the Close of Lord Palmerston's Administration, 25 Feb. 1858.

10. 'If the French will join us in securing the route over the Isthmus, now doubly valuable to us, the U. S. cannot even grumble', Malmesbury wrote. Ibid., Malmesbury to Derby, 8 Oct. 1858.

11. 'Why Clarendon ever sent him [Ouseley] to Washington to eat dirt, I never cd. understand', Malmesbury wrote, and Derby held similar views. Ibid., Malmesbury to Derby, 8 Oct. 1858.

12. Ibid., Malmesbury to Derby, 26 Apr. 1858.

13. As early as 1853 Napoleon III had expressed opposition to the Monroe Doctrine in a conversation with Malmesbury which termed America a 'barbarous Republic'. Malmesbury, *Memoirs*, I, 389, *Diary*, 20 Mar. 1853.

14. 'What is of great importance', Malmesbury wrote to Cowley in September, 'is that France should join us in securing a passage for herself over Nicaragua, and thus act in unison with us on this critical point'. Malmesbury, *Memoirs*, II, 136, Malmesbury to Cowley, 28 Sep. 1858.

15. *Sessional Papers*, LXVIII, 1860 (Coms.), Malmesbury to Ouseley, no. 66, 9 Aug. 1858.

16. *Sessional Papers*, LXVIII, 1860 (Coms.), Malmesbury to Ouseley, no. 94, 16 Oct. 1858. The Foreign Secretary noted that Article XXI, which provided for the passage of British troops over the isthmus, was

very important now that Britain was establishing the new Northwest colony in Canada.

17. *F.O.* 5–689, Malmesbury to Napier, no. 106, 18 Aug. 1858. It is not clear from the despatches just how much information Malmesbury expected his diplomats to divulge to the United States.

18. This seems clear from one of Malmesbury's private letters, which is not wholly legible. He wrote: 'I fear Ouseley is less wise than he ever was. When the treaties were prepared I told Ld. Napier & him to inform the U. S. Govt. of our intentions, but not to consult or ask advice. They did so, but because Napier told the U. S. of the Costa Rican Treaty, wh. is analagous & identical in spirit with the other, Sir W.O. gets up (?). If we cannot treat with an independent country without consulting General Cass or concealing our object in fear of his displeasure we had better strike colours as an independent nation'. *DERP*, 144/2, Malmesbury to Derby, undated.

19. *F.O.* 5–689, Malmesbury to Napier, no. 172, 18 Nov. 1858.

20. Ibid., Malmesbury to Napier, no. 169, 10 Nov. 1858.

21. *DERP*, 144/2, Malmesbury to Derby, 8 Oct. 1858.

22. Ibid., 141/10, Pakington to Derby, 11 Oct. 1858.

23. Ibid., Pakington to Derby, 13 Oct. 1858.

24. *F.O.* 5–689, Malmesbury to Napier, no. 135, 14 Oct. 1858.

25. Malmesbury, *Memoirs*, II, 136, Malmesbury to Cowley, 28 Sep. 1858.

26. *F.O.* 5–689, Malmesbury to Napier, no. 168, 10 Nov. 1858.

27. During the attack on Palmerston's American policy in 1856, Malmesbury wrote Derby that the Conservative Party was 'completely divided in opinion & requires leading. . . . The Peers are much the same. All for Peace, but many very angry at Crampton's rejection'. *DERP*, 144/1, Malmesbury to Derby, Sunday, 1856.

28. Ibid., 180/1, Derby to Malmesbury, 11 Oct. 1858.

29. Ibid., 144/2, Malmesbury to Derby, 17 Dec. 1858.

30. Ibid., 144/2, Malmesbury to Derby, 2 Dec. 1858. Malmesbury was evidently much impressed by the rules of *solidarite*. See also: Malmesbury, *Memoirs*, II, 117–18, Malmesbury to Canning, 10 May 1858.

31. *F.O.* 5–689, Malmesbury to Napier, no. 195, 8 Dec. 1858.

32. *DERP*, 144/2, Malmesbury to Derby, 20 Dec. 1858.

33. Ibid., 186/1, Derby to Malmesbury, 21 Dec. 1858.

34. Ibid., Derby to Hammond, 21 Dec. 1858.

35. Malmesbury, *Memoirs*, II, 148, *Diary*, 17 Jan. 1859.

36. *DERP*, 144/2, Memorandum on the State of Foreign Relations at the Close of the Year 1858.

37. Ibid., 184/1, Derby to Malmesbury, 11 Oct. 1858.

38. Ibid., 144/2, Malmesbury to Derby, 11 Sep. 1858.

39. *F.O.* 5–689, Malmesbury to Napier, no. 130, 5 Oct. 1858.

40. Ibid., Malmesbury to Napier, no. 138, 14 Oct. 1858.

41. Ibid., Malmesbury to Napier, no. 168, 10 Nov. 1858.

42. *RUSP*, PRO 30/22–29, Malmesbury to Russell, 30 June 1859.

43. *DERP*, 144/2, Malmesbury to Derby, 17 Dec. 1858.

44. Ibid., Malmesbury to Derby, 26 Dec. 1858.

45. *Sessional Papers*, LXVIII, 1860 (Coms.). Malmesbury to Ouseley, no. 122, 16 Dec. 1858.

46. Ibid., Ouseley to Malmesbury, no. 136, 3 Jan. 1859.

47. Ibid., Malmesbury to Ouseley, no. 137, 16 Feb. 1859. See also: Williams, *Isthmian Diplomacy*, pp. 256-7.

48. Malmesbury, *Memoirs*, II, 157, *Diary*, 16 Feb. 1859. Malmesbury was convinced Napoleon III feared the Carbonari would assassinate him if he broke his promise, and failed to support the Italian cause. So war was inevitable.

49. *Sessional Papers*, LXVIII, 1860 (Coms.). Malmesbury to Wyke, no. 139, 16 Feb. 1859.

50. The Nicaraguans secured a promise from Britain to prevent filibusters from her territory into their country – a meaningless pledge, but put there so that they could demand a similar pledge in the Cass-Yrissari treaty, and hold up its ratification. Malmesbury also disliked certain changes in the provisions for citizens who died intestate in Nicaragua. Ibid., Malmesbury to Ouseley, no. 154, 23 Mar. 1859.

51. *RUSP*, PRO 30/22-33, Ouseley to Russell, 19 Sep. 1859.

52. *Sessional Papers*, LXVIII, 1860 (Coms.). Malmesbury to Ouseley, no. 175, 10 Apr. 1859.

53. Ibid., Ouseley to Malmesbury, no. 176. 30 Mar. 1859.

54. Ibid., Ouseley to Malmesbury, no. 200, 23 Apr. 1859.

55. *DERP*, 48/4, Memorandum on the State of Foreign Relations at the Close of Lord Derby's Administration, 14 June 1859.

56. Ibid., 'We have no present cause of difference with the United States', the memorandum observed. 'The Cabinet of Washington professes its desire to be on good terms with England, expresses itself satisfied with the course that the latter is pursuing in Central America. . . .'

57. *Hansard*, 3rd ser., CLIV, 880.

58. *RUSP*, PRO 30/22-74, Otway to Russell, 11 Aug. 1859.

59. Malmesbury, *Memoirs*, II, 136, Malmesbury to Cowley, 28 Sep. 1858.

60. *The Times* (London), 5 Nov. 1858.

61. *F.O.* 5-689, Malmesbury to Napier, no. 187, 26 Nov. 1858.

62. Ibid., Malmesbury to Napier, no. 200, 15 Dec. 1858.

63. *Hansard*, 3rd ser., CLII, 4-5.

64. *The Times* (London), 21 Mar. 1859.

65. Ibid., 3 May 1859.

66. *RUSP*, PRO 30/22-74, Otway to Russell, 26 Nov. 1859.

67. 'I saw John Russell yesterday Evening', Palmerston wrote. 'He joins our government, but I am sorry to say claims the Foreign Office. I wish that this had been otherwise'. *CLAR.*, c. 524, Palmerston to Clarendon, 13 June 1859.

68. *RUSP*, PRO 30/22-21, Palmerston to Russell, 15 Mar. 1860.

69. *COB*, BM 43670, Cobden to Baxter, 20 Nov. 1860.

70. Palmerston observed: 'It would be delightful if your utopia could

be realised, and if the nations of the earth would think of nothing but Peace and Commerce, and would give up quarrelling and fighting together. But unfortunately man is a fighting and quarrelling animal, and that this is human nature is proved by the fact that republics where masses govern, are far more quarrelsome, and more addicted to fighting than Monarchies which are governed by comparatively few Persons. But so long as other nations are animated by these human Passions a Country like England, wealthy and exposed to attack must by necessity be provided with means of defence, and however expensive those means may be, they are infinitely cheaper than the war which they tend to keep off.' *PAMP*, BM 48582, Palmerston to Cobden, 8 Jan. 1862.

71. Malmesbury, *Memoirs*, II, 193, *Diary*, 23 June 1859. All communications were to be read by both Palmerston and the Queen. 'I suppose this is to make a contrast with Lord Palmerston's conduct when Foreign Secretary under *him* . . .', Malmesbury wrote.

72. *Sessional Papers*, LXVIII, 1860 (Coms.), Lyons to Russell, no. 222, 19 Jul. 1859.

73. *RUSP*, PRO 30/22–96, Russell to Lyons, 28 Jul. 1859.

74 Ibid., PRO 30/22–29, Malmesbury to Russell, 30 June 1859.

75. 'I had intended', Malmesbury advised him, 'to get rid of the three grievances *tertium* leaving the Bay Islands for the last & taking care that we did not *conclude* that cession until we had a most unqualified recognition from the U.S. that the Clayton Bulwer Treaty was then what we maintain it to be in all respects'. *RUSP*, PRO 30/22–96, Malmesbury to Russell, 30 June 1859.

76. *Sessional Papers*, LXVIII, 1860 (Coms.). Russell to Wyke, no. 226, 15 Aug. 1859.

77. Ibid., Russell to Wyke, no. 227, 15 Aug. 1859.

78. Ibid., Russell to Wyke, no. 228 and no. 229, 15 Aug. 1859.

79. Ibid., Russell to Ouseley, no 231, 15 August 1859.

80. Ibid., Ouseley to Russell, no. 251, 29 Sep. 1859.

81. *RUSP*, PRO 30/22–33, Ouseley to Russell, 17 Sep. 1860. This defence was written after he had seen the final treaties, and after Russell had told him that his dismissal had been a sort of 'official legacy' from Malmesbury. He noted that his instructions had required him to make Costa Rica part of the treaty, and to safeguard her interests in Grey Town, but this *sine qua non* had been abandoned by Russell. He further noted that his six treaties would have been 'concluded in a very short time' had he continued the negotiation. This statement does not agree with one he made in a letter to Russell on 19 Sep. 1859, in which he stated coercion might be needed to force Nicaragua to accept the Mosquito treaty. Ibid., Ouseley to Russell, 19 Sep. 1859. Undoubtedly the exclusion of Costa Rica from the negotiations gave Wyke a great advantage over Ouseley in achieving a quick settlement.

82. *Sessional Papers*, LXVIII, 1860 (Coms.), Lyons to Russell, no. 241, 16 Aug 1859.

83. *BP*, 13327, Lyndhurst to Brougham, 30 Sep. 1859.

84. Buchanan had recently written to Clarendon expressing the hope

that the Prince of Wales would visit the United States. B&E, *Victoria*, III, 476–7, Newcastle to Victoria, 26 Sep. 1859.

85. *RUSP*, PRO 30/22–24, Somerset to Russell, 20 Sep. 1859.

86. *The Times* (London), 25 Oct. and 23 Dec. 1859.

87. *Sessional Papers*, LXVIII, 1860 (Coms.), Wyke to Russell, no. 258, 11 Oct. 1859.

88. Ibid., Treaty between Great Britain and Honduras, respecting the Bay Islands, the Mosquito Indians, and the Rights and Claims of British subjects.

89. Ibid., Wyke to Hammond, no. 261, 28 Nov. 1859.

90. Waddell, 'Bay Islands', pp. 75–6.

91. *Sessional Papers*, LXVIII, 1860 (Coms.), Wyke to Russell, no. 264, 29 Nov. 1859.

92. Ibid., Wyke to Russell, no. 268, 10 Jan. 1860.

93. Ibid., Treaty of Friendship, Commerce, and Navigation between Britain and Nicaragua.

94. Ibid., Treaty Relative to the Mosquito Indians.

10   THE MEXICAN COUP AND THE LAST GREAT CRISIS

1. *CLAR*, c. 524, Palmerston to Clarendon, 13 Jan. 1859.

2. Ibid., Palmerston to Clarendon, 17 May 1859.

3. *RUSP*, PRO 30/22–29, Malmesbury to Russell, 30 June 1859.

4. *Hansard*, 3rd ser., CLIV, 878–881.

5. *RUSP*, PRO 30/22–74, Otway to Russell, 11 Aug. 1859.

6. Ibid., Otway to Russell, 26 Nov. 1859.

7. '. . . with the exception of Bright and Disraeli', Palmerston observed, 'we have not a bitterer enemy than Cobden on any bench in the House of Commons', *GP*, BM 44272, Palmerston to Russell, 4 Dec. 1863.

8. *RUSP*, PRO 30/22–39, Green to Russell, 5 Oct. 1859.

9. Ibid., PRO 30/22–33, Mathew to Russell, 4 Sep. 1861.

10. Carl H. Bock, *Prelude to Tragedy* (Philadelphia: University of Pennsylvania Press, 1966) pp. 38–54.

11. *RUSP*, PRO 30/22–74, Mathew to Russell, 29 May 1860.

12. Ibid., Mathew to Russell, 20 Oct. 1859. An honest governor had attempted to suppress the Pacific smuggling operations of a Mr. Barron, and he therefore provided funds for the uprising.

13. Ibid., Mathew to Russell, 29 May 1860.

14. Bock, *Tragedy*, p. 54.

15. Ibid.

16. *RUSP*, PRO 30/22–74, Mathew to Russell, 29 May 1860.

17. *RUSP*, PRO 30/22–74, Mathew to Russell, 29 May 1860.

18. Bock *Tragedy*, p. 58.

19. *RUSP*, PRO 30/22–95, Russell to Mathew, 1 Nov. 1860.

20. 'You may be assured', Russell wrote on learning of it, 'that so injurious a robbery will not pass without punishment'. *RUSP*, PRO 30/22–95, Russell to Mathew, 1 Jan. 1861.

21. Ibid., PRO 30/22–74, Mathew to Russell, 30 Dec. 1860.

22. Ibid., Mathew to Russell, 18 Aug. 1861.

23. Ibid., Mathew to Russell, 30 Dec. 1861.

24. Ibid., Mathew to Russell, 21 May, 1861.

25. Ibid., PRO 30/22–95, Russell to Mathew, 22 Aug. 1861.

26. See: Bock, *Tragedy*, pp. 64–83.

27. Ibid., p. 66.

28. *RUSP*, PRO 30/22–74, Robertson to Russell, 22 Sep. 1861.

29. See: Jones, *Lord Derby*, pp. 264–9.

30. 'I think that in your communications with Palmerston you cannot be too explicit. He is a gentleman . . .,' Derby wrote Malmesbury, 'I should, however, assure him that, though we might, in debate, object to some of the "sayings and doings" of the Foreign Office (and chiefly the *sayings*, or rather, *writings*), we would not countenance any movement on the subject of foreign policy calculated to defeat the Government, unless it were on the impossible supposition that they should desire us to take an active part in an attack by Sardinia and France on Venetia.' Malmesbury, *Memoirs*, II, 243–4, Derby to Malmesbury, 26 Dec. 1860.

31. *PAMP*, BM 48582, Palmerston to Somerset, 27 Mar. 1861.

32. Ibid., Palmerston to Gladstone, 21 Jul. 1861.

33. *RUSP*, PRO 30/22–21, Palmerston to Russell, 22 Jan. 1861.

34. *PAMP*, BM 48582, Palmerston to Herbert, 3 June 1861.

35. Ibid., Palmerston to Russell, 10 June 1861.

36. Ibid., Palmerston to Somerset, 23 June 1861.

37. *RUSP*, PRO 80/22–21, Palmerston to Russell, 18 Jul. 1861.

38. *PAMP*, BM 48582, Palmerston to Russell, 25 Aug. 1861.

39. Ibid., Palmerston to Lewis, 26 Aug. 1861.

40. Russell stoutly defended the naval building programme in a letter to Richard Cobden. *COB*, BM 43670, Russell to Cobden, 2 Apr. 1861.

41. *RUSP*, PRO 30/22–21, Palmerston to Russell, 7 Oct. 1861.

42. Sir Herbert Maxwell, *The Life and Letters of George William Frederick, Fourth Earl of Clarendon* (London: Edward Arnold, 1913) II, 243, Lewis to Clarendon, 27 Oct. 1861.

43. Clarendon noted it would have been wrong if war against Mexico had been decided upon without the consent of the Cabinet '. . . but it would have been Palmerstonian'. Ibid., pp. 240–1, Clarendon to Lewis, 4 Oct. 1861.

44. See: Bock, *Tragedy*, pp. 122–215.

45. *RUSP*, PRO 30/22–96, Russell to Lyons, 26 Oct. 1861.

46. Bock, *Tragedy*, pp. 164–5.

47. Ibid., pp. 196–7.

48. *RUSP*, PRO 30/22–33, Mathew to Russell, 20 Jul. 1862.

49. Bourne believes that, having failed to check America in Central America, Palmerston looked for an indirect means of containing American power, and this was done by enlisting France at this time. See: Bourne, *Victorian England*, p. 89. The present writer, however, feels the above interpretation seems more likely, though admittedly unproved.

50. *RUSP*, PRO 30/22–21, Palmerston's Memorandum, 11 Dec. 1860.

51. Ibid., PRO 30/22–97, Russell to Baring, 21 Dec. 1860.

52. *PAMP*, BM 48582, Palmerston to Somerset, 29 Dec. 1860.

53. John Morley, *The Life of William Ewart Gladstone* (London: Macmillan, 1903) II, 82.

54. See: *RUSP*, PRO 30/22–74, Mathew to Russell, 30 Dec. 1861 in which Mathew (who often spoke more bluntly than the average British diplomat) averred that the peace of the world would be benefited by cutting down the power of the United States, even though he, himself, did not believe in secession.

55. One of Gladstone's relatives visited Palmerston in 1864, and made the following comment: 'The interview which Lord P. was so gracious as to accord me was not specially noticeable. America is a young country & has rushed into full growth since the time when Lord P.'s mind was plastic & prehensible. He struck me therefore (though of course I should not say this publicly) as a little jaded when carried out of his own groove of European Foreign policy.' *GP*, BM 44402, Hon. Francis C. Lawley to Catherine Gladstone, 18 Feb. 1864.

56. *RUSP*, PRO 30/22–21, Palmerston to Russell, 15 Feb. 1861.

57. *PAMP*, BM 48582, Palmerston to Newcastle, 24 May 1861.

58. Ibid., Palmerston to Somerset, 26 May 1861.

59. Ibid., Palmerston to Herbert, 3 and 4 June 1861.

60. Ibid., Palmerston to Somerset, 23 June 1861.

61. *RUSP*, PRO 30/22–21, Palmerston to Russell, 25 Aug. 1861.

62. *Hansard*, 3rd ser., CLXII, 1830–2.

63. *PAMP*, BM 48582, Palmerston to Russell, 9 Jul. 1861.

64. Ibid., Palmerston to Somerset, 29 Dec. 1860.

65. Ibid., Palmerston to Newcastle, 1 Sep. 1861.

66. Ibid., Palmerston to Newcastle, 9 Nov. 1861.

67. Ibid., Palmerston to Newcastle, 1 Sep. 1861.

68. The Canadians, however, made some vigorous efforts to prepare for their own defence. See: Robin W. Winks, *Canada and the United States: The Civil War Years* (Baltimore: The Johns Hopkins Press, 1960) pp. 71–81.

69. American interpretations of the crisis have moderated vastly since the appearance of Thomas L. Harris's *The Trent Affair* in 1896, which termed Wilkes's error 'entirely excusable', and the British response unwarranted and not consistent with her position as a 'leader of civilisation'. John W. Foster, *A Century of American Diplomacy* (Boston: Houghton, Mifflin, and Co., 1901) was content merely to chide Britain for belatedly accepting the American view of impressment. Bemis and Pratt in their texts in diplomatic history acquit Britain of the charge of overreacting. The British historian, H. C. Allen (*Great Britain and the United States*. New York: St. Martin's Press, Inc., 1955) praises Seward for his diplomacy in the settlement. Detailed accounts of the crisis can be found in E. D. Adams, *Great Britain and the American Civil War* (New York: Longmans, Green and Co., 1925) and F. L. Owsley, *King Cotton Diplomacy: Foreign Relations of the Confederate States of America* (Chicago: University of Chicago Press, 1931). See also: Bourne, *Britain and the Balance of Power*, pp. 218–47.

70. *GP*, BM 44136, Gladstone to Cobden, 13 Dec. 1861.

71. *RUSP*, PRO 30/22–96, Russell to Lyons, 1 Dec. 1861.

72. Ibid., PRO 30/22–21, Palmerston to Russell, 6 Dec. 1861.

73. *PAMP*, BM 48582, Palmerston to Russell, 9 Dec. 1861.

74. *RUSP*, PRO 30/22–96, Russell to Lyons, 1 Dec. 1861.

75. Ibid., PRO 30/22–29, Clarendon to Russell, 4 Dec. 1861.

76. Ibid., Clarendon to Russell, 8 Dec. 1861.

77. Ibid., PRO 30/22–21, Palmerston to Russell, 20 Dec. 1861.

78. *DERP*, 189/1, Derby to Grenville, 3 Jan. 1862.

79. *GP*, BM 44136, Cobden to Gladstone, 11 Dec. 1861; Gladstone to Cobden, 13 Dec. 1861.

80. *BRP*, BM 44390, Sumner to Bright, 27 Dec. 1861.

81. 'When the House meets', Cobden wrote, 'four-fifths of the members will in their hearts be against the Federal Union & glad to see anything occur to weaken the great Republic. There will be parties ready to press the government on false pleas to recognise the South – some will be friends of the poor operatives, others will pretend that it will put an end to a useless war. . . . And who will there be to reply to all this? You & I & half a dozen might play the unpopular part of disregarding the interests of our Country – as will be said of us!' *COB*, BM 43652, Cobden to Bright, 7 Jan. 1862.

82. See: Brooks Adams, 'The Seizure of the Laird Rams', *Massachusetts Historical Society Proceedings*, XLVII (1914).

83. In a stricken sentence in a letter to Milner Gibson written earlier in the year, Palmerston noted that war with the North was 'not a very formidable thing for England & France combined, and possibly the North might shrink from such a contest. . . .' *PAMP*, BM 48582, Palmerston to Gibson, 7 June 1861. Two years later Palmerston observed 'It would not be well to tell France that we could not carry on war in Europe as well as in America. They might take advantage of such a Hint if ever we become embroiled with the Americans'. *RUSP*, PRO 30/22–22, 'Comments on a despatch to France on the Polish situation', 29 Sep. 1863.

84. Early in January 1862, Flahault wrote to Russell: 'What a good prophet you were in your expectations of Mr. Lincoln's determination. I admire it the more, that mine were quite opposite to it. I did not think the President of a mob would show so much sound judgment.' *RUSP*, PRO 30/22–14, Flahault to Russell, 9 Jan. 1862.

85. Ibid., PRO 30/22–21, Palmerston to Russell, 29 Nov. 1861.

86. Theodore Martin, *The Life of His Royal Highness The Prince Consort* (New York: D. Appleton and Co., 1880) v, 348.

87. Ibid., pp. 349–50. By coincidence the Prince's cherished friend, Lord Aberdeen, predeceased him by only three weeks.

88. Palmerston complained it was 'like amending a Bill in a Committee of the Whole House'. *RUSP*, PRO 30/22–21, Palmerston to Russell, 1 Dec. 1861.

89. *RUSP*, PRO 30/22–96, Russell to Lyons, 1 Dec. 1861.

90. *GP*, BM 44594, Lyons to Russell, 9 Jan. 1862.

91. This belief is widely held, and may have some substance to it. Mary

Williams, for example, noted that a major change toward conciliation occurred in British foreign policy in latter 1856, as British trade took precedence over British interests in Central America. Williams, *Isthmian Diplomacy*, pp. 221–3. Bourne shows that Palmerston was frustrated by popular opposition, as well as the newspapers, in his attempts to have a showdown with the United States over the recruitment issue in 1856, and he maintains that the solution of the Central American questions in 1860 marked the end of any British idea of confronting the United States on the American continent. Bourne, *Victorian England*, pp. 88–9. H. C. Allen notes that in the decade of the 1850's Britain came to realise that the United States was destined to be a great power, and began to realise the importance of having her as a friend, rather than as an enemy. H. C. Allen, *Britain and the United States*, p. 441. In almost all cases when Britain opposed American expansion, however, it was in support of traditional British interests. Lord Aberdeen, as we have seen, specifically rejected creating a sudden British interest in California simply to keep the Americans out. His Texas venture was motivated more by his French than his American policy.

Index

Morocco, 38

Mosquitia: See Mosquito Protectorate

Mosquito Protectorate, origins of, 65–72; first British attempt to abandon, 91–2; second attempt, 96–8, 104–7; third attempt, 124, 127, 131–2; fourth attempt, 148; fifth attempt, 154–8; sixth attempt, 158–60, 166–8, 173–5; final solution, 180–5. Mentioned, 82, 84–8, 90, 102. *Notes*, ch. 4 n. 64; ch. 4 n. 65

Mountcashell, 3rd Earl (Stephen Moore), 4

Musquitos: See Mosquito Protectorate

Napier, Sir Charles (R.N.), 50

Napier, Sir Charles James, 50, ch. 3 n. 93

Napier, 9th Baron (Francis Napier), appointed to Washington, 156; seeks American aid in China, 156–8; Mosquito negotiations, 158–60; sent to Spain, 172. Mentioned, 165–6, 176–7, ch. 9 n. 18

Napier, George, 50

Napoleon III, becomes permanent President, 93–4; friend of Malmesbury, 101; and Numeral Question, 102–3; attempt on his life, 161; hostile toward the Conservatives, 162; ambitions in Mexico, 197. Mentioned, 179, 208. *Notes*, ch. 9 n. 7; ch. 9 n. 13; ch. 9 n. 48

Napoleonic Wars, 8

Narrow Strip, 15, 25, 28, ch. 2 n. 48

Naval Race (Anglo–French), 45, 56–8, 94, 163, 188, 194–6, ch. 5 n. 34

Navigation Acts, 63–4, 76, 78, 82

Near Eastern Crisis (1840–1), 2, 4, 8

Negroes (British), 60–1, 207

Neufchatel, 102

New Brunswick, 130

Newcastle, 5th Duke of (Henry Clinton), 120–1, 125, 140–1, 179, 200. *Notes*, ch. 6 n. 40; ch. 7 n. 38

Newfoundland Fisheries, 80–1, 109–18, 126, 130

New Orleans, 93, 116

New York, 4, 7, 141–2

New York Herald, 31, 112–13

New York Times, 112

New Zealand, 203

Nicaragua, 65–6, 68, 71, 75, 84–5, 87–8, 91–2, 96–7, 105–7, 124, 132, 150, 156, 166–8, 170, 173, 175, 181, 184–5

Nicholas I (Tsar of Russia), 123

Nile, Battle of the, 193

Nova Scotia, 130

Numeral Question: See Napoleon III

Oldenburg, 16

Orange Free State, 203

Oregon Dispute, x, ch. 3, 56, 60, 64–5, 95, 119, 128, 156, 170, 183, 188, 207–9. *Notes*, ch. 3 n. 45; ch. 3 n. 77; ch. 4 n. 2; ch. 5 n. 2

Orthodox Christian (Ottoman Empire), 120

Ottoman Empire, 120

Otway, Loftus C., 172, 175–6, 180, 182, 186–7

Oudh, 159

Ouseley, William Gore, 159, 164–8, 170, 172–4. *Notes*, ch. 9 n. 18; ch. 9 n. 81

Pacific Area, 55, 69, 73

Pakenham, Richard, sent to Washington, 36; instructions regarding Oregon, 37–8; diplomatic blunder, 44–5; replaced, 78. Mentioned, 40–1, 44, 46–7, 49, 52, 54, 58–62, 70

Pakington, Sir John Somerset, 109, 111–12, 153, 168, 203

Palmerston, 3rd Viscount (Henry John Temple), views on national personalities, 1; and Near Eastern Crisis, 2; and McLeod Crisis, 4–8; and Webster–Ashburton Treaty, 13–16, 31–2; returns to Foreign Office (1846), 55; opinion of Oregon Treaty, 55; and Spanish Marriages, 55–6; and national defense, 56–8; projects entente with America, 58–9; during the Revolutionary Year, 59; policies during Mexican War, 59–61; and Free Trade, 63–5; Central

Palmerston, 3rd Viscount – *contd.*
American policy, 1846–50, 65–8;
successes, 1848–50, 77–8; his
opposition, 77–8; disinterest in
Bulwer mission, 77, 82–3; censure
in the Lords, 89; triumph in Brazil,
90; dismissed by Russell, 93–4;
forms Government (1855), 138;
political position, 139; American
policy, 139; deserted by Peelites,
144–5; and Foreign Enlistments,
146; alleged American plot against,
148–9, 153; signs peace, 150; and
Crampton crisis, 152–3; opinion of
United States, 160; falls from
power, 161; split with Russell, 162;
approach to Russell, 178; becomes
Prime Minister (1859), 178; fear of
France, 179, 194–9; involvement
of France in Mexico, 196–8;
attitude toward American Civil
War, 198; and Canadian Defence,
199–202; and *Trent* Crisis, 202–6.
Mentioned, 11, 17, 25, 28–9, 39, 41,
53, 99–101, 104, 115, 119–21, 126,
137, 156–8, 175, 192–4. *Notes*, ch.
1 n. 3; ch. 2 n. 3; ch. 2 n. 4; ch. 2
n. 5; ch. 4 n. 1; ch. 4 n. 2; ch. 4 n.
24; ch. 4 n. 32; ch. 4 n. 93; ch. 9 n.
67; ch. 9 n. 70; ch. 9 n. 71; ch. 10 n.
7; ch. 10 n. 55; ch. 10 n. 83
Panama, 159
Papal Aggression, 90
Paraná River, 108
Peel, Sir Robert (2nd Bt.), becomes
Prime Minister, 7; defence of
Webster–Ashburton Treaty, 32;
loss of confidence in the United
States, 34, 37, 41, 47; resigns and
returns, 47–8; death of, 90.
Mentioned, 4, 6, 10–11, 16–17, 29,
31, 36, 39, 43, 45–6, 50, 52, 68, 79,
99–100. *Notes*, ch. 2 n. 5; ch. 2 n.
9; ch. 2 n. 12; ch. 2 n. 39; ch. 3 n.
20
Peelite Section (Parliament), 58, 64,
78, 89–90, 99, 118, 120–1, 138, 144,
157, 161, 179, 200. *Notes*, ch. 4 n.
36; ch. 8 n. 53; ch. 8 n. 77
Pembroke, 147
Perkins, Emanuel C., 147
Perry, Oliver Hazard (U.S.N.), 157
Philadelphia, 141

Philippe, Louis (King of France), 6,
10, 24, 40, 55, 59
Pickett, Capt. George Edward, 183
Pierce, Franklin (14th President of
the U.S.), 126–7, 130, 133, 137, 143,
149, 155–6
Plumper, 183
Plymouth, 56
Plymouth, 168
Point Arenas, 133, 168
Polk, James Knox (11th President of
the U.S.), 42–3, 46–7, 51, 53, 72,
126, 148
Portugal, 80, 162, ch. 2 n. 22
Powerful, 147
Preble, William P., 27, ch. 3 n. 24
Prince Consort, 35, 93, 95, 101–2,
128, 163, 205, ch. 10 n. 87
Prince Edward Island, 130
Principalities, The, 122–3
Prometheus Affair, 96
Prussia, 1–2
Puget's Sound, 40

Quarterly Review, 52
Quebec, 24–5, 28, 201

Radical Section (Parliament), 58, 64,
78, 89, 118, 122, 137, 157, 178, ch.
1 n. 23
Reciprocity Treaty (United States
and Canada), 109–18, 124–5,
129–31, 170, 178, 209
Red Line Map, 26. *Notes*, ch. 2 n. 3;
ch. 3 n. 20
Red River, 50, 95
Reform Bill (1859), 178
Reform Club, 10
Right of Visit, 21, 30
Ripon, 1st Earl of (Frederick John
Robinson), 16–17, 34, 50. *Notes*,
ch. 1 n. 1; ch. 1 n. 8; ch. 2 n. 9;
ch. 2 n. 12
Rives, William Cabell, 74
Roanoke, 168
Roatan (Ruatan), 66, 84, 86, 90, 107,
117, 131–2, 154–5. See also Bay
Islands
Roebuck, John, 89, 137, 145, 153
Rome, 9
Rosamond, 147
Rosas, Juan Manuel, 40, 104, 107
Rothschild Bankers, 10